Mac® OS X, v10.4 Tiger™

Kate Binder

Contents

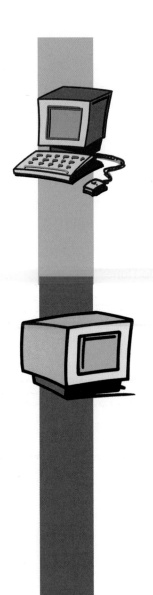

Associate Publisher
Greg Wiegand

Acquisitions Editor
Laura Norman

Development Editor
Laura Norman

Managing Editor
Charlotte Clapp

Project Editor
Tonya Simpson

Production Editor
Megan Wade

Indexer
Ken Johnson

Technical Editor
Amy Hoy

Publishing Coordinator
Sharry Lee Gregory

Designer
Anne Jones

Easy Mac® OS X, v10.4 Tiger™
Copyright © 2005 by Que Publishing

International Standard Book Number: 0-7897-3313-7

Library of Congress Catalog Card Number: 2004099098

Printed in the United States of America

First Printing: April 2005

08   07   06   05   4   3   2

Trademarks

Warning and Disclaimer

Bulk Sales

Que Publishing offers excellent discounts on this book when ordered in quantity for bulk purchases or special sales. For more information, please contact

U.S. Corporate and Government Sales
1-800-382-3419
corpsales@pearsontechgroup.com

For sales outside the United States, please contact

International Sales
international@pearsoned.com

We Want to Hear from You!

As the reader of this book, *you* are our most important critic and commentator. We value your opinion and want to know what we're doing right, what we could do better, what areas you'd like to see us publish in, and any other words of wisdom you're willing to pass our way.

As an associate publisher for Que Publishing, I welcome your comments. You can email or write me directly to let me know what you did or didn't like about this book—as well as what we can do to make our books better.

Please note that I cannot help you with technical problems related to the topic of this book. We do have a User Services group, however, where I will forward specific technical questions related to the book.

When you write, please be sure to include this book's title and author as well as your name, email address, and phone number. I will carefully review your comments and share them with the author and editors who worked on the book.

Email: feedback@quepublishing.com

Mail: Greg Wiegand
          Associate Publisher
          Que Publishing
          800 East 96th Street
          Indianapolis, IN 46240 USA

For more information about this book or another Que title, visit our Web site at www.quepublishing.com. Type the ISBN (excluding hyphens) or the title of a book in the Search field to find the page you're looking for.

About the Author
Kate Binder is a longtime Mac lover and graphics expert who works from her home in New Hampshire. She has written articles on graphics, publishing, and photography for magazines including *Publish*, *PEI*, and *Desktop Publishers Journal*. Kate is also the author of several books, including *The Complete Idiot's Guide to Mac OS X* and *Easy Adobe Photoshop 6*, and coauthor of books including *Microsoft Office: Mac v.X Inside Out*, *SVG for Designers*, and *Get Creative: The Digital Photo Idea Book*. To those interested in a successful career as a computer book writer, Kate recommends acquiring several retired racing greyhounds (find out more at www.adopt-a-greyhound.org)—she finds her four greyhounds extraordinarily inspirational.

Dedication
With all my love, this book is dedicated to my husband, partner, and sine qua non, *Don Fluckinger.*

Acknowledgments
Thanks to Mike Shebanek at Apple for making sure I received the beta OS releases I needed to get this book out on time. And to Laura Norman for shepherding me through another one. And even to Mack the Former Baby, for his bizarre ability to be both the boat anchor of my longest days and the fizzy bubbles in my happiest days. Thanks, too, to the awesome editorial, design, and production people at Que—and especially tech editor Amy Hoy—for making it happen once again.

Introduction to *Easy Mac OS X, v10.4 Tiger*
Mac OS X is like no operating system, Macintosh or otherwise, that came before it. It's incredibly stable and powerful, and it looks sleek and new and very unfamiliar to long-time Mac users. But underneath, it has the same old friendly nature that Mac lovers have always enjoyed.

With *Easy Mac OS X, v10.4 Tiger*, you'll learn how to take advantage of powerful and useful Mac OS X features such as the built-in instant messaging program iChat, automatic file and printer sharing with Windows PCs, and the ability to find just about anything you could want online with Sherlock. Along the way, you'll get used to being able to run a dozen programs at one time on a stable system that doesn't crash. This book's step-by-step approach tells you just what you need to know to accomplish the task at hand, quickly and efficiently. All the skills you need to get the most out of Mac OS X, both online and on the desktop, are covered here.

If you want, you can work through the tasks in *Easy Mac OS X, v10.4 Tiger* in order, building your skills steadily. Or, if you prefer, use this book as a reference to look up just what you need to know *right now*. Either way, *Easy Mac OS X, v10.4 Tiger* lets you see it done and then do it yourself.

① Each step is fully illustrated to show you how it looks onscreen.

It's as Easy as 1-2-3

Each part of this book is made up of a series of short, instructional lessons, designed to help you understand basic information that you need to get the most out of your computer hardware and software.

② Each task includes a series of quick, easy steps designed to guide you through the procedure.

③ Items that you select or click in menus, dialog boxes, tabs, and windows are shown in **bold**.

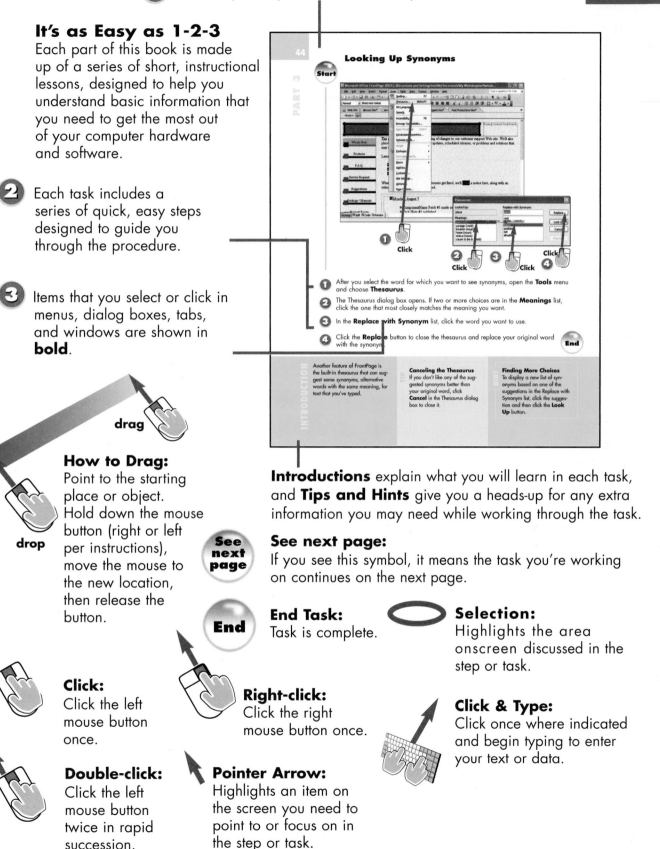

Introductions explain what you will learn in each task, and **Tips and Hints** give you a heads-up for any extra information you may need while working through the task.

How to Drag:
Point to the starting place or object. Hold down the mouse button (right or left per instructions), move the mouse to the new location, then release the button.

drag

drop

See next page:
If you see this symbol, it means the task you're working on continues on the next page.

See next page

End Task:
Task is complete.

End

Selection:
Highlights the area onscreen discussed in the step or task.

Click:
Click the left mouse button once.

Double-click:
Click the left mouse button twice in rapid succession.

Right-click:
Click the right mouse button once.

Pointer Arrow:
Highlights an item on the screen you need to point to or focus on in the step or task.

Click & Type:
Click once where indicated and begin typing to enter your text or data.

Getting Started

Mac OS X was introduced, after much anticipation and even more hype, in the spring of 2001. Surprisingly, it has lived up to its hype. With Mac OS X, users have an operating system that is many times more powerful than older systems, completely modern, capable of handling the latest innovations in hardware, and as easy to use as any Mac system that has gone before.

And it just keeps on getting better. Every new version of Mac OS X—including this one, Tiger—has brought with it features that are exciting, fun, and useful. Tiger includes Dashboard, a new way of using myriad small programs called *widgets*; Spotlight, the best file search system ever; and an updated version of iLife that includes GarageBand, a fun new application that makes it easy to write your own music. But first things first....

The starting point for any exploration of Mac OS X is the desktop: what you see when your Mac has finished starting up. The desktop is operated by a program called the Finder, and it's a central location where you'll gain access to your disks and their contents, move files around, and keep track of what your computer's up to—sort of like a hotel or office building lobby. This section covers the basics of working with the Finder, as well as other functions that work the same no matter what program you're using.

Mac OS X's Desktop

Control your Mac with the Apple menu's commands

Set System Preferences

Drag the title bar to move a window

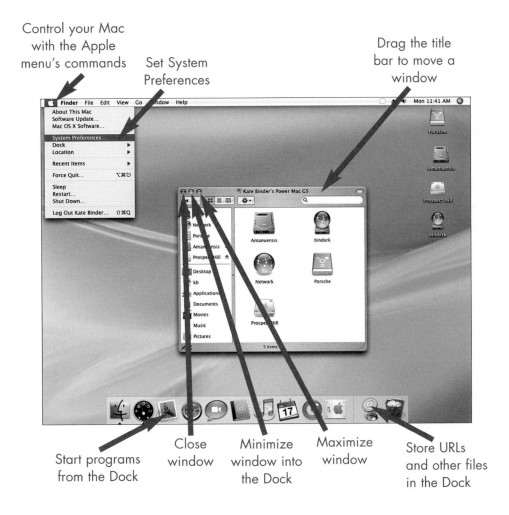

Start programs from the Dock

Close window

Minimize window into the Dock

Maximize window

Store URLs and other files in the Dock

Touring the Desktop

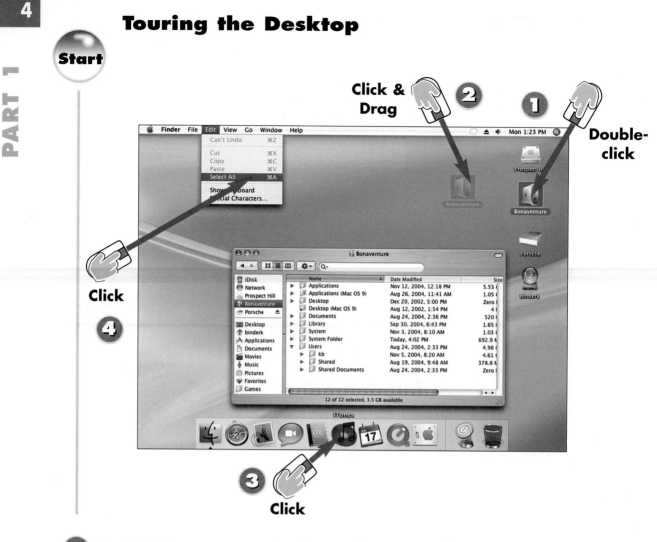

1. Double-click to view a window showing the contents of a drive or folder.

2. Click and drag to move icons on the desktop.

3. Click objects in the Dock to activate them.

4. Click a menu name, drag the mouse down, and release the mouse button on the menu item you want to use.

If you've used a Mac before, Mac OS X's desktop won't look completely new to you—just a bit unfamiliar. On the other hand, if you're new to computers, concepts like *windows*, *icons*, and *menus* might need a little explanation. Either way, this tour of the Mac OS X desktop should set you on your way.

It's Okay to Explore
HINT
If you're not sure what something on the desktop does, try clicking or double-clicking it. Mac OS X will let you know before it does anything destructive to your system, so it's safe to explore and experiment.

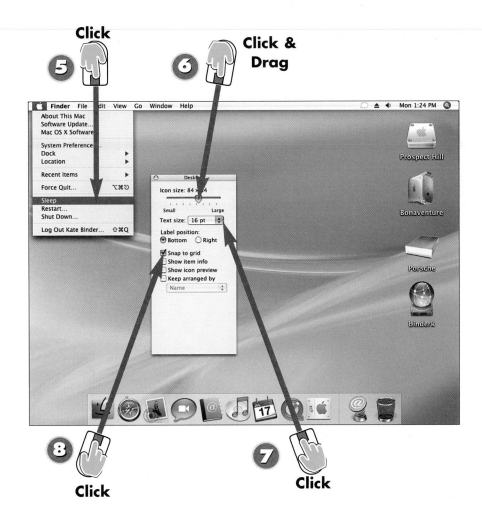

Click 5

Click & Drag 6

Click 8

Click 7

5. Use the **Apple** menu to perform tasks that affect your whole computer.

6. Choose **View**, **Show View Options** to open the View Options dialog box. Drag the **Icon size** slider to change the size of desktop icons.

7. Change the **Text size** and **Label position** to change the appearance of icon labels.

8. Check any of the other options to display more information about files, folders, and drives on the desktop.

End

Where's the Trash?
If you've used pre-OS X Macs before, you're probably looking for the Trash, which used to live on the desktop. It's in the Dock now, but you can put it back on the desktop if you like by using a little program called Trash X (www.northernsoftworks.com).

Cleaning Up the Place
When your desktop gets cluttered with downloaded files and the like, so that it's impossible for you to find anything, choose **View**, **Clean Up** to line up all the icons on the desktop in neat rows, so you can see what you've got.

Making the Desktop Your Own
Turn to the task called "Changing Your Desktop Picture" in Part 5, "Customizing the Mac," to learn how to change the desktop picture so you'll truly feel at home when you sit down in front of your Mac.

Using the Dock

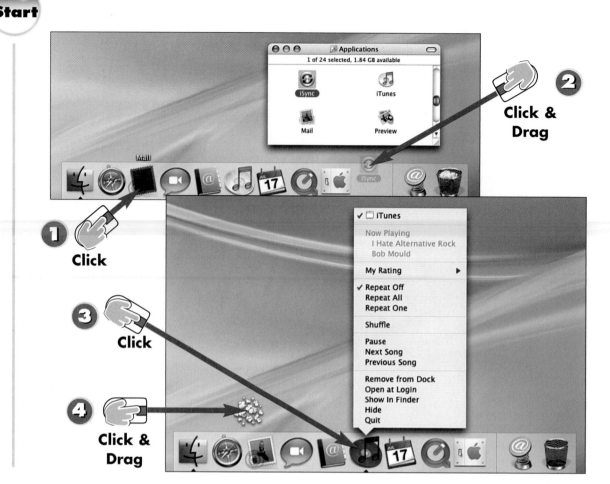

Start

Click & Drag ②

Click ①

Click ③

Click & Drag ④

① Click a program icon in the Dock to switch to that program (if it's running) or to start it up (if it's not running).

② Drag programs from the desktop into the Dock's left side and documents or folders from the desktop into the Dock's right side to store them for easy access.

③ Click and hold an icon in the Dock to see a menu of actions you can perform on that object or a list of folder contents.

④ Drag icons of files, folders, and inactive programs off the edge to remove them from the Dock in a puff of virtual smoke.

End

The *Dock* serves more than one function. First, it's where you can see which programs are running and switch among them. The Dock contains an icon for each active program at any given time. Second, it's a good place to store things you use often, whether they're programs, folders, or documents. And finally, it's where you'll find the Trash (you'll learn how to use the Trash in Part 2, "Working with Disks, Folders, and Files"). The Dock has a vertical line dividing its two sides. Program icons are stored on the left side, whether the programs are running or not, and folders and documents you add to the Dock yourself are stored on the right side. You'll find that you aren't able to drag a program onto the right side of the Dock or a document onto the left side.

HINT

Disappearing Act
When you drag programs or documents off the Dock, they disappear in a puff of smoke. But don't worry about the original files—they're still on your hard drive right where you left them. Dock icons are just pointers to the files, not the files themselves.

Moving and Resizing Windows

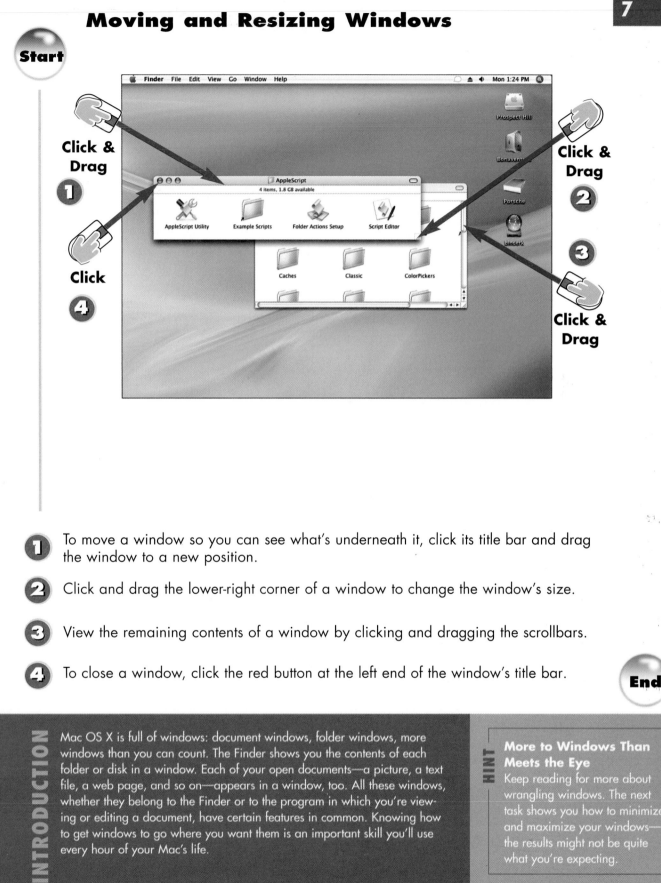

Start

Click & Drag ❶

Click ❹

Click & Drag ❷

Click & Drag ❸

❶ To move a window so you can see what's underneath it, click its title bar and drag the window to a new position.

❷ Click and drag the lower-right corner of a window to change the window's size.

❸ View the remaining contents of a window by clicking and dragging the scrollbars.

❹ To close a window, click the red button at the left end of the window's title bar.

End

INTRODUCTION

Mac OS X is full of windows: document windows, folder windows, more windows than you can count. The Finder shows you the contents of each folder or disk in a window. Each of your open documents—a picture, a text file, a web page, and so on—appears in a window, too. All these windows, whether they belong to the Finder or to the program in which you're viewing or editing a document, have certain features in common. Knowing how to get windows to go where you want them is an important skill you'll use every hour of your Mac's life.

HINT

More to Windows Than Meets the Eye
Keep reading for more about wrangling windows. The next task shows you how to minimize and maximize your windows—the results might not be quite what you're expecting.

Minimizing and Maximizing Windows

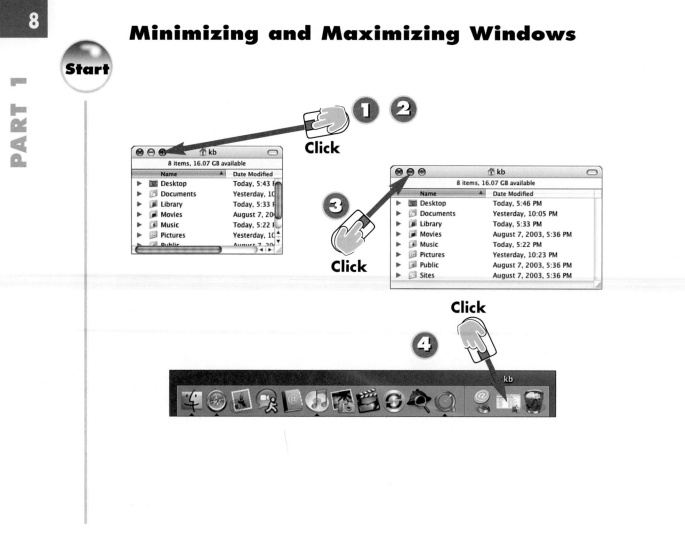

 Click the green button at the left end of a window's title bar to size the window so that it shows its entire contents.

 Click the green button again to return the window to its previous size.

3 Click the yellow button at the left end of a window's title bar to shrink the window downward into the right side of the Dock.

4 Click the window's thumbnail image in the Dock to put it back onto the desktop.

End

INTRODUCTION

Although windows are a great way to look inside folders, they never seem to open at just the right size for what you're trying to see. Getting the most from your windows requires learning to maximize their size and minimize them out of sight.

Window Identification
Each minimized window in the right side of the Dock has a small icon attached to its lower-right corner that identifies the program to which the window belongs. Folder and disk windows belong to the Finder, so they have a Finder logo.

The Wonders of Windows
The Dock continuously updates the appearance of minimized document windows. For example, if you minimize a QuickTime movie window while the movie's running, you can continue to monitor the movie's progress while its window is in the Dock.

Managing Multiple Windows

Start

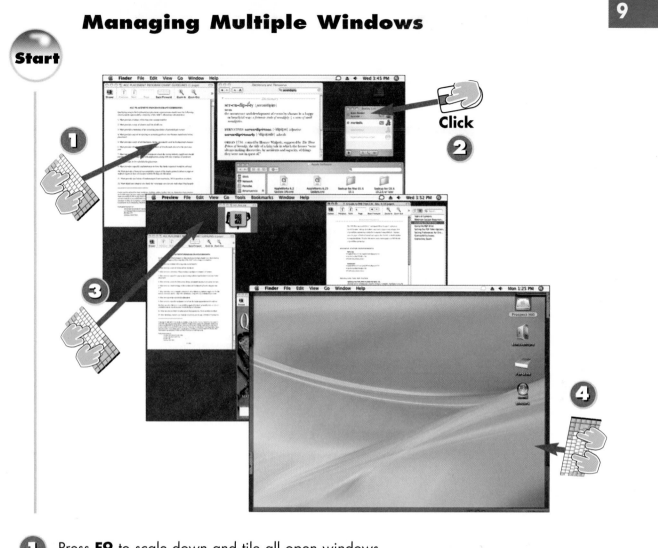

Click

1. Press **F9** to scale down and tile all open windows.

2. Click to select the window you're looking for and return all the windows to their normal size.

3. Press **F10** to tile all the windows in the current program and shade other windows.

4. Press **F11** to hide all windows so you can see the desktop.

End

INTRODUCTION

Mac OS X Tiger introduces a new feature called Exposé. It's a way to cut through window clutter instantly, no matter what program you're using. And if you tend to use a lot of programs at the same time, you'll definitely find Exposé's three functions very useful. They use the function keys, the row of *F* keys at the top of your keyboard.

TIP

For Those Who Prefer the Mouse
If you prefer to use the mouse, choose **Apple menu**, choose **System Preferences**, and click **Exposé** to assign the Exposé functions to three of the corners of the screen. Then perform any of these magical actions by simply positioning your mouse in the appropriate screen corner.

Using Contextual Menus

Start

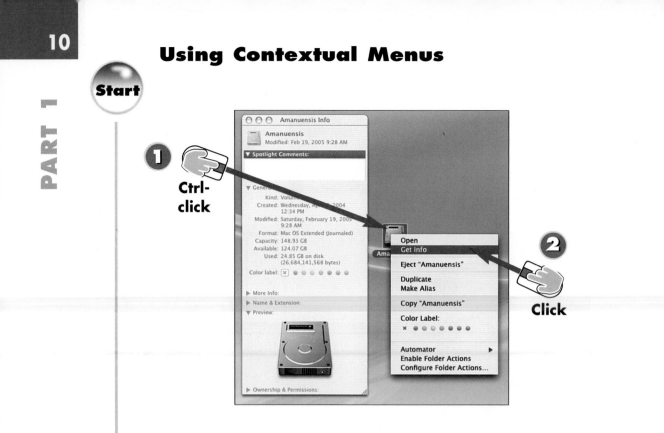

Ctrl-click

Click

① Press **Ctrl** and click any object on the desktop.

② Click the contextual menu command you want to perform.

End

Taking a Screenshot

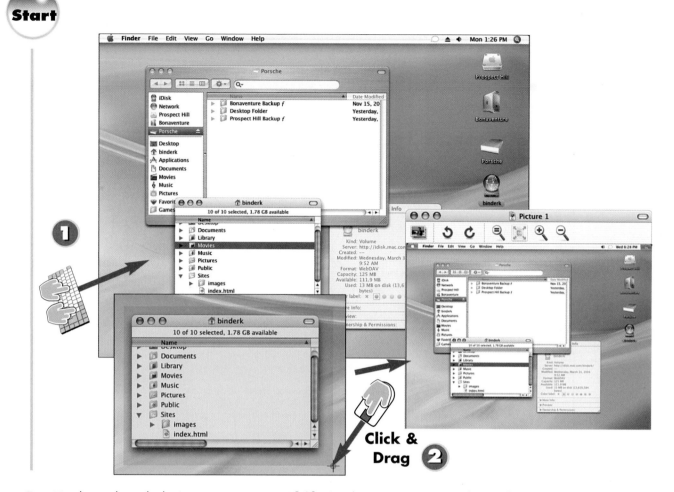

Start

1

Click & Drag **2**

1 To shoot the whole screen, press ⌘-**Shift-3**. The picture is saved in a file called **Picture 1** in your home folder.

2 To shoot part of the screen, press ⌘-**Shift-4**. Click and drag the mouse to select the area you want to shoot.

End

There will come a time when you'll want to take a shot of your Mac's screen for one reason or another. Maybe you need to show a technical support person exactly what's going wrong with your web browser, or perhaps you just want to preserve a picture of an amazing high score list in your favorite game.

TIP

In the Window

To shoot a single window, press ⌘+Shift+4, and then press the spacebar. Your cursor turns into a giant camera. Click the camera in any window to shoot a picture of just that window.

HINT

Open, Sesame

Mac OS X saves screenshots in PNG format. If you double-click one, it opens in Preview. You can also open PNG images in any graphics program, such as Adobe Photoshop.

Getting Help

Start

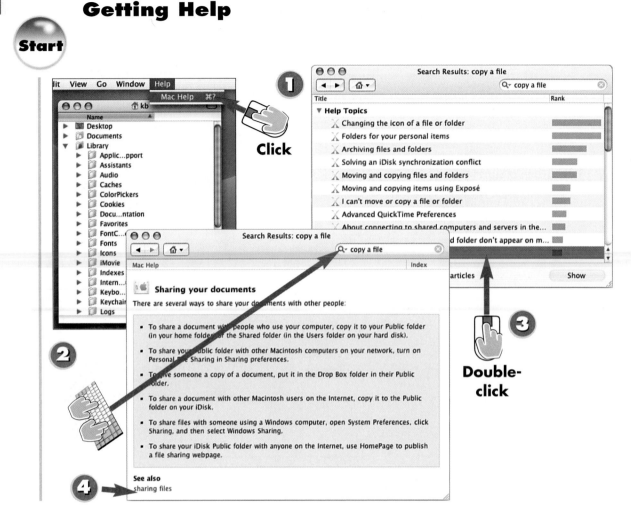

Click

Double-click

1. Choose the command you want from the **Help** menu. In the Finder, choose **Help**, **Mac Help**.

2. Type a phrase or question in the text entry field and press **Enter**.

3. Double-click a line in the search results to see that Help section.

4. The Mac Help window opens showing the information. Click a link at the bottom of the window to get additional information.

End

INTRODUCTION

In Mac OS X, the Help Viewer offers access to help for the Mac system and all your programs. No matter what you're doing when you start up the Help Viewer, you can see help for any program, whether it's running or not.

More and More Help

HINT

Some programs have several commands in the Help menu. Usually, the first command or two opens the Help Viewer, or that program's equivalent. The other commands take you places like the software developer's website, where you can find helpful information.

Restarting or Shutting Down the Mac

Start

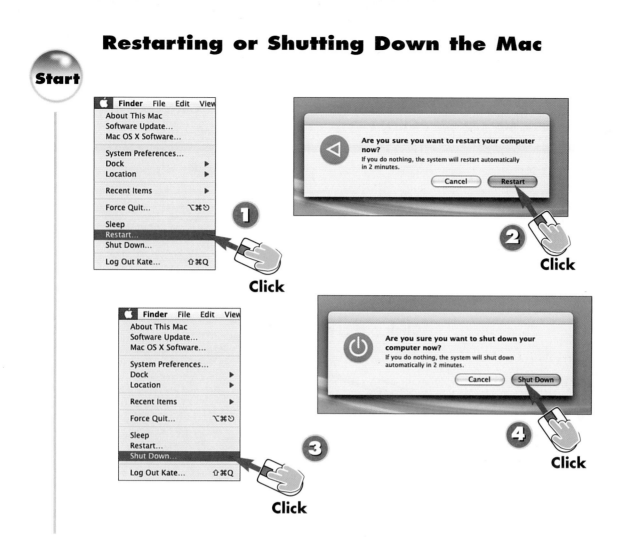

Click

Click

Click

Click

1. To restart the Mac, choose **Apple menu**, **Restart**.

2. In the dialog box, click **Restart**. Click **Cancel** to exit the dialog box without restarting.

3. To shut down the Mac, choose **Apple menu**, **Shut Down**.

4. In the dialog box, click **Shut Down**. Click **Cancel** to exit the dialog box without shutting down.

End

INTRODUCTION

As commands that affect the entire system, Restart and Shut Down are located in the Apple menu, so you can access them from any program rather than having to switch to the Finder, as in previous versions of the Mac OS. You'll use Restart most often after installing new software, and you'll use Shut Down when you want to turn your computer off.

TIP

No Fresh Start Needed
You don't have to restart the Mac if you only want to switch users. Choose **Apple menu**, **Log Out** instead; this command quits all running programs and presents you with the login screen, but it doesn't require the computer to completely reboot.

Setting Basic System Preferences

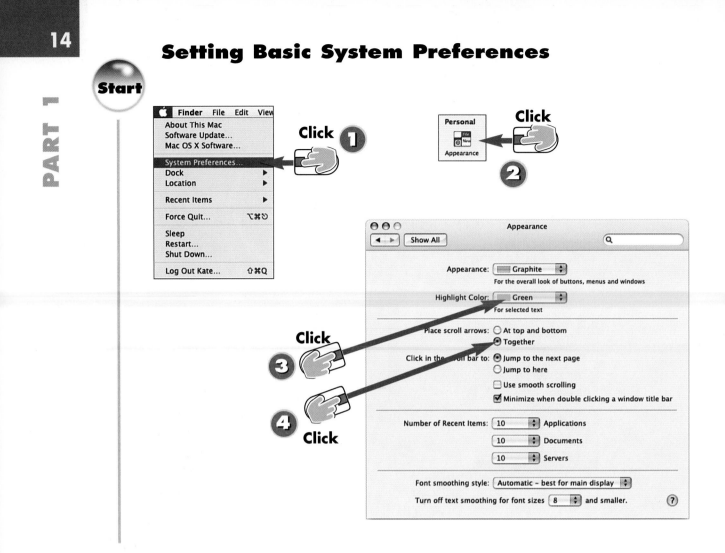

1. Choose **Apple menu**, **System Preferences**.

2. Click **Appearance** to display the Appearance preferences.

3. Choose colors from the **Appearance** pop-up menu (for scrollbars, buttons, and menus) and the **Highlight Color** pop-up menu (for selected text and objects in list view).

4. Click a radio button to put scrollbar arrows together or at the top and bottom of each window.

You can't customize everything about your Mac, but you can get darn close (for more customization techniques, turn to Part 5). Here's a look at the most basic preferences you'll want to set on a new Mac.

HINT

Blue Versus Graphite
Your Appearance color preference starts out set to Blue. If you switch it to Graphite, all your dialog box buttons, menu highlights, and window components turn graphite gray. The only problem you might encounter with that setting is that the Close, Minimize, and Maximize buttons—normally red, yellow, and green, respectively—also turn gray. You can still tell them apart by placing the cursor over them; an X appears in the Close button, a minus sign in the Minimize button, and a plus sign in the Maximize button.

Appearance

Appearance: [Graphite ▲▼]
For the overall look of buttons, menus and windows

Highlight Color: [Green ▲▼]
For selected text

Place scroll arrows: ○ At top and bottom
⦿ Together

Click in the scroll bar to: ○ Jump to the next page
⦿ Jump to here

☐ Use smooth scrolling
☑ Minimize when double clicking a window title bar

Number of Recent Items: [10 ▲▼] Applications
[20 ▲▼] Documents
[10 ▲▼] Servers

Font smoothing style: [Medium – best for Flat Panel ▲▼]

Turn off text smoothing for font sizes [8 ▲▼] and smaller. ⑦

Click ⑤

Click ⑥

Click ⑦

System Preferences	Edit	View
About System Preferences		
Services		►
Hide System Preferences		⌘H
Hide Others		⌥⌘H
Show All		
Quit System Preferences		⌘Q

Click ⑧

⑤ Click a radio button to choose how far clicking in the scrollbar scrolls the window.

⑥ Choose the number of recently used applications and documents that will appear in the Apple menu.

⑦ Choose a font smoothing style and size from the pop-up menus.

⑧ Choose **System Preferences**, **Quit System Preferences** to apply your changes.

End

TIP
Scroll, Scroll, Scroll Your Window
Choosing a scrollbar setting might be a little confusing unless you've used different operating systems in the past. Here's the scoop: Jump to the next page moves the view up or down one screenful when you click in the scrollbar. With long documents, you might prefer Jump to here, which moves the view to the location within the document that approximates the location of your click. In other words, click halfway down the scrollbar to see the document's midpoint. These settings apply within both application windows and folder windows in the Finder.

HINT
Font Smoothing
If font smoothing is off, be aware that some dialog boxes can look odd. You'll still be able to use those dialog boxes, but button labels and the like might be positioned a bit oddly and you might see a dialog box warning you of this fact on occasion.

Using Universal Access

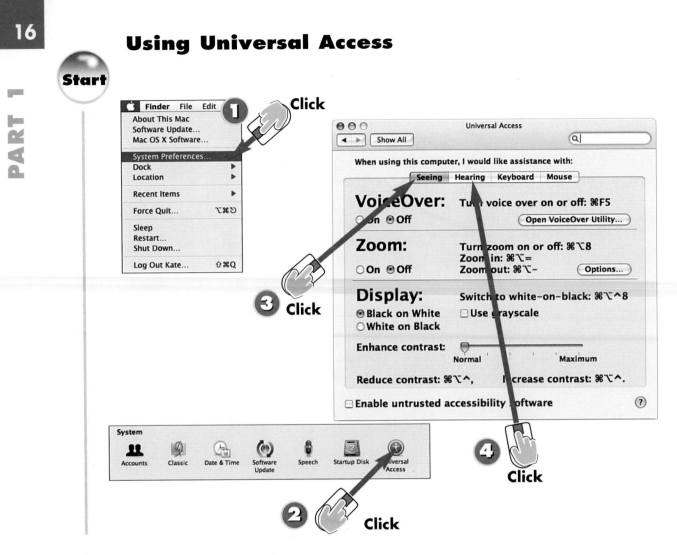

Start

1 **Click**

3 **Click**

2 **Click**

4 **Click**

1 Choose **Apple menu**, **System Preferences**.

2 Click **Universal Access**.

3 Click the **Seeing** tab and click the buttons to turn on the Zoom feature or switch to white text on a black background.

4 Click the **Hearing** tab and click the check box to flash the screen when an alert sound is played.

INTRODUCTION

Universal Access provides alternative ways of viewing the Mac's screen, hearing the sounds it makes, using the keyboard, and using the mouse. For example, if you can't hear alert sounds, you can set the screen to flash instead, calling your attention to what's happening just as clearly as an alert sound would.

TIP

Shortcuts to Access
No matter which Universal Access settings you want to use, you should click **Allow Universal Access Shortcuts**. This option activates the keyboard shortcuts shown on each tab of the Universal Access preferences pane.

HINT

Yakkety Yak
VoiceOver is the first setting in the Seeing section of the Universal Access preferences. This new Tiger feature enables you to control your Mac with voice commands. Turn to the next task to learn more.

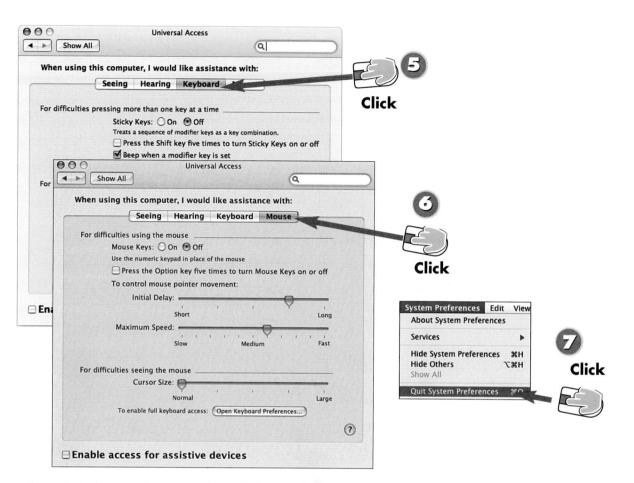

Click the **Keyboard** tab and choose from the various keyboard options.

Click the **Mouse** tab and choose from the various mouse options.

Choose **System Preferences**, **Quit System Preferences** to apply your changes.

End

Special Assistance

The **Enable Access for Assistive Devices** setting at the bottom of the Universal Access preferences pane enables you to use special equipment to control your Mac, such as head tracking devices with which you can move the cursor by moving your head.

Setting Up VoiceOver

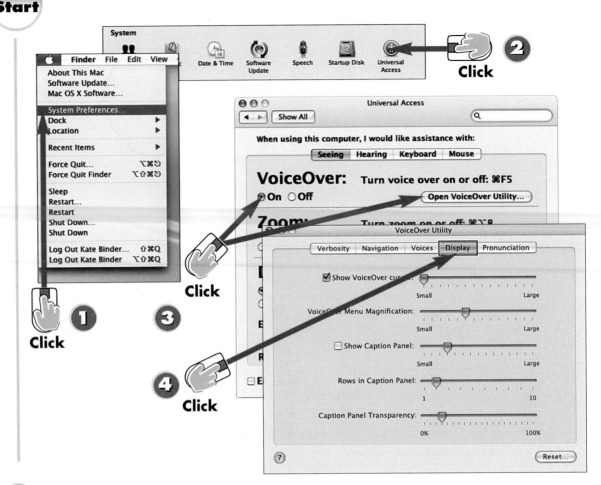

1 Choose **Apple menu**, **System Preferences**.

2 Click **Universal Access**.

3 Click **On** to enable VoiceOver and click **Open VoiceOver Utility** to configure VoiceOver settings.

4 Click the **Display** tab to control which VoiceOver features are used.

With VoiceOver, you can use the keyboard and Mac speech features to control your computer. Standard keyboard commands are augmented by special commands to enable you to start up, switch, and control programs and to move around your hard drive.

More or Less

The Display settings determine how evident VoiceOver is as you use your Mac. For example, you can turn on the VoiceOver cursor to hear spoken descriptions of the objects and dialog boxes under your cursor, or you can turn off the cursor to hide this feature.

VoiceOver Utility

Verbosity | Navigation | Voices | Display | Pronunciation

5 — **Click**

6 — **Click**

7 — **Click**

8 — **Click**

Punctuation: Some
Repeated Punctuation: First Three Times
When text attributes change: Do Nothing
While typing speak: Every Character
☐ Speak text under mouse after delay:
Short — Long
Login Greeting: Welcome to Macintosh.
VoiceOver is running.

☐ Announce when mouse cursor enters a window
☐ Announce w
☑ Announce w

VoiceOver Utility

Verbosity | Navigation | Voices | Display | Pronunciation

Voices		Rate	Pitch	Volume
▼ Default Voice	Fred	35	50	100
Content	Default Voice	35	50	100
Status	Default Voice	35	50	100
Type	Default Voice	35	50	100
Attributes	Default Voice	35	50	100
VoiceOver Menu	Default Voice	35	50	100

Reset...

5 Click the **Verbosity** tab to control how much VoiceOver talks.

6 Click the **Navigation** tab to control how VoiceOver moves around your screen.

7 Click the **Voices** tab to change the voice VoiceOver uses.

8 Click the **Pronunciation** tab to add terms you want VoiceOver to speak a particular way.

End

PatienceOver
The level of your Verbosity settings should be inversely proportional to your patience. If you want to get moving without listening for very long, turn down the **Item Description** and **Punctuation** settings.

Teach VoiceOver Your Language
Use the **Pronunciation** tab of the VoiceOver Utility to enter special terms you want VoiceOver to pronounce in a particular way. For example, you could add **:-(** under **Text** and **Frown smiley** under **Substitution**.

Working with Disks, Folders, and Files

The tasks in this part might not be glamorous or exciting, but they're the foundation of everything you do on your Mac. It's all about files, folders, and the disks that hold them. Every time you create a new document or receive an email attachment, that information is stored in a file on your hard drive, and the file is in turn stored within a folder. Mac OS X provides many ways for you to view and modify folder contents and file attributes, so you're in control of your Mac.

The tasks in this part teach you how to create new folders and view their contents in different ways, how to move and copy files, how to organize your hard drive and keep it uncluttered, and how to use Apple's .Mac online service to perform regular backups of your important files and synchronize your vital information across multiple computers.

You might notice that windows on your Mac OS X desktop have two distinct guises—a "plain" dress that looks like any document window and a "fancy" version that includes racks of buttons down the side and across the top. These are, respectively, multiwindow mode and single-window mode. Don't be deceived, though—you can have windows of both types open at the same time. This important aspect of Mac OS X is covered in the first task in this part.

Exploring the OS X File System

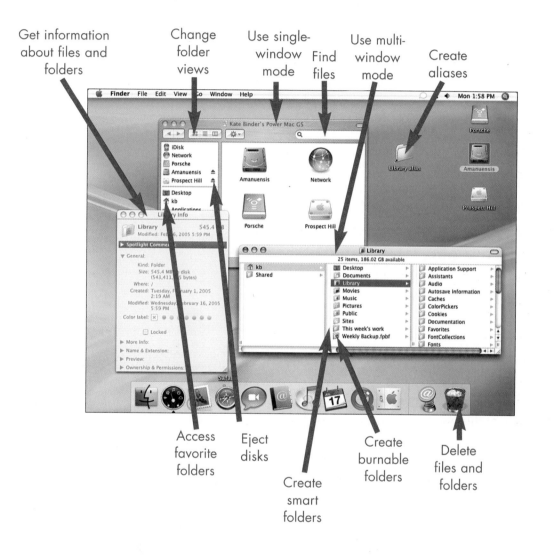

Get information about files and folders

Change folder views

Use single-window mode

Find files

Use multi-window mode

Create aliases

Access favorite folders

Eject disks

Create smart folders

Create burnable folders

Delete files and folders

Using Single-Window Mode

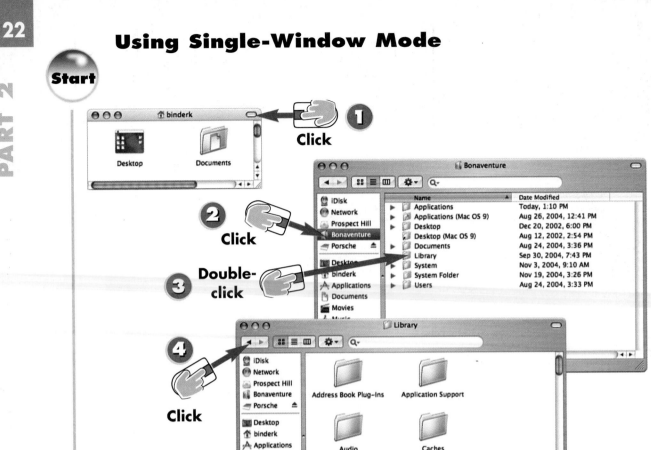

1 If you're using multiwindow mode, click the transparent button in the upper-right corner of the window to switch to single-window mode.

2 Click a folder or disk in the Places sidebar to see its contents.

3 Double-click folders in the main window to see their contents.

4 Click the left and right arrows to go back and forward in the series of windows you've viewed (similar to the Back and Forward buttons in a web browser window). **End**

INTRODUCTION

Traditionally, the Mac has spawned a new window for each folder or disk you open. Mac OS X introduced single-window mode, in which the contents of each folder or disk appear in the same window, like each successive page in a web browser displays in the same window. It takes a little getting used to, but it's a better way of working.

Single Versus Multi
Single-window mode is at its most useful when you need to see the contents of only one window. If you're copying or moving files from one folder to another, you'll probably find good old-fashioned multiwindow mode a better bet.

More Fun
Don't forget that you can switch window views in single-window mode by clicking the Icon, List, and Column view buttons at the top of the window. A special button next to these three summons up a contextual menu for any selected file in the window.

Using Multiwindow Mode

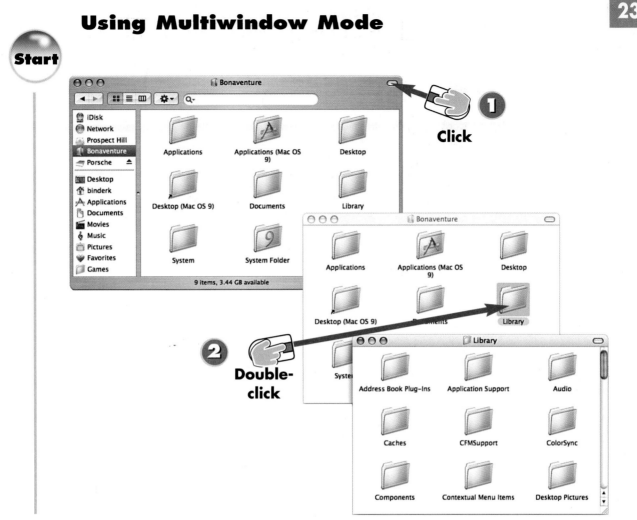

Start

① Click

② Double-click

① If you're using single-window mode, click the transparent button in the upper-right corner of the window to switch to multiwindow mode.

② Double-click a folder in the window to open a new window showing its contents.

End

INTRODUCTION

Sometimes you need to see the contents of two windows at once, and it's easier to focus on what you need to look at without the sidebar and toolbar of single-window mode. Multiwindow mode makes copying or moving files from one folder or disk to another easier.

TIP

Quick Switch
Even without the single-window mode toolbar, you can switch quickly from one window view to another. Click in a window and press ⌘-**1** for icon view, ⌘-**2** for list view, and ⌘-**3** for column view.

Using the Toolbar

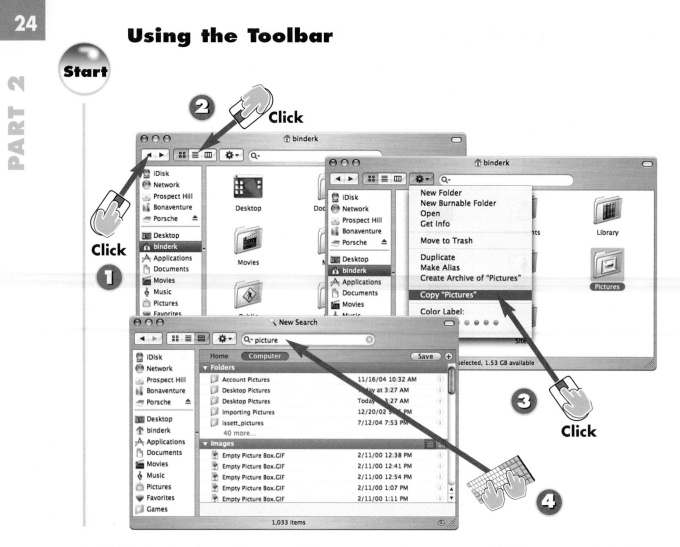

1. Click the **Back** and **Forward** buttons to see the contents of folders you've looked at before in this window.

2. Click the **Icon View**, **List View**, or **Column View** button to change your folder view.

3. Choose an option from the **Action** menu to perform one of several common tasks.

4. Type in the **Search** field to search for files and folders by name.

End

INTRODUCTION

In single-window mode, each window contains a toolbar that provides shortcuts to common tasks in the Finder, such as switching folder views and searching for files. After you get to know the toolbar, it will quickly become your best friend. You can even customize it with your favorite buttons, too—see the next task.

Action Figures

HINT
The commands available in the Action menu vary depending on what's selected. For example, if you click a disk icon, the Action menu adds an Eject command. Be sure to explore your Action menu options by checking the menu with a single file, multiple files, a folder, and a disk selected.

Customizing the Toolbar

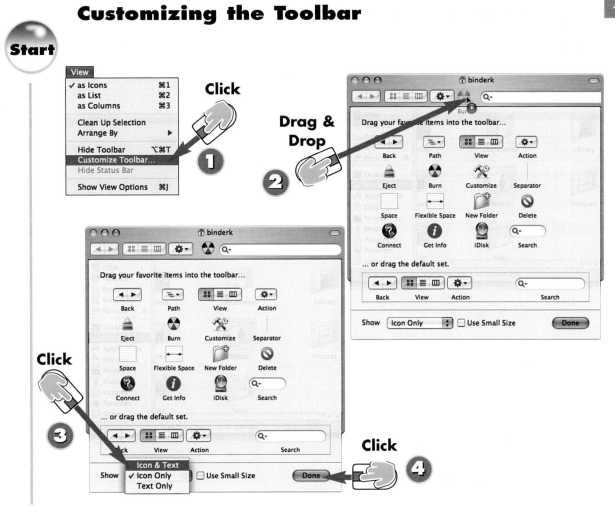

Start

Click ①

Drag & Drop ②

Click ③

Click ④

End

① Choose **View**, **Customize Toolbar**.

② Drag buttons onto the toolbar to add them.

③ Choose an option from the **Show** pop-up menu.

④ Click **Done**.

The row of buttons across the top of a window when you're in single-window mode is called the *toolbar*. These buttons offer you quick access to the most common functions in the Finder, such as changing window views and creating new folders. You can choose which buttons you want to display.

TIP

Back Where You Started
When you're customizing your toolbar, you can restore the default set of buttons by dragging the whole set from the bottom of the Customize dialog box up to the toolbar.

TIP

Cutting Back
To remove buttons from the toolbar, choose **View**, **Customize Toolbar** and drag the buttons you don't want off the toolbar.

Using Different Folder Views

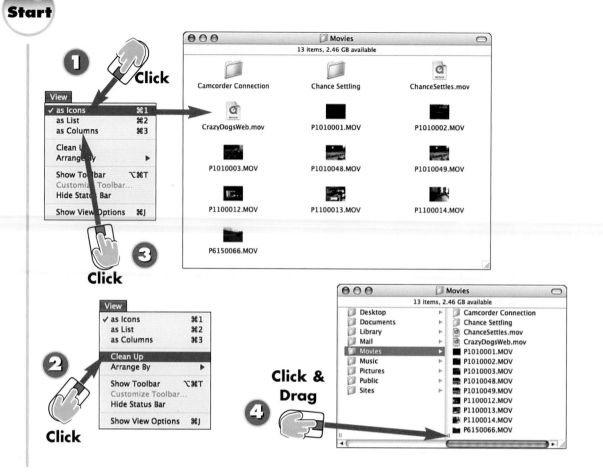

① To switch to Icon view, choose **View**, **as Icons**.

② If the icons are stacked on top of each other, choose **View**, **Clean Up** to space them out so you can see them all.

③ To switch to Column view, choose **View**, **as Columns**.

④ Drag the bar between two columns to adjust the columns' width.

Wide Angle View
To adjust column widths in column view, drag the small double line at the bottom of the column divider. It's only visible if the column contains a list of files and folders; you can't adjust empty columns.

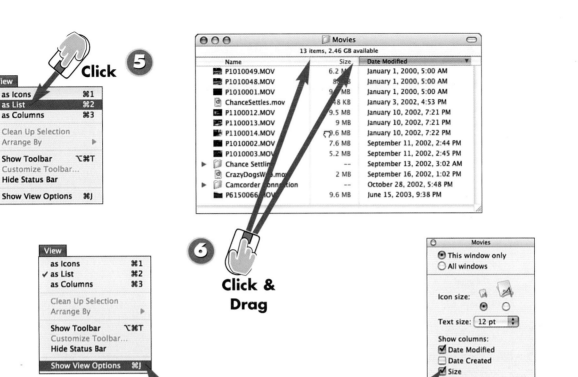

5 To switch to List view, choose **View**, **as List**.

6 Drag the right edge of a list column header to change that column's width, or drag a column header to a different position to change the order of the columns.

7 Choose **View**, **Show View Options** to select which list columns are visible.

8 Check boxes to choose which columns are visible in the active window.

End

Using the Go Menu

Start

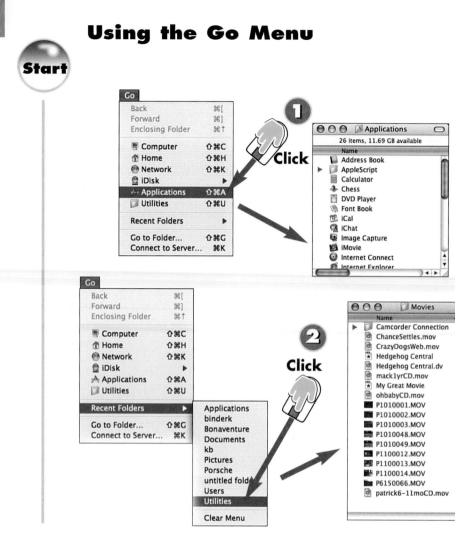

1 To go to one of Mac OS X's special folders, choose **Go** and choose **Computer**, **Home**, **Applications**, or **Utilities**.

2 To go to one of the folders you've opened recently, choose **Go**, **Recent Folders** and choose a folder.

End

INTRODUCTION

To make getting around your system easier, the Go menu contains commands that instantly take you to specific locations, including any of the special folders Mac OS X creates for your programs and documents. The Go menu also keeps track of the last several folders you've opened so you can return to any of them with a single click.

TIP

Using the Keyboard
You can also go to the special folders with keyboard commands. Press ⌘-**Shift-C** to see the Computer window; press ⌘-**Shift-H** to open your home folder; press ⌘-**Shift-A** to open the Applications folder; and press ⌘-**Shift-U** to open the Utilities folder.

Using Folder Pathnames

Start

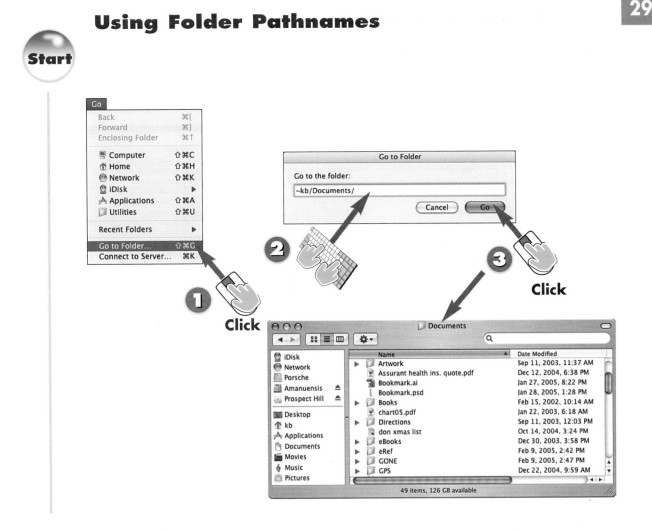

Click

Click

1 In the Finder, choose **Go**, **Go to Folder**.

2 Type the pathname of the folder you want to go to.

3 Click **Go** to open the folder.

End

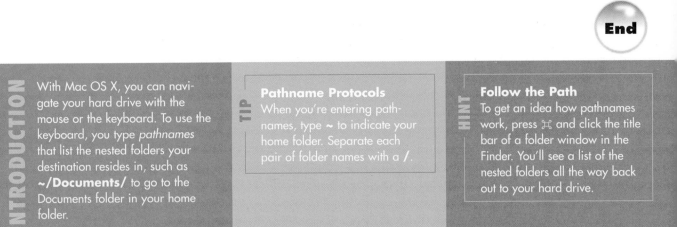

INTRODUCTION

With Mac OS X, you can navigate your hard drive with the mouse or the keyboard. To use the keyboard, you type *pathnames* that list the nested folders your destination resides in, such as **~/Documents/** to go to the Documents folder in your home folder.

TIP

Pathname Protocols
When you're entering pathnames, type ~ to indicate your home folder. Separate each pair of folder names with a /.

HINT

Follow the Path
To get an idea how pathnames work, press ⌘ and click the title bar of a folder window in the Finder. You'll see a list of the nested folders all the way back out to your hard drive.

Selecting Files

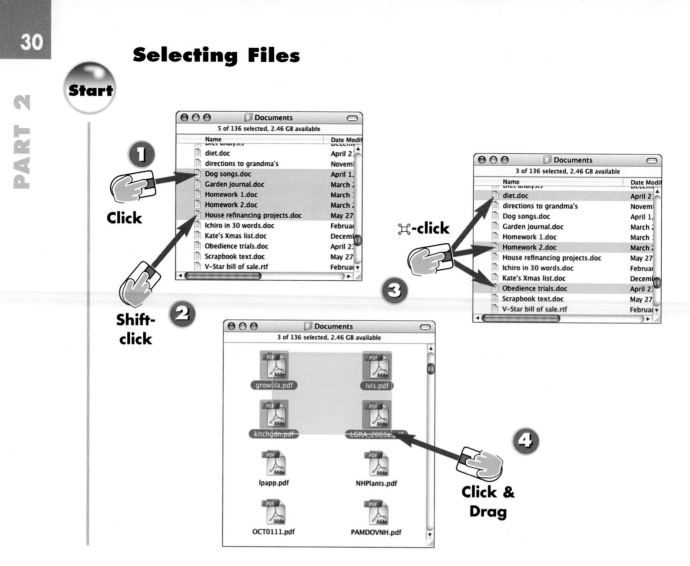

1. In any folder view, click a file or folder to select it.

2. **Shift**-click another file or folder to select it along with all the items between it and the first object you selected.

3. ⌘-click to select noncontiguous items.

4. In icon view, click and drag to select a group of icons.

TIP

Selecting Everything at Once
To select all the items in a folder (or on the desktop), click the folder's title bar to make sure it is the active folder; then either press ⌘-**A** or choose **Edit**, **Select All**.

Moving and Copying Files and Folders

Start

1. To *move* an item to another folder on the same disk, drag and drop it into the folder's window.

2. To *copy* an item to a location on a different disk, drag and drop it into the folder's window.

3. To copy an item to a different location on the same disk, press **Option** while you drag and drop it into the folder's window.

End

TIP

Another Way to Copy
To make a copy of an item in the same place, press **Option** and drag the icon a little away from its current location or choose **File**, **Duplicate**.

TIP

Using Copy and Paste to Copy Files
Ctrl-click the file you want to copy and choose **Copy** from the menu. **Ctrl-click** in an open area of the folder's window where you want to copy the item and choose **Paste Item**.

Making a New Folder

Start

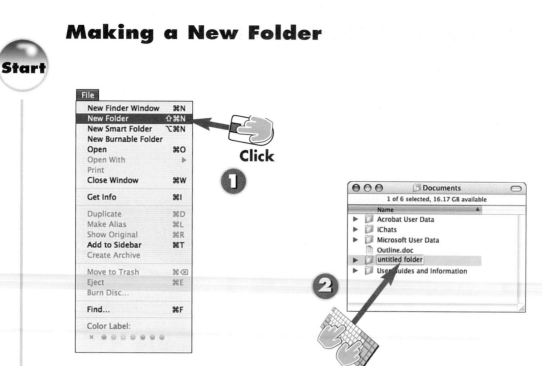

Click

1 To create a new folder, choose **File**, **New Folder** (or press ⌘-**Shift-N**).

2 Type a name for the untitled folder; to change the name, see the next task.

End

INTRODUCTION

This is one task that often trips up long-time Mac users, who are used to pressing ⌘-N to create a new folder. That keyboard shortcut brings up a new Finder window now, instead of creating a new folder. You'll get used to the change, and you'll find that being able to create new Finder windows this way is pretty useful, too.

TIP

You Don't Have to Start from Scratch
If you need several folders with the same name and, perhaps, a different number tacked onto the end of each, create the first one and create copies of it as described earlier in the task "Moving and Copying Files and Folders." Then replace **"copy"** in the folder name with the numbers or text you want.

Renaming Folders and Files

Start

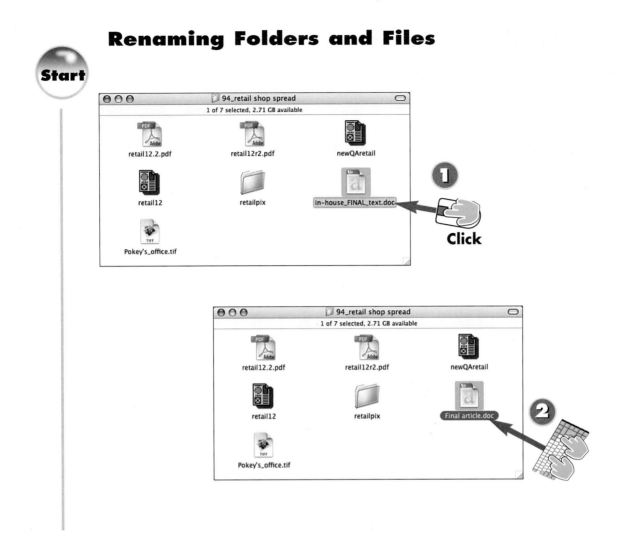

Click

① Click to select the item whose name you want to change and keep the mouse cursor positioned over the name.

② When the item's name becomes highlighted, type to replace the old name with the new one. Press **Enter** when you're done.

End

Some people like to include dates and similar information in filenames so anyone can tell what's inside; others don't care if anyone else can make sense of their filenames. Whichever camp you fall into, you'll need to know how to change the names of files and folders.

Adding Extensions

Don't you hate documents with blank, white icons? You can't open them by double-clicking because your Mac doesn't know which program to use. If you know which kind of document it is, add the correct filename extension so it will open.

Extended Filenames

Filenames have two components: the name and the extension, such as **.pdf** or **.doc**. Mac OS X uses extensions to determine which program can open which files, so don't change an extension unless you know what you're doing.

Handling Files with Automator

Start

Double-click

Click

Drag **Drop**

Drag **Drop**

1 Double-click to start **Automator** (located in the Applications folder).

2 Click **Finder** in the **Library** column to narrow down the available actions.

3 Drag **Get Selected Finder Items** into the workflow area.

4 Drag **New Folder** into the workflow area.

INTRODUCTION

Remember how computers were supposed to make our lives simpler? Well, Automator really does that. With Automator, you can set up a series of steps once, save them as a workflow, and then set that task in motion any time with a mere double-click or drag and drop. Here's how to create a workflow that backs up selected files.

TIP

Running Workflows
Saving a workflow as an application enables you to run it without starting Automator. While it's running, you see a message to that effect in the menu bar; click the red stop sign button to cancel the series of actions.

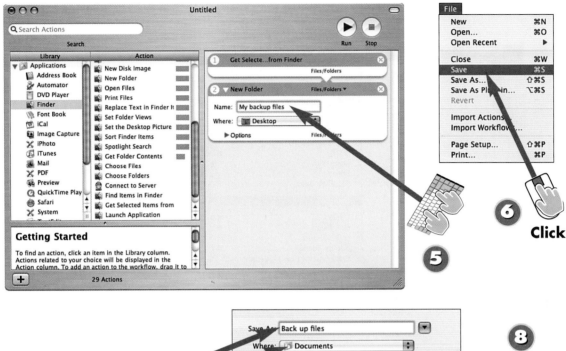

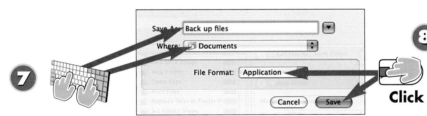

5 Enter a name for the folder the action will create.

6 Choose **File**, **Save**.

7 Give the workflow a name and specify where to save it.

8 Select **Application** from the **File Format** pop-up menu and click **Save**.

End

The Endless Possibilities
You can add other steps to make this workflow more useful. For example, you might add an Archive action to compress the backup folder after the files are copied into it. Another possibility is a Copy action to back up the files to another disk or server.

Making It Happen
To run this workflow, select the files you want to back up and drag them onto the icon of the saved workflow file.

Viewing File Information

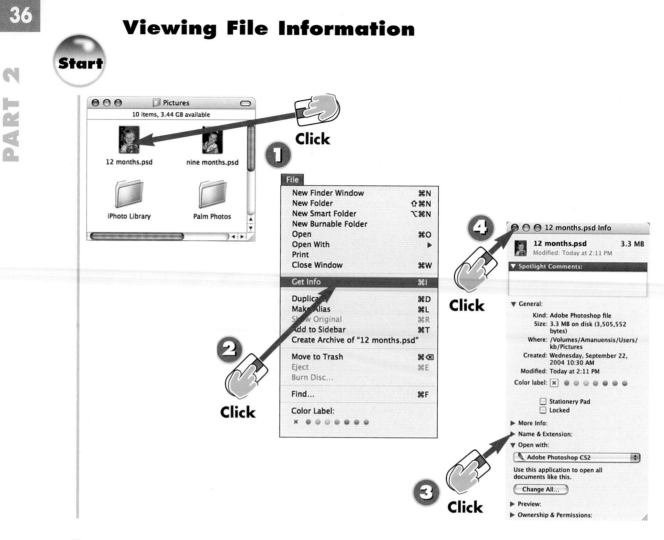

Start

Click

Click

Click

Click

End

1. Click a file to select it.

2. Choose **File**, **Get Info**.

3. The Info window opens to the General pane; to see the contents of another pane, click the gray triangle next to its name.

4. Click the red **Close** button to close the Info window when you're done.

INTRODUCTION

Each file or folder on your computer has a lot of information associated with it—not just the data it contains, such as recipes or pictures or programming code, but data about the file, such as when it was created, the last time it was modified, and which program made it.

TIP

Avoiding a Trip to the Menu Bar

You can also press ⌘-I or use a contextual menu to get information about an item.

HINT

Getting Info

Some file information can be changed in the Info window, if you're the owner of a file. You can change the name and extension, the program that opens a document, and the file's ownership (if you're an *admin user*), and you can add comments.

Opening a File

Start

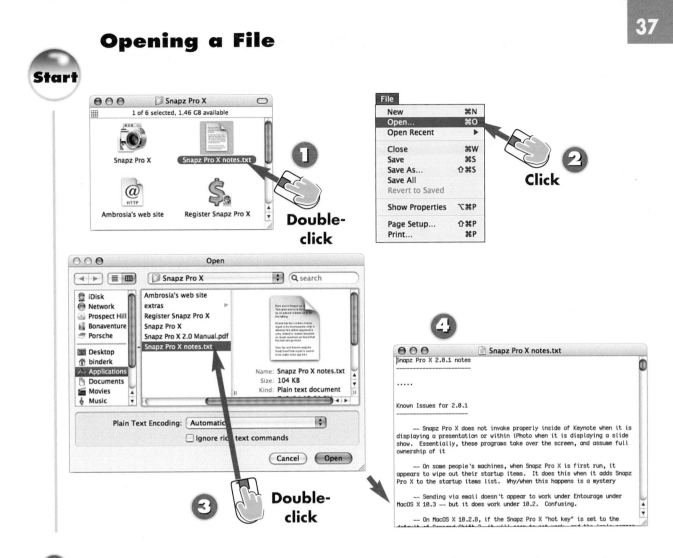

1 Double-click

2 Click

3 Double-click

4

1 In the Finder, double-click the file's icon. The file opens in the program that created it.

2 Or, to open a file from within a running program, choose **File**, **Open**.

3 Navigate to the file in the pick list and double-click it or click **Open**.

4 The file opens in the program window.

End

Choosing a Program to Open a File

Start

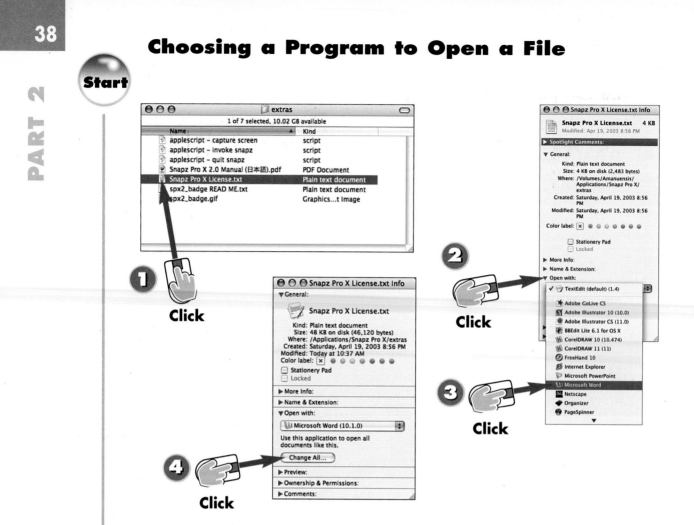

Click

Click

Click

Click

 Click to select the file and press ⌘-I to see its Info window.

 Click the gray triangle next to **Open with** in the Info window.

 Choose an application from the pop-up menu, or choose **Other** to navigate to the program you want if it's not listed.

 Click **Change All** if you want to make the same change for all documents with the same extension.

End

Sometimes you disagree with your Mac about which program it should use to open a file you double-click. For example, perhaps you want to open PDF files in Adobe Reader instead of Preview, or RTF word processor files in Microsoft Word instead of TextEdit. You have the power to make the change—here's how.

TIP

There's More than One Way
The directions here enable you to open a file in the right program by double-clicking its Finder icon. But if you're in a hurry, you can just start the program, choose **File**, **Open** as described earlier in the task "Opening a File."

Deleting a File

Start

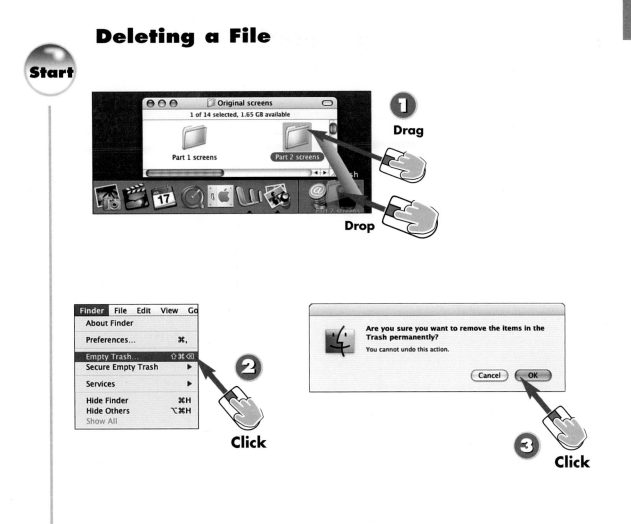

Drag

1

Drop

Click

2

3

Click

1 Drag the file to the **Trash** icon on the Dock and drop it when the Trash icon is highlighted.

2 To delete all the objects in the Trash, choose **Finder**, **Empty Trash**.

3 Click **OK** in the confirmation dialog box or **Cancel** to keep the items in the Trash.

End

Finding Files with Spotlight

 Start

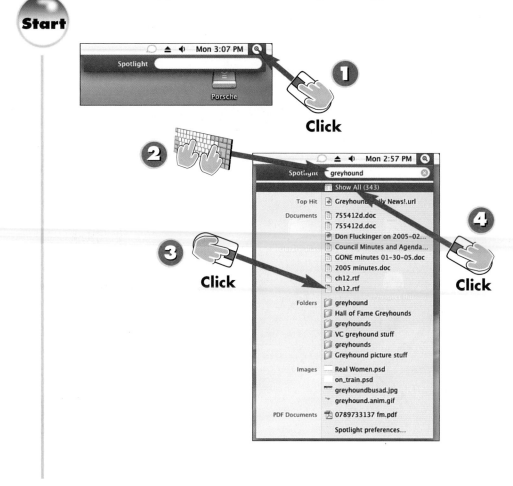

Click

Click

Click

1. Click the **Spotlight** menu to display the search field.

2. Enter search terms in the field.

3. Click a document in the menu to open it.

4. Click **Show All** to see more results.

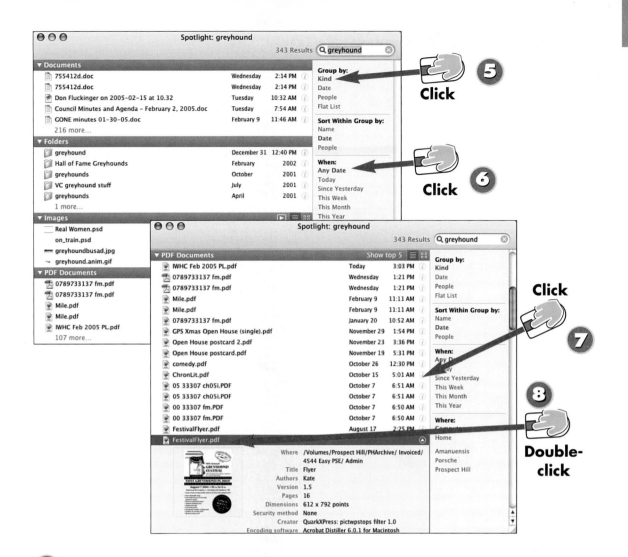

5 Click an option in the sidebar to sort the results differently.

6 Click an option in the sidebar to filter the search results by time or location.

7 Click the **Info** button next to an item in the list to see more information about that file.

8 Double-click an item in the list to open the file.

End

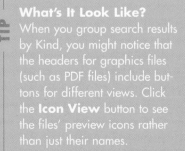

TIP

What's It Look Like?
When you group search results by Kind, you might notice that the headers for graphics files (such as PDF files) include buttons for different views. Click the **Icon View** button to see the files' preview icons rather than just their names.

HINT

Flat Find
The Flat List grouping option eliminates the categories in your search results. In effect, it enables you to throw all the found documents into one pot, so to speak, and then sort them in any order you want.

Creating a Smart Folder

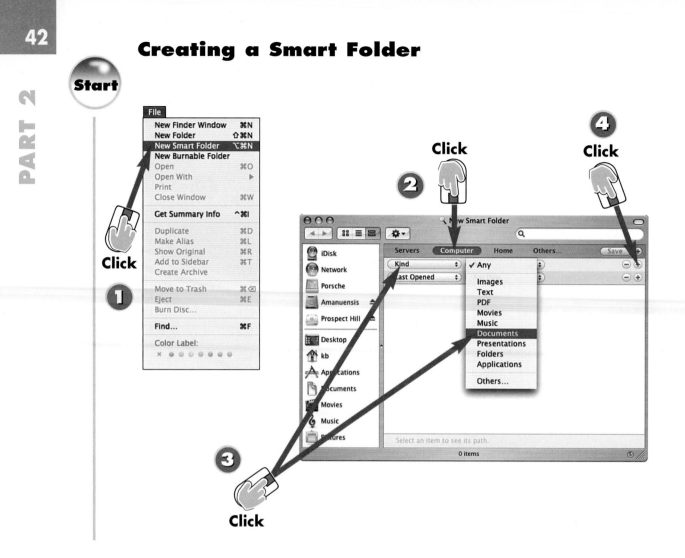

Start

Click ①

Click ②

Click ③

Click ④

1 Choose **File, New Smart Folder**.

2 Click to specify a location for the files you want to track in this folder.

3 Select a search criteria category and make a setting within that category.

4 Click **Add** to add another search criterion, or click **Remove** to remove one.

HINT

On-the-Fly Smarts

The system adds files to the smart folder as soon as you start setting search criteria. Don't worry about ending up with the wrong files in your smart folder, though; as you change the criteria, the folder's contents are updated to reflect the new criteria.

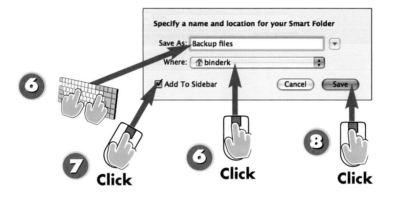

5 Click **Save**.

6 Enter a name and select a location for the folder.

7 Check **Add To Sidebar** if you want the folder to appear in the sidebar when you're using single-window mode.

8 Click **Save**.

End

Creating a Burnable Folder

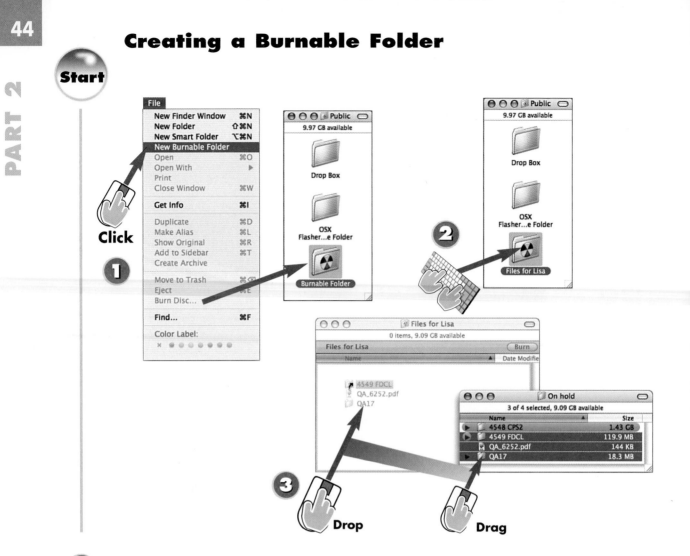

Start

Click

Drop

Drag

1 Choose **File**, **New Burnable Folder**.

2 Type a new name for the folder; this name is also given to the CD you burn from this folder.

3 Drag files and folders into the burnable folder's window to add them to the CD.

But What's It For?
Burnable folders are useful for keeping track of files you regularly transfer to another person or location. Because the file you see in the burnable folder is really just a marker for the real file, you can edit the file in its original location and the changed version is burned to the CD. The burnable folder sticks around after you burn the CD, so you can use it to create regular backups of the same set of files.

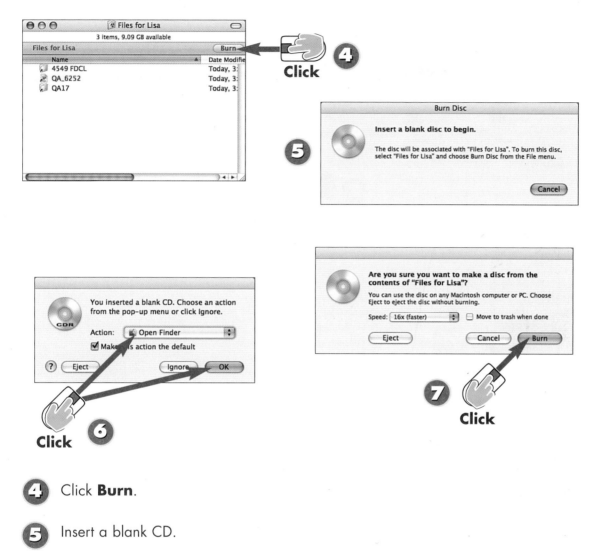

4 Click **Burn**.

5 Insert a blank CD.

6 If the system asks how to handle the CD, choose **Open Finder** and click **OK**.

7 Click **Burn**.

Accessing Your Favorite Files and Places

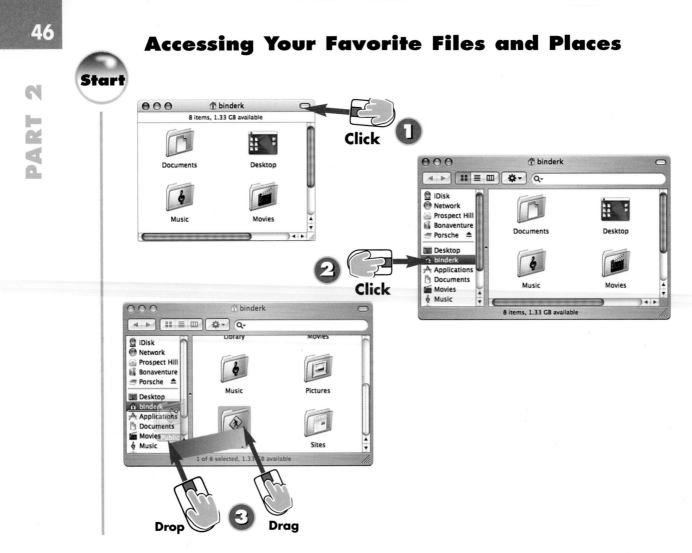

 If you don't see the Places sidebar, click the transparent button at the upper-right corner of the window to enter single-window mode.

 Click a disk or folder to view its contents in the window.

 Drag files or folders into or out of the lower section of the Places sidebar to customize it.

INTRODUCTION

Mac OS X offers a way to store and access your favorites. They're visible in a column called the Places sidebar at the left side of every window when you're using single-window mode. The top section of the Places list contains disks attached to your Mac, and the lower section contains anything you want.

HINT

Quick Copy, Quick Move
You can move or copy files to disks or folders in the Places sidebar by dragging them from the main section of the window over a disk or folder icon in the sidebar.

HINT

Customizing the Custom List
To change the order of items in the bottom half of the Places sidebar, just drag and drop them into the order you prefer. Drag folders out of the lower section of the Places sidebar to remove them from the list.

Organizing Files and Folders with Labels

Start

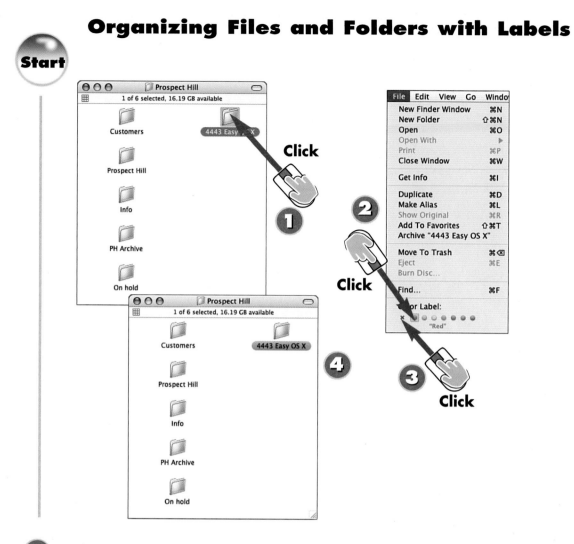

Click **1**

2

Click **3**

4

Click

File Edit View Go Windo
New Finder Window ⌘N
New Folder ⇧⌘N
Open ⌘O
Open With ▶
Print ⌘P
Close Window ⌘W

Get Info ⌘I

Duplicate ⌘D
Make Alias ⌘L
Show Original ⌘R
Add To Favorites ⇧⌘T
Archive "4443 Easy OS X"

Move To Trash ⌘⌫
Eject ⌘E
Burn Disc...

Find... ⌘F

or Label:
✕ ● ● ● ● ● ●
"Red"

1 In the Finder, select a file or folder to label.

2 Open the **File** menu, scroll to the bottom, and choose a label color.

3 To remove a label, choose the **X** at the left end of the color list.

4 The name of the item appears in the chosen color.

End

INTRODUCTION
You can think of labels as actually being color coding. With a label, you can assign a color to a file or folder so that it jumps out at you when you're digging through a folder for it, or you can search for files by label color.

TIP
Sorting by Labels
Choose **View, Show View Options** and click the **Labels** check box to add a Labels column to the window. Then return to the window and click the **Labels** column header to sort by the value in that column.

HINT
Labeling the Fast Way
Adding a label color is one of the things you can do to a file or folder via a contextual menu. Turn to "Using Contextual Menus" in Part 1, "Getting Started," to learn more.

Making an Alias

Start

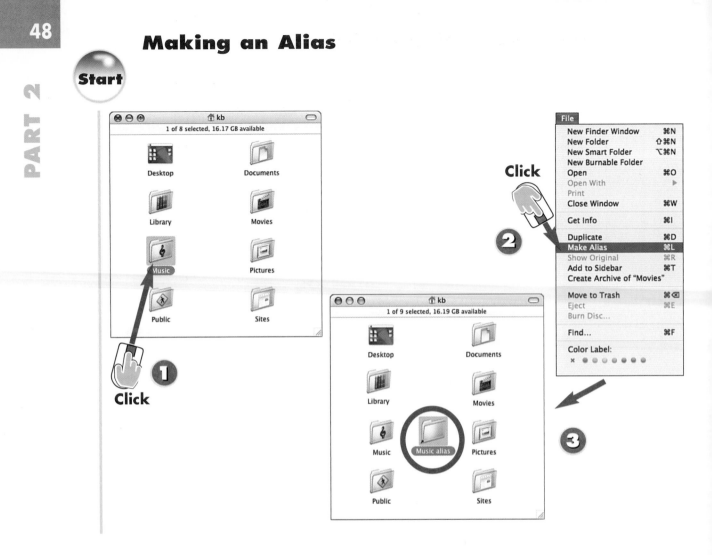

Click

Click

1 Click the original file or folder to select it.

2 Choose **File**, **Make Alias**.

3 Move the alias wherever you want it; you can recognize it by the small arrow in the icon's lower-left corner.

End

An *alias* is a file that links to another file, folder, or program. To make locating and opening an item you've stored several folder levels deep in your home folder or anywhere else on your Mac easier, you can put an alias of that file on your desktop. Deleting an alias does not delete the item it points to.

TIP

Avoid Dock Obesity
One way to put a lot of files in your Dock is to put aliases in a folder, put the folder in your home folder, and drag it into the Dock. When you click and hold the folder's icon in the Dock, you see a list of files from which you can choose.

HINT

One, Two, Many Aliases
You can make as many aliases of an item as you want, and you can store them anywhere that makes sense to you, even on another disk. If your Mac can't find the alias's original when you double-click the alias, it will politely let you know.

Archiving a File or Folder

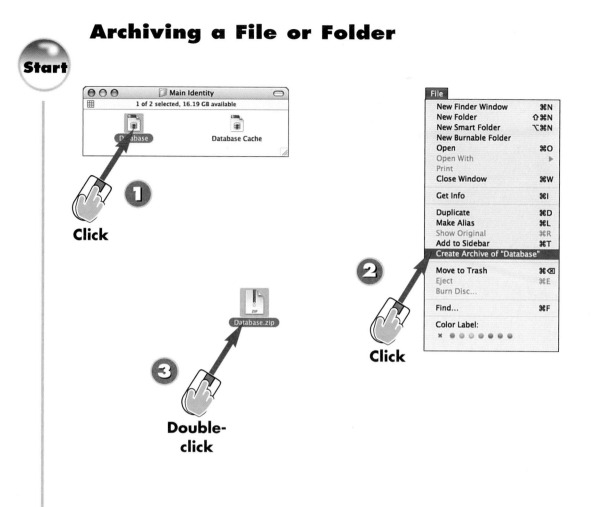

Start

Click ①

Click ②

Double-click ③

① In the Finder, select a file or folder to archive.

② Choose **File**, **Create Archive**.

③ To de-archive a file, double-click the archive.

End

HINT

Watch Out for Archive Clutter
When you de-archive a file, the archive is left intact, so you end up with two copies of the file: the archive and the decompressed version. Watch out for these extra files so that you don't lose track of which is the version you're working on.

Ejecting a Disk

Start

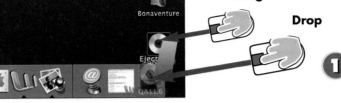

Drag

Drop

①

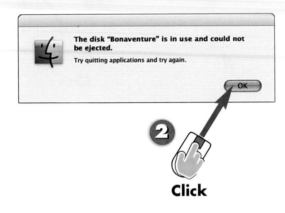

②

Click

① Drag the disk icon to the Dock and drop it on the Eject button to eject the disk.

② If files are open on the disk, the Mac lets you know. Click **OK**, close the open files, and try again.

End

TIP

Alternative Ejection Methods
Don't want to drag a disk to the Dock? Select the disk on the desktop and choose **File**, **Eject**. Or choose **Eject** from its contextual menu. In single-window mode, select the disk in the Places sidebar and click the Eject button next to the disk's icon or choose **Eject** from the Action menu in the window's title bar. Most Mac keyboards also have an Eject key with the same symbol you see in the Places sidebar.

Undoing a Finder Action

Start

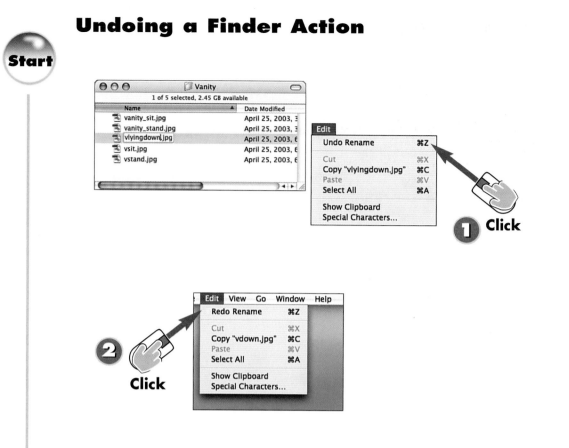

1 Click

2 Click

1 If you mistakenly rename, copy, delete, or move a file or folder, choose **Edit**, **Undo** to restore the item to its original state.

2 To redo the change after undoing it, choose **Edit**, **Redo**.

End

HINT

Fools Rush Ahead
You can't undo some actions, such as duplicating a file or folder or applying a label. In that case, however, you can just drag the unwanted item to the Trash or remove the label via the File menu. Watch out for actions that are harder to reverse, such as actually emptying the Trash, burning a disc, or even rearranging file and folder icons.

Tidying Up Your Folders

Start

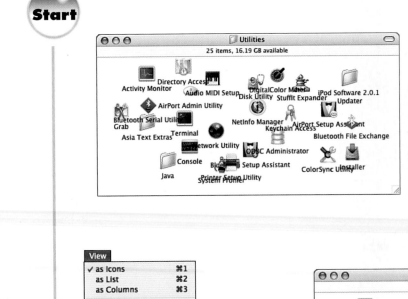

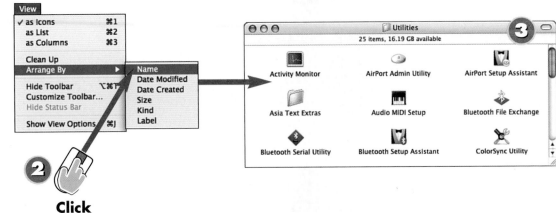

Click

Click

1. With a window open, choose **View**, **Clean Up** to line up the window's icons neatly.

2. Choose **View**, **Arrange** and an option from the submenu to re-sort the icons in your preferred order.

3. The icons are then arranged in the desired order.

End

Constant Organization
To keep the folder organized all the time, choose **View**, **View Options** and click the **Keep arranged by** check box; then choose an option from the pop-up menu. To keep icons lined up on a grid, click the **Snap to Grid** check box.

Bigger Is Better
If you want to enjoy your icons more, try viewing them at a larger size. Choose **View**, **View Options** and drag the slider at the top of the View Options palette to scale icons up to as large as 128 pixels square.

Using Your iDisk

Start

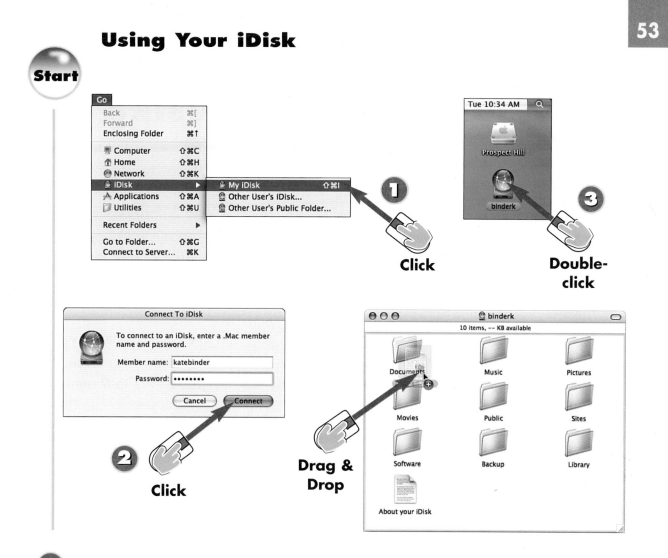

Click

Double-click

Click

Drag & Drop

1 In the Finder, either choose **Go**, **iDisk**, **My iDisk** or press ⌘-**Shift-I**.

2 If you haven't entered your .Mac username and password in System Preferences, type that information into the dialog box that appears and click **Connect**.

3 Double-click the iDisk's icon to view its contents.

4 Drag files into the iDisk's folders to copy them to the iDisk.

End

INTRODUCTION

Apple's special online services for Mac users, referred to collectively as .Mac (dot-Mac), include the use of an *iDisk*—an online storage area. You can mount your iDisk right on your desktop, where it appears along with your hard drive and any removable disks you insert (Zip disks, DVDs, or CDs).

TIP

Keeping Your iDisk at Home
For easy access to your iDisk, go to the **.Mac** pane in **System Preferences**. Click **iDisk** and click the **Create a local copy of your iDisk** check box. The iDisk copy appears on your desktop all the time; changes you make to it are automatically made to the real iDisk.

Installing and Using Applications

The programs make using your Mac worthwhile, whether it's the applications that come with Mac OS X (such as Preview, TextEdit, and Safari) or the ones you buy and install yourself (such as Microsoft Word, Adobe Photoshop, or your favorite games). Most of the software you'll use every day runs natively in Mac OS X, but you can still use older programs that require Mac OS 9 by running them in Classic.

Classic is like a computer within your computer; with this system feature, you can start up a Mac OS 9 "bubble" in which Mac OS 9 programs can run. When you're using a Classic program, you'll see the gray Mac OS 9 menu bar and the rainbow-colored Apple menu icon instead of the white Mac OS X menu bar and blue Apple menu icon.

In this part you'll learn how to use a couple of the system's built-in programs, how to install new programs, how to switch among multiple programs running at the same time, and more techniques to make your Mac day run smoothly. You'll also learn how to start up and run Classic so you can use those older applications.

Mac OS X's Programs

Create text documents with TextEdit

Apply text formatting with the Font Panel

Force programs to quit

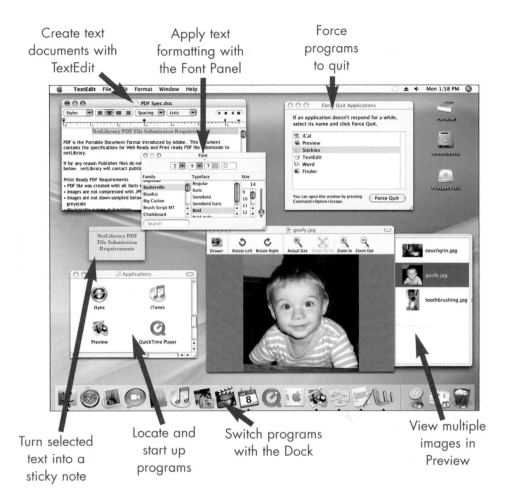

Turn selected text into a sticky note

Locate and start up programs

Switch programs with the Dock

View multiple images in Preview

Installing Programs

Start

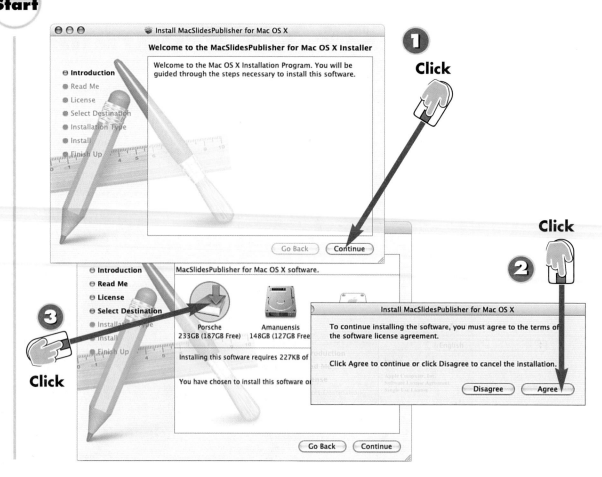

① After you read each screen of the installer, click the **Continue** button at the bottom of the window to move to the next screen.

② Read the program information and the license agreement; then click **Agree** to agree to the license terms (or **Disagree** if you don't want to install the program after all).

③ If you have more than one hard drive, choose the drive where you want to install the software.

Some Mac programs are small enough that you can drag them off their disks right into the Applications folder, but others require an installer program to make sure all their pieces get to the right places. When you run Apple's Installer, you have to enter an admin password to authorize the installation.

Applications in the Applications Folder

You can install programs anywhere you want, but it's best to put them in the Applications folder on your startup drive. That way all users of your Mac can run the programs.

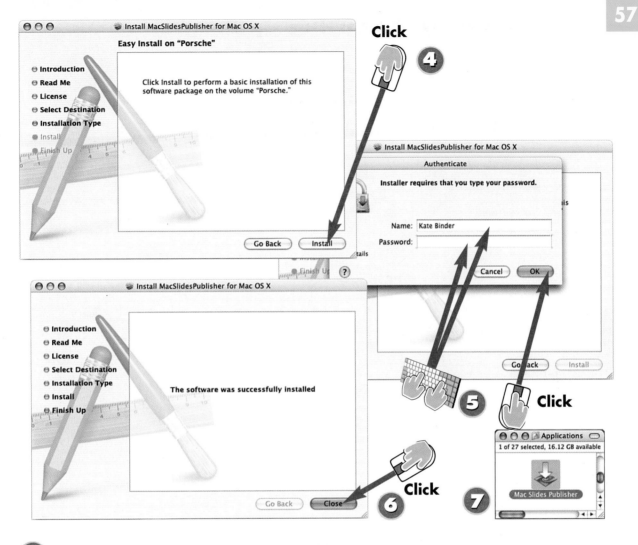

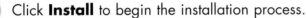

4 Click **Install** to begin the installation process.

5 Enter an admin username and password to authorize the installation and click **OK**.

6 When the installation is complete, click **Close** to quit Installer.

7 The application's icon now appears in the Applications folder (or whatever folder you chose).

End

Installation Options

Many installer scripts ask you to choose whether to install optional software such as sample files, fonts, or bonus features. The Easy Install or Full Install option usually installs everything that's available.

Easy Uninstalling

Some installer programs have an Uninstall option in case you decide you no longer want the software installed on your Mac. Using an installer to uninstall programs ensures that all the extra pieces scattered through your system are uninstalled.

Finding and Starting Up Programs

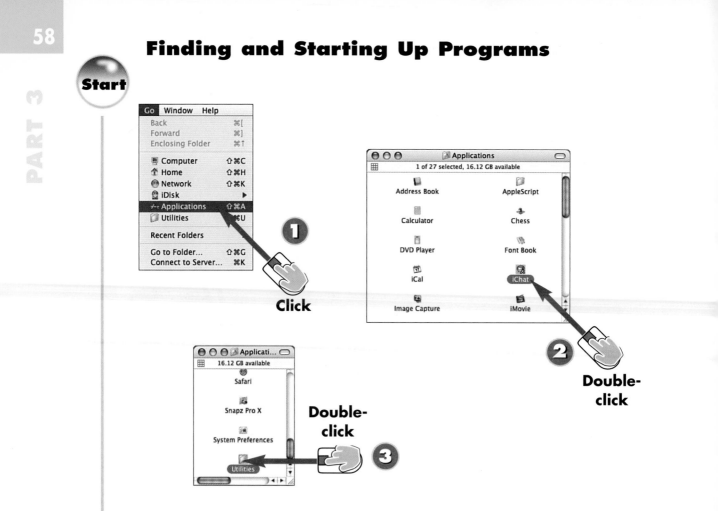

Click

Double-click

Double-click

1. In the Finder, either press ⌘-**Shift-A** or choose **Go**, **Applications** to open the Applications folder.

2. Locate the program you want to use and double-click its icon to start it up.

3. If you can't find a program, look in the Utilities folder within the Applications folder.

End

Mac OS X is a very structured operating system, with a place for everything and everything in its place. Applications are no exception to this rule; all your programs live in the Applications folder where you and other users of your Mac can find them easily.

Control Your Programs

If the wrong program starts up when you double-click a document in the Finder, you need to specify a different program to open that type of document. Press ⌘-**I** to see the document's information and select an application in the **Open with** section of the Info window. Click **Change All** if you want the new program to open all documents of this type.

Saving Files

Start

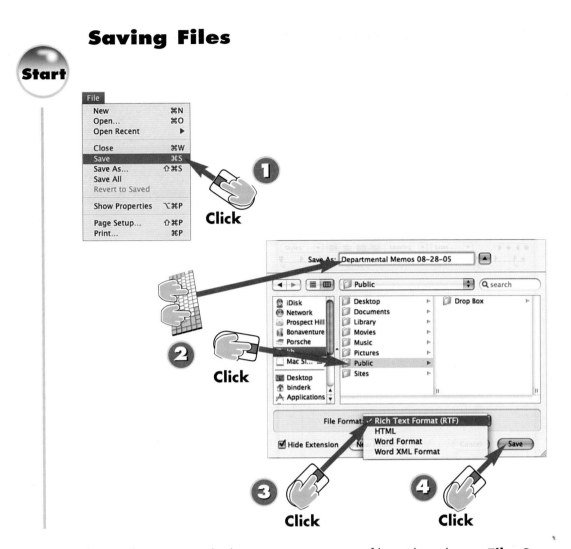

End

1 In the application in which you want to save a file, either choose **File**, **Save** or press ⌘-**S**.

2 Give the file a name and choose a location in the pick list. If you don't see the pick list, click the blue arrow button next to the Save As field.

3 Choose file options such as format and compression (the available options vary depending on the program).

4 Click **Save**.

Writing with TextEdit

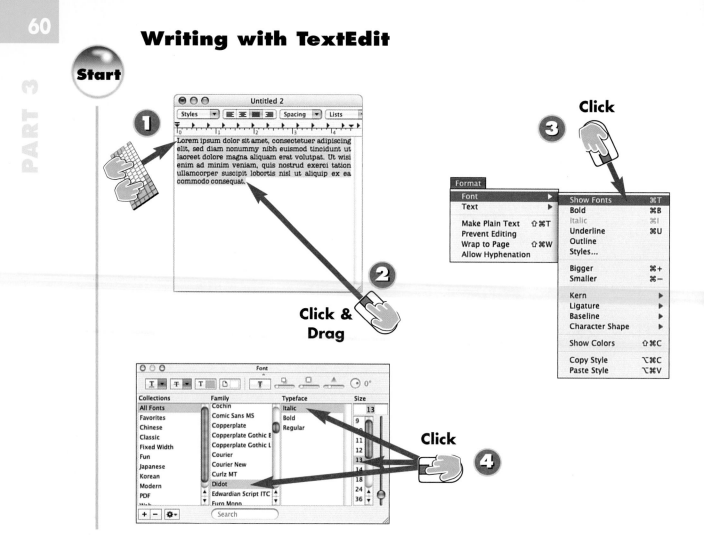

1. Start **TextEdit** (located in the Applications folder) and begin typing in the new document window.

2. To copy text to another location, click and drag to select the text and press ⌘-**C**; place the cursor where you want the text to appear and press ⌘-**V** to paste it.

3. To change the font, select the text and choose **Format**, **Font**, **Show Fonts**.

4. Choose a new font, typeface, and size in the Font panel. The change is applied immediately.

INTRODUCTION

Successor to TeachText and SimpleText, Mac OS X's TextEdit program can do a lot more than either of its ancestors. It's really a very compact, fast word processor with a lot of formatting options and tools as well as the capability to read and write Microsoft Word documents.

HINT

What's *Not* in There
TextEdit is capable, especially with new features such as automatic bulleted lists, but it's not a full-featured word processor. If you need to use paragraph styles, outlining, or HTML conversion, you should use a program such as Microsoft Word.

TIP

Learning How to Spell
TextEdit gives questionable words a red underline; **Control-click** each and choose an option from the contextual menu. The Learn Spelling command adds the word to a systemwide dictionary, so all your built-in applications will know it in the future.

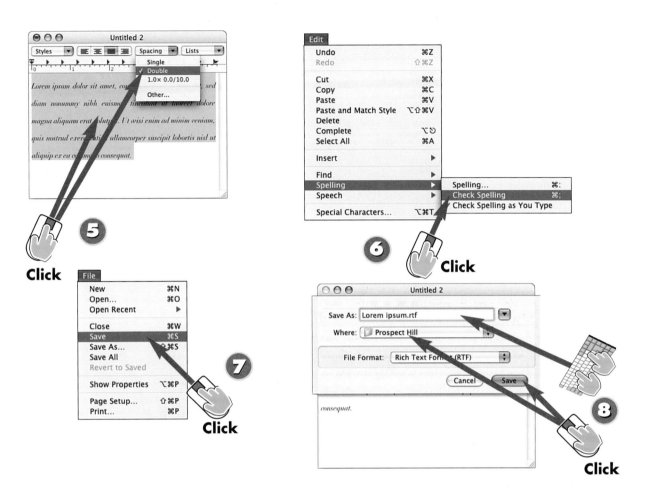

Click

Click

Click

Click

5 To change the text alignment or spacing, click and drag to select the text and choose an option from the controls at the top of the document window.

6 To run a spell check, choose **Edit**, **Spelling**, **Check Spelling**.

7 Choose **File**, **Save** to save the file.

8 Give the file a name and choose a location to save it in; then click **Save**.

End

Getting What You Pay For
TextEdit's capability to open and save files in Microsoft Word format could keep you from having to invest in Word. TextEdit doesn't support Word's entire feature set, however, so some advanced features such as tables and hyperlinks can be lost when you edit a Word file in TextEdit.

Word Compatibility
When you're saving your document in step 8, you can choose RTF (Rich Text Format) or Word format. Either way, your document can be opened in Microsoft Word and retains all its formatting.

Using the Font Panel

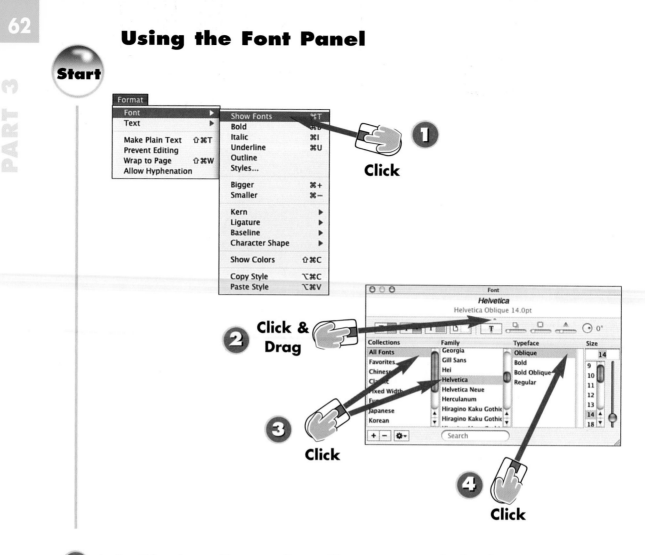

Start

Click

Click & Drag

Click

Click

1. In TextEdit, choose **Format**, **Font**, **Show Fonts** to display the Font panel.

2. Click the dot below the window's title bar and drag downward to reveal the preview area.

3. Click **All Fonts** in the Collections column and choose a font family from the Family column.

4. Choose a style from the Typeface column.

Mac OS X handles fonts very well. A lot of thought went into designing ways to make excellent typography more accessible to the average Mac user. The Font panel, which is the same in all the built-in applications, is part of that effort—it contains a wide variety of settings, from basic to advanced, for modifying the way text is formatted.

Favorite Type Styles

If you create a combination of type settings you plan to use again, click the **Action** menu at the bottom of the Font panel and choose **Add to Favorites**. Then you can apply this style to other text selections by choosing **Font**, **Style** from the menu bar.

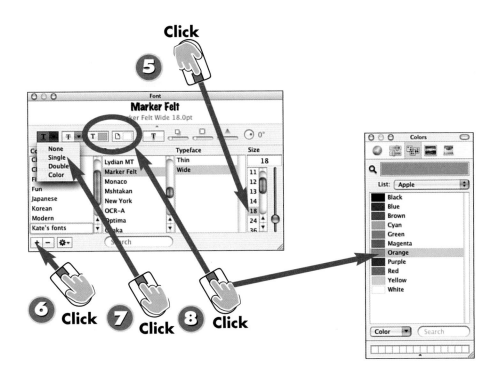

Click 5

Click 6 **Click** 7 **Click** 8

5 Choose a size from the Size column, or enter a value above the column.

6 Click the **Add** button to create a new font collection.

7 Click the **Strikethrough** or **Underline** button and choose an option to add strikethrough or underline style to the selected text.

8 Click the **Text Color** and **Paper Color** buttons to open the Colors panel; then choose a color for the text or the background.

Beyond the Font Basics
If you're interested in working more specifically with type, check out the Font Book program (located in the Utilities folder within Applications). This utility helps you install and manage fonts.

Collectible Fonts
Collections of your corporate fonts or the fonts for a particular project enable you to access those fonts without digging through a long list of fonts. To add a font to a collection, just drag its name from the Family column on top of the collection name.

Sending Text to TextEdit

Start

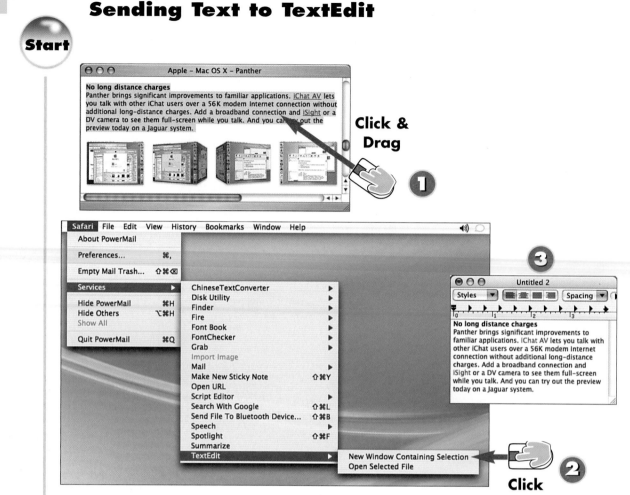

Click & Drag

1

3

2

Click

1 Select the range of text you want to move into TextEdit.

2 From the Application menu, choose **Services**, **TextEdit**, **New Window Containing Selection**.

3 The text appears in an untitled TextEdit window. Save the file as directed earlier in the task "Writing with TextEdit."

End

In each program's Application menu (the menu named after the program), you'll find a Services command with submenus named after other programs. You can use this service to copy text from Mail, Safari, or another program into a brand-new document in TextEdit.

Why Services Rule
Why use this service when you could just copy and paste the text? Because it's less intrusive; you stay in the program you're using, and the text is sent to TextEdit in the background to await your attention.

Turning Text into a New Sticky Note

Start

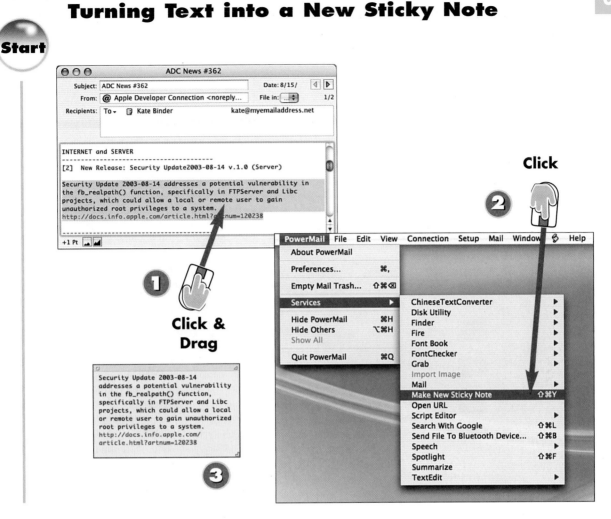

Click

2

1

Click & Drag

3

1 Click and drag to select the range of text you want to make into a sticky note.

2 From the Application menu, choose **Services**, **Make New Sticky Note**.

3 The selected text appears in a sticky note on your desktop.

End

INTRODUCTION

This is one of the most convenient services in Mac OS X. It works the same way as the text to TextEdit service described in the previous task, only it starts up Stickies and creates a new note to hold the text. If you're like most Mac users, you'll use this task a dozen times a day.

HINT

Making Stickies Less Obtrusive
If you use Stickies a lot but the millions of floating stickies drive you crazy, try keeping it hidden by choosing **Stickies**, **Hide Stickies**. You can switch quickly to Stickies using the Dock, so they're always there when you need them, just not in your way.

Viewing Images with Preview

Start

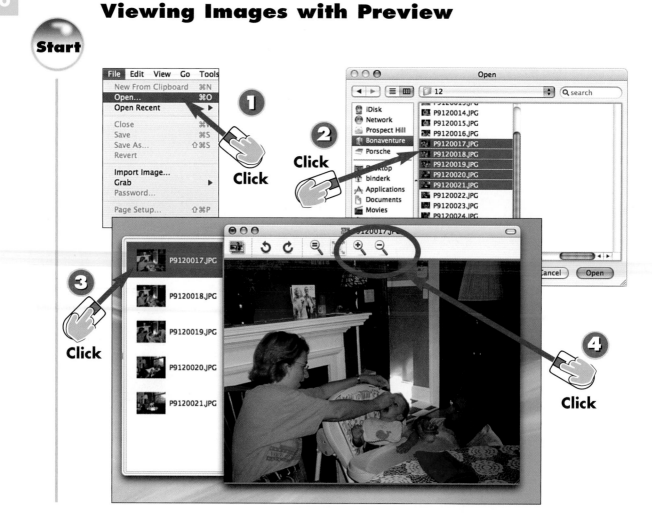

Click

Click

Click

Click

1. Start up Preview (located in the Applications folder) and choose **File**, **Open**.

2. Choose the images you want to open in the pick list and click **Open**.

3. Click a thumbnail to switch images.

4. Click the **Zoom In** and **Zoom Out** buttons to view the image at a different magnification (press ⌘-**B** if you don't see the toolbar).

Preview is a handy program designed for two purposes: looking at pictures and opening PDF files. It works well for both of those jobs. You can't edit either graphic images or PDFs with Preview, but that's not what it's for. Preview's drawer feature makes it particularly useful for reviewing several images at once, all in a single window.

Converting Formats
To save an image in a different format from within Preview, choose **File**, **Export**. In the Export dialog box, give the file a new name and select a location and a format; then click **Save**.

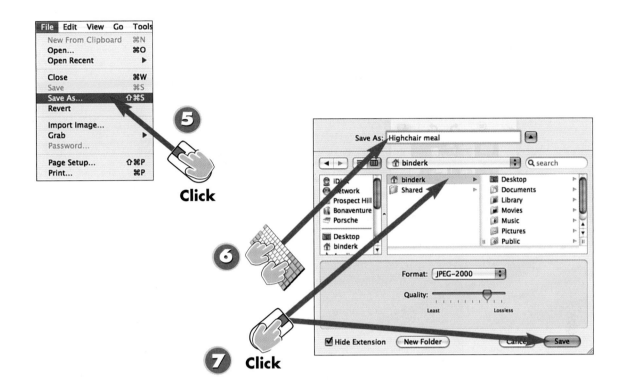

⑤ Choose **File**, **Save As** to save the file with a different name.

⑥ In the Save As dialog box, give the file a new name.

⑦ Choose a location; then click **Save**.

End

Getting Your Thumbnails in Order
Preview's drawer shows you largish thumbnails accompanied by the images' filenames. But you can change the size of the thumbnail images or get rid of them and just view the filenames. Choose **Preview, Preferences** and click **General** to make the change.

PDFs in Preview
Mac OS X is set to automatically open PDF files in Preview. When you're viewing a PDF file, the arrows at the left end of the window's toolbar enable you to move from page to page.

Playing DVDs

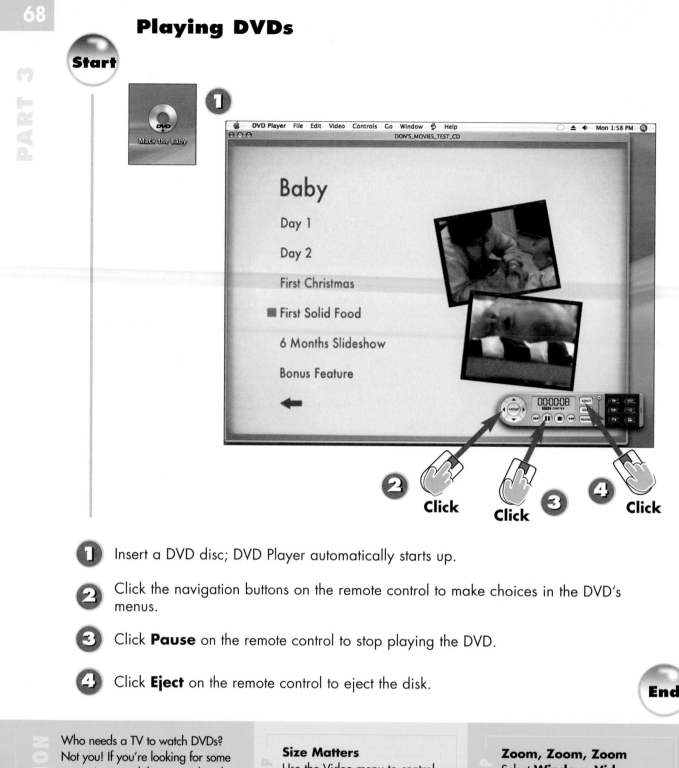

1. Insert a DVD disc; DVD Player automatically starts up.

2. Click the navigation buttons on the remote control to make choices in the DVD's menus.

3. Click **Pause** on the remote control to stop playing the DVD.

4. Click **Eject** on the remote control to eject the disk.

Who needs a TV to watch DVDs? Not you! If you're looking for some entertainment while you work in the office, or if you just don't feel like getting up and moving to the living room, you can play DVDs right on your Mac. Mac OS X includes a full-featured DVD Player program that can do at least as much as your living room DVD player.

Size Matters
Use the Video menu to control the size of the virtual TV screen. Select **Half Size**, **Normal Size**, **Maximum Size**, or **Enter Full Screen** (to get rid of the window and hide the desktop entirely).

Zoom, Zoom, Zoom
Select **Window**, **Video Zoom** to zoom in on an area of the screen as the video plays or while it's paused.

Watching QuickTime Movies

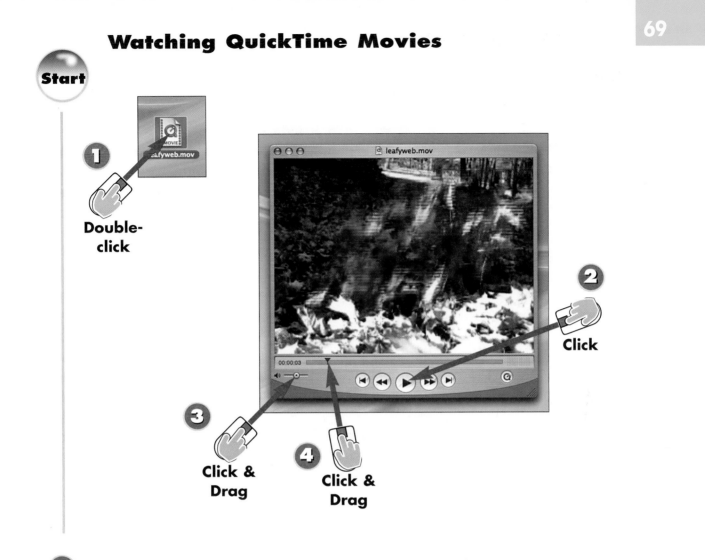

Start

1 Double-click

2 Click

3 Click & Drag

4 Click & Drag

① Double-click a QuickTime video file to start up QuickTime Player.

② Click **Play** to begin playing the movie.

③ Click and drag the **Volume** slider to adjust the sound volume.

④ Click and drag the scrubber slider to move to a different part of the movie.

End

INTRODUCTION

You can think of QuickTime Player as your personal filmstrip viewer. It's not for making movies (use iMovie for that); it's just for watching them. It starts up quickly, plays several types of movie files, and is easy to control with buttons at the bottom of each movie window.

HINT

Going Pro
The QuickTime Player has Pro features you can access if you're willing to drop $29.99 on a registration number. With Pro, you can save movies in different formats and edit movies to some degree. Select **QuickTime Player**, **Buy QuickTime Player Pro** to upgrade.

Switching Programs with the Dock

Start

1 **Click**

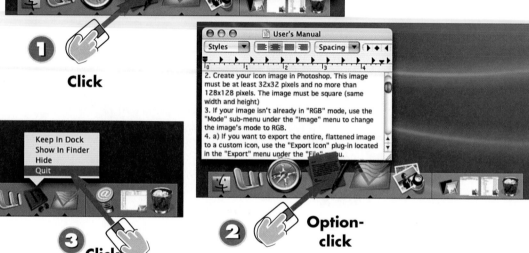

2 **Option-click**

Keep In Dock
Show In Finder
Hide
Quit

3 **Click**

 Move your mouse to the bottom of the screen and click a program icon on the Dock.

 To hide windows belonging to the current program when you switch to the new program, press **Option** as you click.

 To quit a program you're not using, click and hold its Dock icon (or **Control**-click) and choose **Quit** from the contextual menu.

End

The Dock acts as central storage for running programs and frequently used programs, but it has other functions, too. One of those is as an application switcher—a method of bringing different programs to the foreground so you can use them in turn. The Dock's location at the bottom of the screen makes it the most convenient way to switch applications.

Don't Touch That Mouse!
If you prefer to use the keyboard to switch programs, press ⌘-**Tab** to see a list of the currently running programs in the center of the screen. Press ⌘-Tab as many times as needed to cycle through the list to the program you want.

Hiding Programs

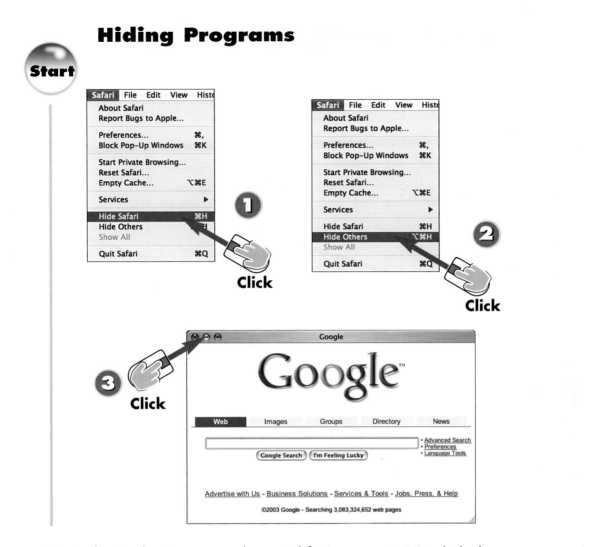

Start

Click

Click

Click

1 In the Application menu, choose **Hide** (or press ⌘-**H**) to hide the program you're currently using.

2 In the Application menu, choose **Hide Others** (or press ⌘-**Option-H**) to hide all other programs that are currently running.

3 To get one window out of the way instead of hiding the program, double-click its title bar or click the yellow **Minimize** button to send it to the Dock.

End

INTRODUCTION

Mac OS X enables you to run many programs at the same time because it hands over memory to each program as it's needed. But if you do like to run multiple programs, your screen can get pretty cluttered. Hiding program windows and palettes is a lifesaver for people who never quit programs until they shut down their Macs.

TIP

Another Way to Hide
Another way to hide programs is to **Option-click** the desktop or a window from another program to simultaneously switch to the Finder or the other program, respectively, and hide the previous program.

HINT

A Window Exposé
Yet another way to maneuver among running programs and open windows is to use a feature introduced with Panther: Exposé. Turn to "Managing Multiple Windows" in Part 1, "Getting Started."

Forcing Programs to Quit

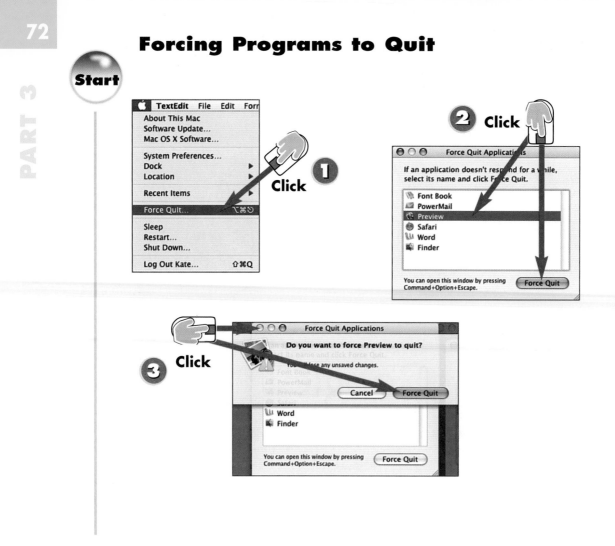

Start

Click ①

Click ②

Click ③

① Choose **Apple menu**, **Force Quit** or press ⌘-**Option-Esc**.

② In the Force Quit Applications dialog box, choose the program you want to quit and click **Force Quit**.

③ Click **Force Quit** again and click the **Close** button to dismiss the dialog box.

End

Macs are great, but that doesn't mean they're perfect. From time to time, a program might act up, refusing to do what you want or perhaps refusing to do anything at all. When this happens and the regular Quit command doesn't work, you can force that program to quit.

Red Alert
If a program's name appears in red in the Force Quit Applications dialog box, that program is being particularly uncooperative. This indicates that the program is not only ignoring your wishes, but also not responding to the system.

Quitting Safely
In earlier Mac systems, force quitting a program disrupted the entire system, so it was a good idea to restart your Mac, but that's no longer the case. Force quitting is now entirely safe, guaranteed not to crash your Mac.

Starting and Stopping Classic

Start

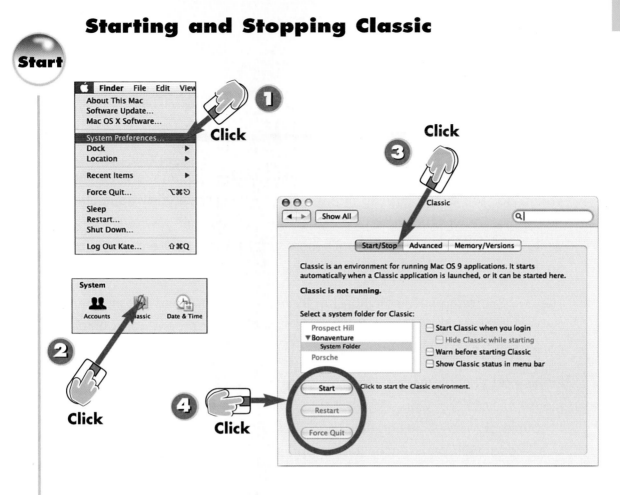

Click

Click

Click

Click

1. Choose **Apple menu**, **System Preferences**.

2. Click **Classic** to open the Classic pane.

3. Click **Start/Stop**, and then click the **Start** button to run Classic.

4. Click **Stop** to shut down Classic, **Restart** to start Classic up again, or **Force Quit** if it has crashed.

End

INTRODUCTION

Classic is a special environment inside your system where you can run Mac OS 9. If you want to use software that doesn't run in Mac OS X, Classic is the way to do that. Normally, double-clicking a Classic application or document starts up Classic, but you can start it up independently if you need more control over it.

Classic for Experts

The Advanced pane in Classic preferences enables you to perform system maintenance on Classic as you would on a free-standing Mac OS 9 system. You can control how it starts up or rebuild its desktop as well as putting it to sleep when it's not being used.

Setting System Preferences

Preferences make the world go round—or, at least, they make your Mac more *your* Mac. You can control so many aspects of your everyday computing experience that it's worth a trip to the System Preferences window every once in a while just to remind yourself what's there. Be sure to explore all the tabs of each preference pane, too, to make sure you know what all your options are.

The System Preferences command in the Apple menu opens a command center for preferences. It contains buttons for each preference pane, organized into categories.

In this part you'll learn how to set preferences for everything from how your mouse or trackpad works to what size objects are displayed on your monitor. A couple of tasks—"Setting Trackpad Preferences" and "Monitoring Battery Use"—deal with preferences for laptop users only; if your Mac isn't an iBook or a PowerBook, you won't even see these settings, so don't worry about them.

The System Preferences Window

Automatically open the right program for each type of disc

Change monitor settings

Minimize energy consumption

Customize mouse and keyboard settings

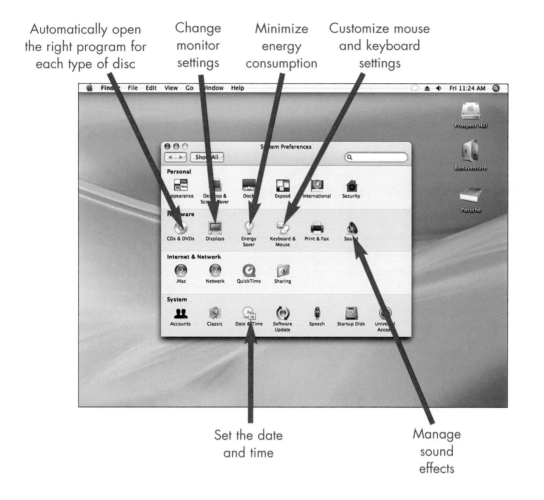

Set the date and time

Manage sound effects

Setting System Preferences

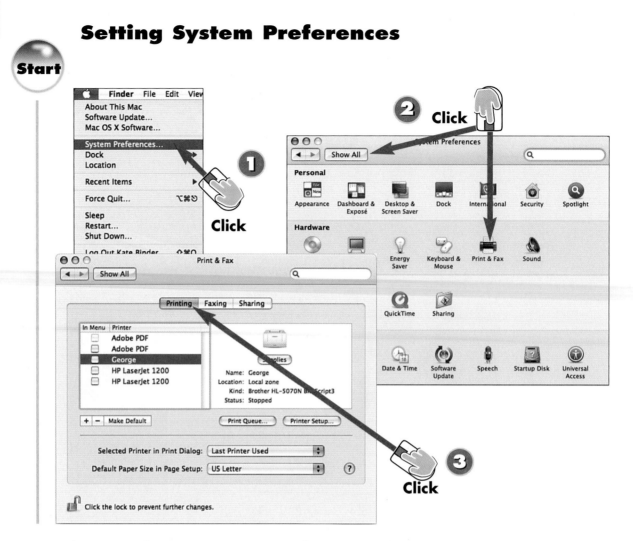

1 Choose **Apple menu**, **System Preferences** to display the System Preferences window.

2 Click **Show All** to see all the icons; then click the icon for the preferences you want to change.

3 Click buttons across the top of the preference pane to access various settings.

In a flashback to the days of the Mac's System 6, Mac OS X stores all its preferences in a central window called System Preferences. It's accessible via the Apple menu, so you can reach it from any program. Third-party preference panes can also be found in System Preferences.

Haven't I Been Here Before?
To go back to a preference pane you've just visited, click the left arrow at the top of the System Preferences window. The left and right arrows work like the ones in a web browser to take you forward and back.

Asking for Directions
Not sure which preferences pane to head for? Type a word or two into the search field in the upper-right corner of the System Preferences window, and you'll get a task menu that takes you to the right place for each possible setting.

Print & Fax

Show All

Printing Faxing Sharing

In Menu | Printer
☐ Adobe PDF
☐ Adobe PDF
☐ George
☐ HP LaserJet 1200
☐ HP LaserJet 1200

Supplies

Name: George
Location: Local zone
Kind: Brother HL-5070N BR-Script3
Status: Stopped

+ − Make Default   Print Queue...   Printer Setup...

Selected Printer in Print Dialog: Last Printer Used
Default Paper Size in Page Setup: US Letter (?)

🔓 Click the lock to prevent further changes.

4 Click

Authenticate

System Preferences requires that you type your password.

Name: Kate Binder
Password: ••••••••
▶ Details

(?)   Cancel   OK

5 Click

4 Lock the preferences by clicking the **padlock** icon.

5 If the preferences are locked (indicated by a closed padlock icon in the lower-left corner of the window), enter an admin name and password when prompted and click **OK**.

End

Down by the Dock
If you haven't changed what's in your Dock since you got your Mac or installed Mac OS X, you'll find System Preferences there. You don't have to leave it there, but if you make many trips to the System Preferences, the Dock can be quicker.

Now You Know Your ABCs
If the System Preference categories don't make sense to you, so that you're always hunting for the icon you want, choose **View**, **Organize Alphabetically**. This command reorders the icons in good old alphabetical order, instead of dividing them by category.

Changing Your Alert Sound

Start

Click **①**

Click **②**

Click **③**

Click & Drag **④**

① Click the **Sound** icon in the System Preferences window to display the sound preferences.

② Click the **Sound Effects** tab to see your choices.

③ Click a sound in the pick list to hear it.

④ Click and drag the **Alert volume** slider to set the volume level for alert sounds. **End**

The alert sound is that annoying beep you hear when you do something your Mac doesn't like or when you tell it to do something it can't do. The nice part about this is that you can change the sound that's played, as well as adjusting its volume independently of the system's overall volume level.

HINT

Blowing Your Own Horn
If you don't like any of the alert sound choices, you can add your own. They must be in AIFF format, and you need to store them in the Sounds folder within the Library folder within the System folder on your main hard drive.

Changing Display Settings

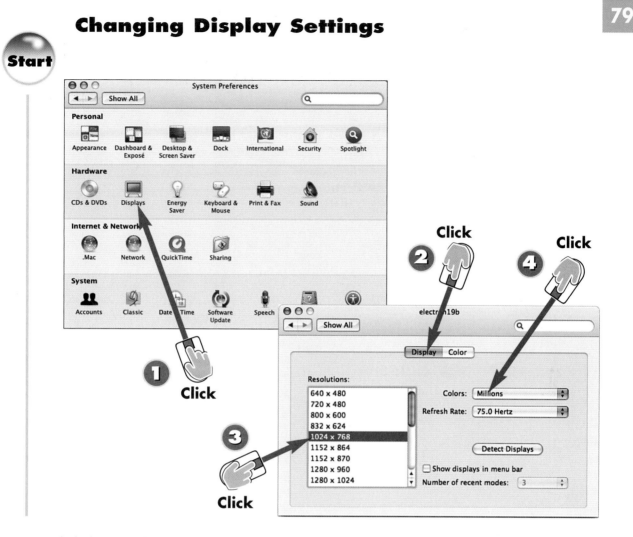

Start

Click

Click

Click

Click

1. Click the **Displays** icon in the System Preferences window to display monitor preferences.

2. Click the **Display** tab to see your choices.

3. Click a setting in the **Resolutions** pick list to determine the scale of the images on your monitor.

4. Choose an option from the **Colors** pop-up menu to change the number of colors displayed on your monitor.

End

Changing the Mouse Speed

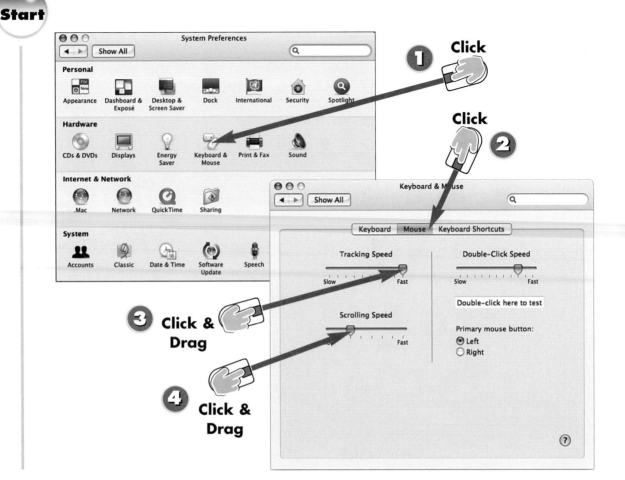

Click

Click

Click &
Drag

Click &
Drag

1 Click the **Keyboard & Mouse** icon in the System Preferences window to display mouse preferences.

2 Click the **Mouse** tab to see the mouse settings.

3 Click and drag the **Tracking Speed** slider to change how quickly the mouse moves across the screen.

4 Click and drag the **Scrolling Speed** slider to change how fast windows scroll when you use a mouse with a scroll wheel.

End

When you're in a hurry, there are few things more annoying than a slow mouse, or one that's so fast you can't keep track of it. Whether your mouse moves too slowly or too quickly for your taste, you can adjust its setting until it's just where you like it. You can also change the speed at which you must click for two clicks to register as an official double-click.

Scrolling, Scrolling, Scrolling
If you haven't tried a mouse with a scroll wheel yet, you should make a point of checking one out. This handy little control makes scrolling through long documents or long Web pages a breeze.

Changing Keyboard Settings

Start

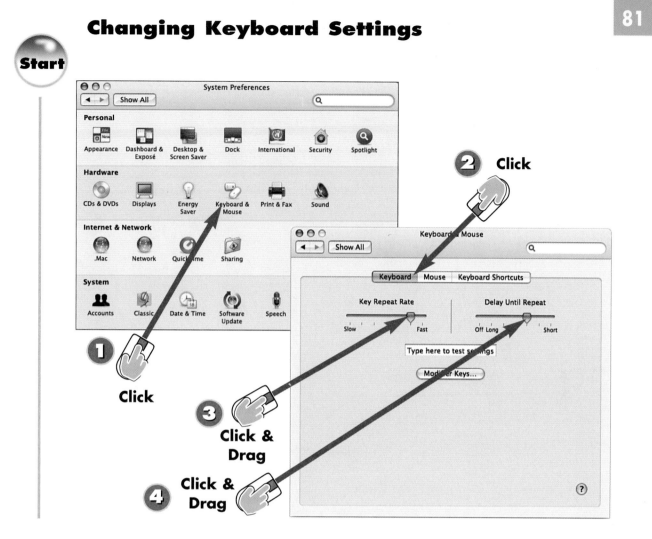

② Click

① Click

③ Click & Drag

④ Click & Drag

① Click the **Keyboard & Mouse** icon in the System Preferences window to display keyboard preferences.

② Click the **Keyboard** tab to see the keyboard settings.

③ Click and drag the **Key Repeat Rate** slider to control how quickly keys repeat when you hold them down.

④ Click and drag the **Delay Until Repeat** slider to control how long the Mac waits before starting to repeat keys when you hold them down.

End

INTRODUCTION

Most aspects of the way a keyboard works are determined by the hardware—in other words, the keyboard itself. However, there are a couple of keyboard settings you can adjust, having to do with how quickly your Mac repeats keys when you hold down a key.

TIP

Another Cool Extra Menu
Like many preference panes, the keyboard settings include a useful menu that you can opt to display, or not, as you wish. In this case, the option puts an Eject menu in the menu bar, which enables you to eject disks in removable drives such as CD or DVD drives.

Setting Energy Saver Options

Start

Click

Click & Drag

Click

Click

Click

1. Click the **Energy Saver** icon in the System Preferences window to display energy preferences.

2. Click the **Sleep** tab to display sleeping options.

3. Click and drag the top slider to choose when your Mac will sleep and the bottom slider to set a separate time for when your monitor will sleep.

4. Click the check box if you want the hard drive to sleep.

INTRODUCTION

You might not think your quiet little computer, sitting over there in the corner not even moving, could eat up that much electricity—but think again. That's why the Energy Saver settings are important; they enable you to reduce your Mac's power consumption during times when you're not using it. Be sure to take as much advantage of Energy Saver as possible.

HINT

Hurry Hurry
If you're always in a hurry when you come back to your computer, don't set the hard drive to sleep. The monitor wakes up from sleep instantly, but it takes a few moments for the hard drive to spin back up to speed when it wakes up.

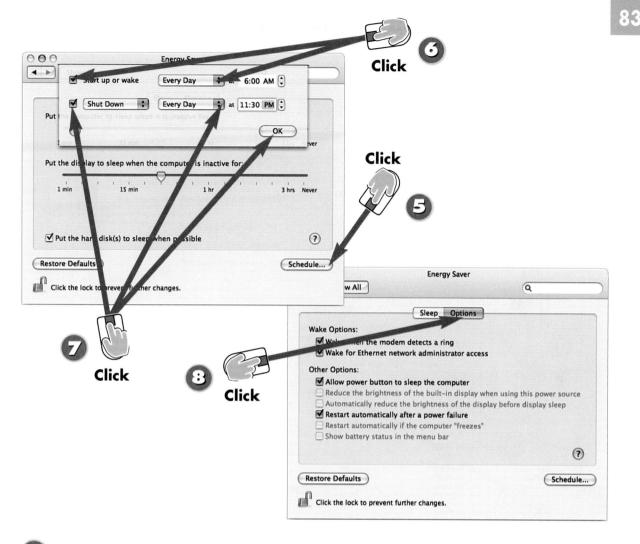

Click 6

Click 5

Click 7

Click 8

5 Click the **Schedule** button to display scheduled startup and shutdown options.

6 Check the box and choose when to start up the Mac automatically.

7 Check the box and choose when to shut down the Mac automatically; then click **OK**.

8 Click the **Options** tab if you want to change the circumstances under which the Mac will sleep and wake up.

End

Are You Getting Sleepy?

TIP

For computers, sleep is a state between powered up and powered down. A sleeping computer consumes much less power, but it's not completely turned off. Of course, it wakes up much more quickly than it boots up from a powered-down state.

Sleepy Time

HINT

In step 7, you can also set your Mac to sleep at a particular time instead of shutting down. This is a good choice if you keep programs running all the time that you don't want to have to start up again every day.

Setting Options for Inserted Discs

Start

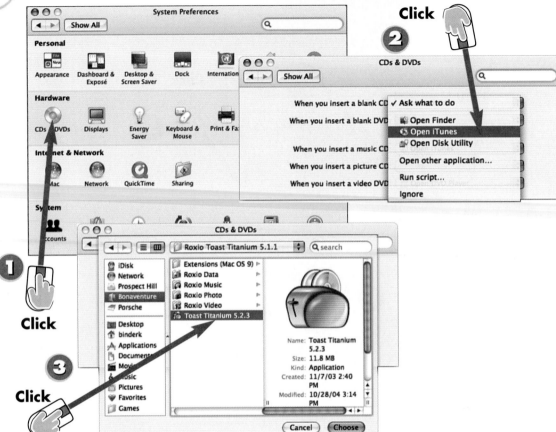

1 Click the **CDs & DVDs** icon in the System Preferences window to display removable disc preferences.

2 Choose an option for blank CDs.

3 If you have a CD-burning program such as Toast, choose **Open other application** and navigate to the program in the Applications folder.

Wouldn't it be nice if your Mac knew just what to do when you inserted a CD or DVD into its drive? The CDs & DVDs preferences enable you to have your Mac start up a specified program when you insert a blank disc that you're going to write yourself or when you insert a prewritten data, music, or movie disc.

Ignore Me, Please
HINT
Sometimes, the Ignore option is the best choice. If you set the Mac to ignore discs you insert, you'll be able to decide what to do with each disc at the time, without having to quit a program that started up when you didn't want it to. You might do this if you use multiple methods to burn CDs—for example, using Toast or the Finder, depending on the circumstances.

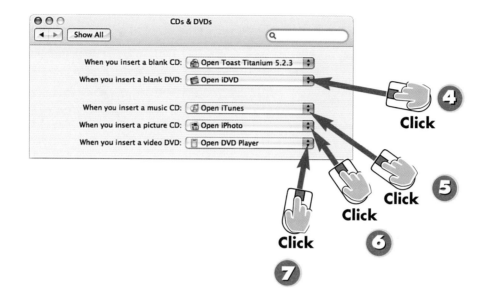

4 Choose an option for blank DVDs; if you use iDVD, choose **Open**; otherwise, choose **Open other application**.

5 Choose an option for music CDs; **Open iTunes** is the best choice unless you prefer a different program for playing music.

6 Choose an option for picture CDs; **Open iPhoto** is the best choice unless you prefer a different program for viewing photos.

7 Choose an option for video CDs; **Open DVD Player** is the best choice unless you prefer a different program for viewing movies.

End

TIP

It Never Hurts to Ask
If you're not sure what you want to happen when you insert a particular type of disc, just choose **Ask what to do**.

HINT

Burn, Baby, Burn
You can burn CDs and DVDs using the Finder's Burn Disc command. But if you want a choice of formats to ensure you can send the right type of disc to various customers, you'll need a program such as Toast (www.roxio.com).

Setting the Time and Date

Start

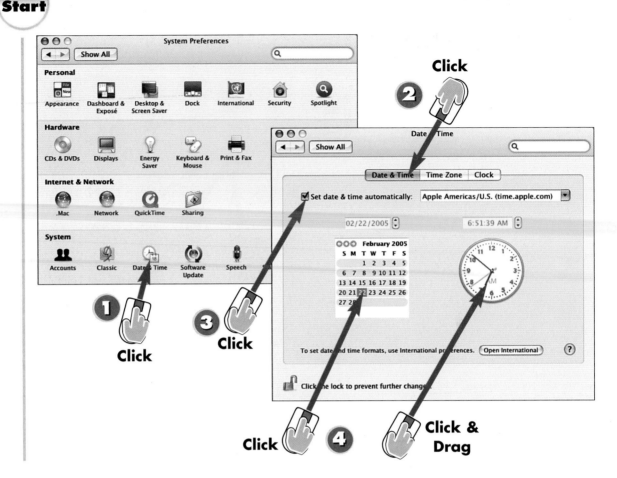

Click

1 Click the **Date & Time** icon in the System Preferences window to display time and date preferences.

2 Click the **Date & Time** tab to see your choices.

3 If the **Set Date & Time automatically** box is checked, click to remove the check mark.

4 Click a day on the calendar to set the date, or type in the date; drag the hands on the clock to set the time, or type in the time.

End

If you opt to set the date and time yourself, you can do it by clicking a calendar or dragging clock hands—no messy typing needed! If you have a constant or frequent online connection, you can choose instead to have your Mac's clock set automatically over the Internet.

HINT

Do You Have the Correct Time?
If you use a timeserver to set your Mac's clock automatically over the Internet, be sure you've chosen the correct time zone in the Time Zone tab of the Date & Time preferences.

HINT

A Clockwork Preference
The third tab in the Date & Time preferences pane is the Clock tab, where you'll find settings for the menu bar clock. You can even choose an analog clock with hands instead of the regular digital display.

Adjusting the System Volume

Start

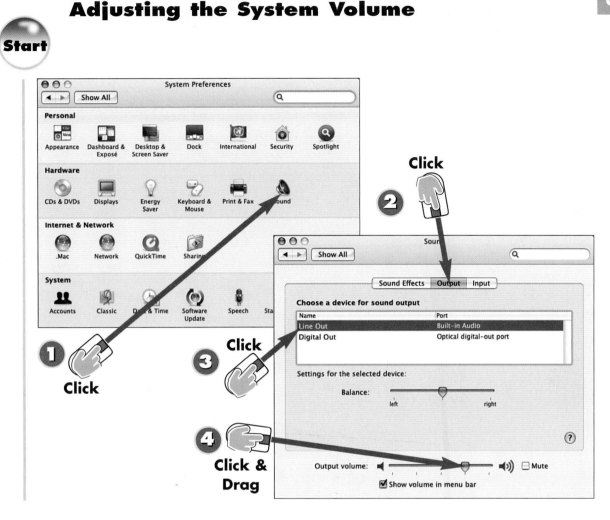

Click (2)

Click (1)

Click (3)

Click & Drag (4)

1. Click the **Sound** icon in the System Preferences window to display sound preferences.

2. Click the **Output** tab to see your choices.

3. If you have more than one output method (internal speaker and external speakers), choose the device you want to use from the pick list.

4. Click and drag the **Output volume** slider to change the volume for all sounds produced by your Mac.

End

A small thing such as the volume of the sounds your Mac plays can have such an impact on your experience while using the computer. You can always increase the volume when you're working in the next room or you want to turn up the radio and sing along, or lower it when you don't want to wake the baby.

TIP

Muting for Discretion's Sake
Click the **Mute** check box next to the Output volume slider if you want to turn the volume all the way down. When the sound is muted, you'll see a screen flash instead of hearing an alert sound.

TIP

Getting Louder (or Softer) Faster
Click the **Show volume in menu bar** check box to put an extra menu in your menu bar that's simply a volume slider. To use it, click its icon, release the mouse button, and click and drag the slider.

Setting Trackpad Preferences

Start

Click ②

System Preferences

Personal
Appearance | Dashboard & Exposé | Desktop & Screen Saver | Dock | International | Security | Spotlight

Hardware
CDs & DVDs | Displays | Energy Saver | Keyboard & Mouse | Print & Fax | So...

Internet & Network
.Mac | Network | QuickTime | Sharing

System
Accounts | Classic | Date & Time | Software Update | Speech | Startu...

Keyboard & Mouse

Keyboard | Trackpad | Keyboard Shortcuts

Tracking Speed — Slow / Fast
Double-Click Speed — Slow / Fast

Double-click here to test

Use trackpad for:
☐ Clicking
☐ Dragging
☐ Drag Lock (tap again to release)
☑ Ignore accidental trackpad input
☐ Ignore trackpad when mouse is present

① **Click**

③ **Click & Drag**

④ **Click**

① Click the **Keyboard & Mouse** icon in the System Preferences window to display mouse preferences.

② Click the **Trackpad** tab to see the trackpad settings.

③ Click and drag the **Tracking Speed** slider to set how fast the trackpad cursor moves; click and drag the **Double-Click Speed** slider to set how fast you must double-click.

④ In the **Use trackpad for** section, click the check boxes to change your click and drag settings.

End

Trackpads—those snazzy touch-sensitive pads laptops use instead of trackballs these days—are funny creatures. Because they don't feel the same as a mouse, you might want to use different speed and double-clicking settings than you would for a mouse. Feel free to experiment until you're comfortable with the settings you have.

Trackpad Settings
Don't overlook the last two check boxes: Ignore accidental trackpad input reduces the sensitivity of the trackpad so you don't click or drag accidentally, and Ignore trackpad when mouse is present turns off the trackpad when you plug in a mouse.

A Trackpad but no Laptop
If you love trackpads but don't use a PowerBook, you can still satisfy your craving. Try a standalone trackpad such as the Cirque Easy Cat—the USB version plugs right into your Mac—and your fingertips will be cruising along in no time.

Monitoring Battery Use

Start

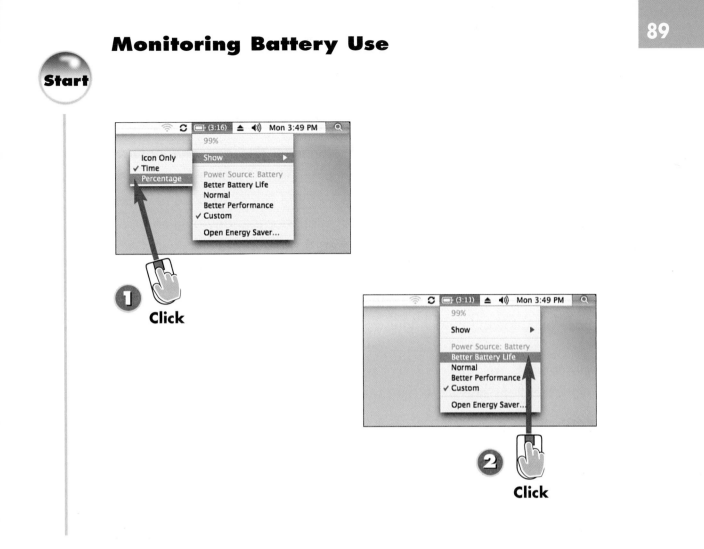

1 Click

2 Click

1 Click the battery display in the menu bar to see the **Battery** menu; then choose a display option, such as **Percentage**.

2 In the **Battery** menu, choose a performance option to quickly change all your Energy Saver settings.

End

INTRODUCTION

If you're a laptop user, you know how important it is to keep track of the charge in your PowerBook's battery. Running out of power at a crucial moment could be a disaster—you'll definitely want to keep an eye on the Battery menu to make sure the worst never happens to you.

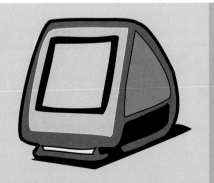

Saving More Power

Look at the Energy Saver functions in the System Preferences—you can save a lot of power by setting the right preferences. See the task "Setting Energy Saver Options" earlier in this part to learn more about Energy Saver settings.

Customizing Your Mac

It's your Mac—why not have some fun with it? There are myriad ways to make your Mac your own, from changing its desktop picture, its icons, and even your own login icon to changing the way the Finder works and responds to you. You can even change the Finder's language to any of a couple dozen alternatives, including Asian languages, or you can set up your Mac to talk to you—and listen for your responses.

Your custom settings are associated with your login name, so they're automatically put into action each time you log in. When other users log in, their own settings are activated. That means a single Mac can offer each user a custom experience. Your custom settings can include useful preferences such as network locations and more fun preferences such as your desktop wallpaper.

In this part you'll learn how to customize the Finder, the Dock, the desktop, your screen saver, and your security preferences. You'll also learn about using Speakable Items to give voice commands to your Mac and how to make your Mac talk to you. If you move your computer around or switch networks a lot, you'll benefit from the "Creating Custom Network Locations" task, which shows how to create custom location settings that change all your network preferences with a single click.

Taking Advantage of Custom Settings

Magnify Dock icons

Set Finder preferences

Choose your desktop wallpaper

Choose a screen saver

Set language preferences

Secure your files

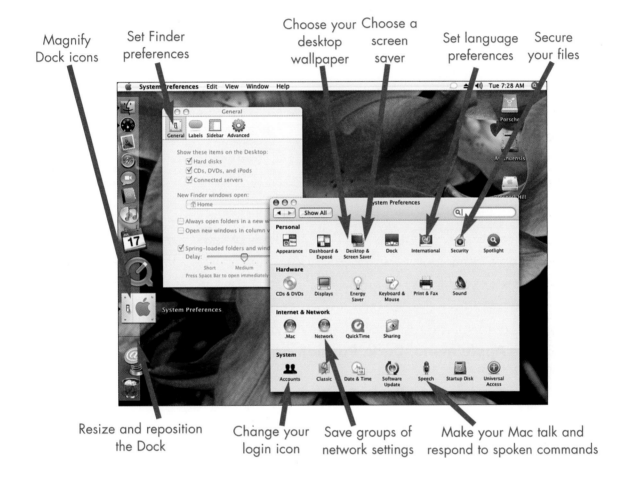

Resize and reposition the Dock

Change your login icon

Save groups of network settings

Make your Mac talk and respond to spoken commands

Moving the Dock Around

Start

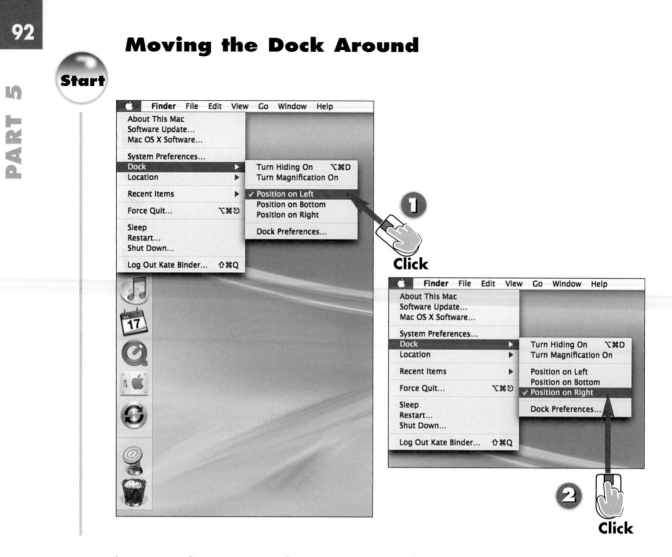

Click

Click

1. Choose **Apple menu**, **Dock**, **Position on Left** to move the Dock to the left edge of the screen.

2. Choose **Apple menu**, **Dock**, **Position on Right** to move the Dock to the right edge of the screen.

End

INTRODUCTION

Although the Dock normally lives at the bottom of your screen, it doesn't have to stay there. If you prefer, you can put it on the left or right side of the screen instead. No matter which edge of the screen it's on, the Dock works the same way and you can set its preferences to suit your tastes.

TIP

Hide and Go Dock
To hide the Dock, choose the **Apple** menu, **Dock**, **Turn Hiding On**; the Dock sinks off the edge of the screen whenever you're not using it. Move your mouse back to that edge, and the Dock pops back up.

HINT

Dock Substitutes
The Dock can get crowded if you store everything there. Some users use the Dock as an application switcher, with inactive programs and documents stored in a third-party Dock substitute such as DragThing (www.dragthing.com).

Changing the Dock's Size

Start

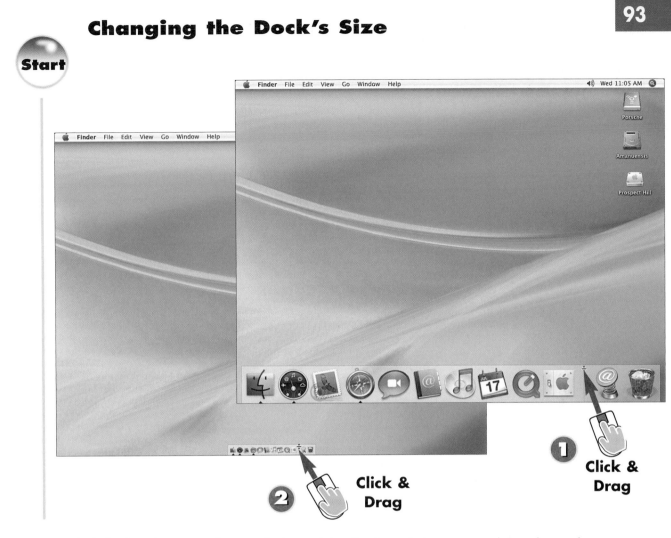

Click & Drag ❶

Click & Drag ❷

❶ Click the line between the two halves of the Dock and drag upward to enlarge the Dock.

❷ Drag downward to reduce the Dock's size.

End

INTRODUCTION

The more stuff you stash in the Dock, the more room it takes up on your screen. If it gets too full, you can shrink it to give you more room onscreen—or, if you prefer, you can make it larger so it's easier to see what it contains.

TIP

There's Always Another Way
You can also use the Dock Size slider in the Dock preferences (choose the **Apple** menu, **Dock, Dock Preferences**) if you happen to be going there to change other preferences as well.

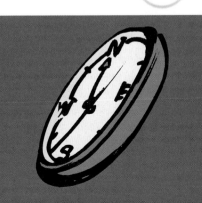

Customizing the Dock's Behavior

Start

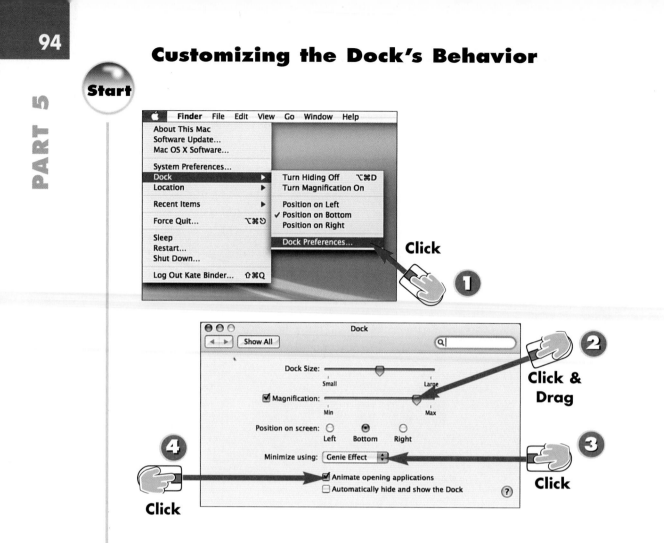

Click **1**

Click & Drag **2**

Click **3**

Click **4**

1 Choose **Apple menu**, **Dock**, **Dock Preferences**.

2 Click and drag the **Magnification** slider toward Max if you want Dock icons to be enlarged as you pass the mouse cursor over them.

3 Choose an option from the **Minimize using** pop-up menu.

4 Click the **Animate opening applications** check box to make Dock icons bounce as their programs start up.

End

INTRODUCTION

As if moving the Dock around and changing its size weren't enough, there's yet more you can do to make the Dock work just the way you want it to. The Dock preferences enable you to control the way the Dock moves—or, more precisely, the way its icons move and change size and the way windows enter the Dock.

TIP

Dock Behavior in Another Context
You can control Dock Preferences by Ctrl-clicking the dividing line between the halves of the Dock. The contextual menu has controls for magnification, hiding, position, and the minimization effect, as well as a Dock Preferences command.

Changing the Way the Finder Works

Start

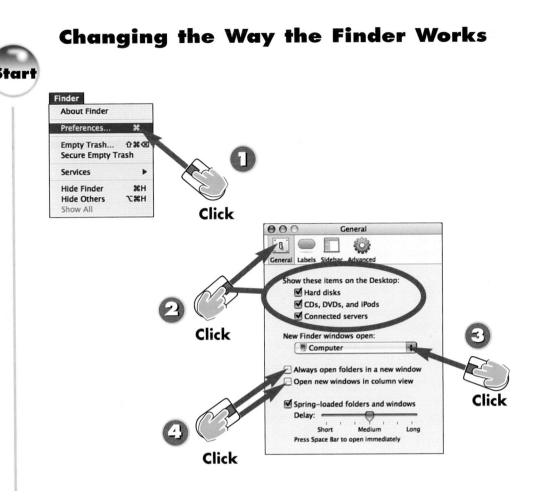

1. In the Finder, choose **Finder**, **Preferences**.

2. Click the **General** button to see basic Finder preferences, and then click check boxes to set the kinds of disks to appear on the desktop.

3. Choose an option from the **New Finder windows open** pop-up menu to determine which folder or disk location appears in new Finder windows.

4. Click the check boxes to set whether each folder generates a new window and whether new windows start out in Column view.

End

INTRODUCTION

The Finder—the program that generates the desktop and enables you to explore your hard drive and network drives visually via windows—is where you'll spend a lot of time while using your Mac. You have several choices about the way it operates; here's how to set up the Finder to suit your tastes.

TIP

Finding Files with the Finder
The Finder got its name for its capability to find files. To find files in the Finder, choose **File**, **Find** or press ⌘-**F** and type in the search criteria.

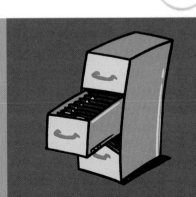

Changing Your Desktop Picture

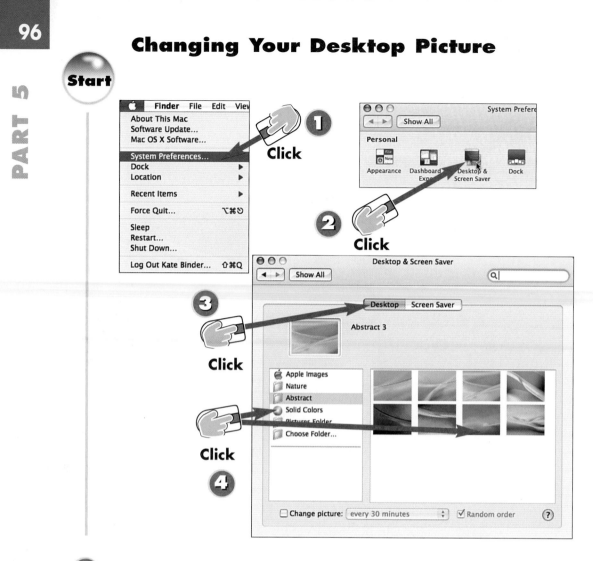

Start

Click ①

Click ②

Click ③

Click ④

①　Choose **Apple menu**, **System Preferences**.

②　Click the **Desktop & Screen Saver** icon to see your choices.

③　Click the **Desktop** tab.

④　Click a folder and an image from within the folder to apply that image to the desktop.

End

TIP

Surprise Me
If you want your desktop picture to change automatically, click **Choose Folder** in the Desktop tab and pick a folder full of your favorite images. Then check **Change picture** at the bottom of the Desktop tab and choose a time interval.

HINT

The Mother Lode
Looking for more desktop pictures to relieve your boredom? You can download hundreds of high-quality desktop images at MacDesktops (www.macdesktops.com).

Changing Your Login Icon

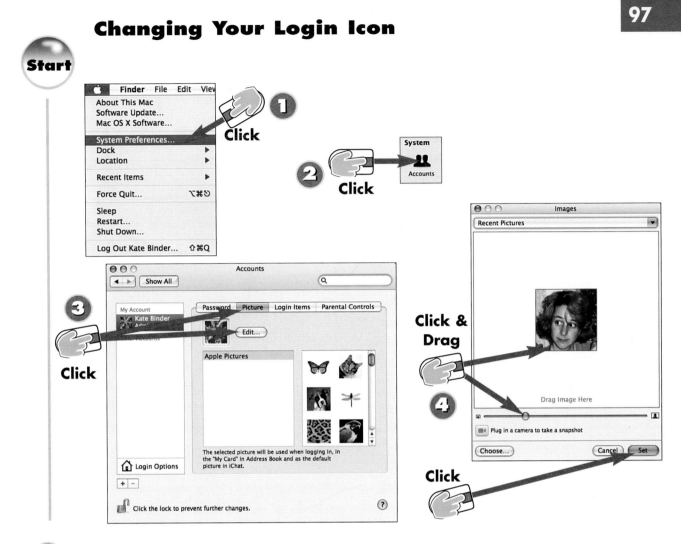

1 Choose **Apple menu**, **System Preferences**.

2 Click the **Accounts** icon to see your choices.

3 Click the **Picture** tab; then click the **Edit** button next to your picture.

4 Drag or paste an image file into the Images window, drag the image and the scaling slider until the square shows the area you want for the icon, and click **Set** to make it your login picture.

INTRODUCTION

Your login item represents your face within the world of your Mac. It's used as your buddy icon for online messaging in iChat, it appears next to your personal information in the Address Book, and you see it every time you log in. You can use one of the built-in pictures, or you can add any picture you like—your photo or anything else.

HINT

Using Your Own Picture
There are some reasons it might not be wise to use your own photo as a login icon. If people you don't know will see the photo—as an iChat icon, for instance—you might want to reconsider using it and substitute a personal logo of some type.

Changing Your Mac's Language

Start

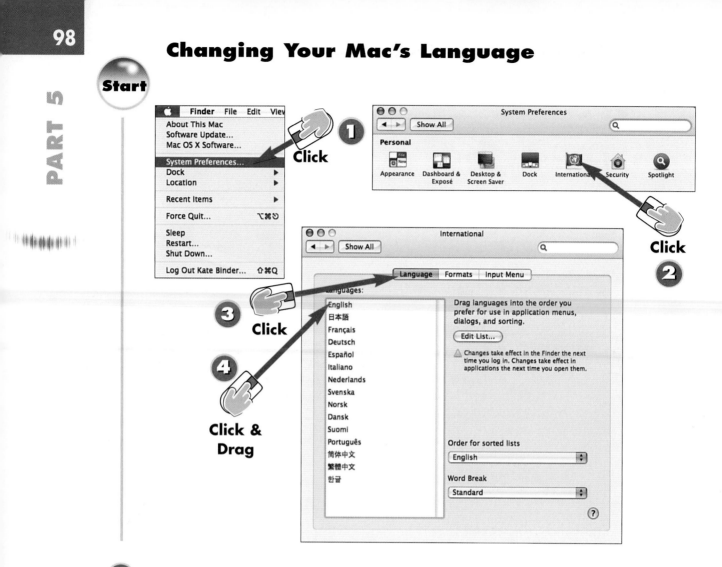

Click

Click

Click & Drag

1. Choose **Apple menu**, **System Preferences**.

2. Click the **International** icon to see your choices.

3. Click the **Language** tab.

4. Click and drag your preferred language to the top of the pick list.

End

INTRODUCTION
You might have thought that you would need to buy a special version of Mac OS X if you want your Mac's interface to use a language other than English. Actually, Mac OS X ships with the capability to display menus, dialog boxes, and other interface elements in a couple dozen languages, including those with special alphabets.

TIP

Making a Menu
When you switch languages, you should also switch keyboard layouts to activate each language's special characters. In the International preferences' Input Menu tab, you can create a menu of the languages you use so you can switch keyboard layouts quickly.

Changing Your Screen Saver

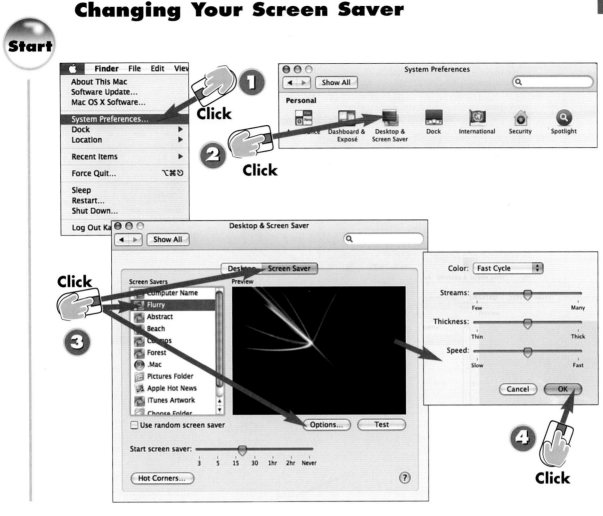

Start

Click ①

Click ②

Click ③

Click ④

① Choose **Apple menu**, **System Preferences**.

② Click the **Desktop & Screen Saver** icon to see your choices.

③ Click the **Screen Saver** tab and then click a screen saver in the list to select it. Click the **Options** button.

④ Use the settings in this dialog box to change settings specific to each screen saver. Click **OK** when finished.

End

INTRODUCTION

Originally invented to stop the kind of screen burn-in that you see on automatic teller machines, screen savers are actually little more than a pretty entertainment these days. But that shouldn't prevent you from using them; screen savers provide some privacy, shielding your screen from casual observers, as well as being fun to look at.

TIP

Got Savers?
If you're not satisfied with the built-in selection of screen savers—or if you've run through them all and are desperately in need of new ones— check out www.macscreensavers.com. There you can download more screen saver modules than you could ever need.

Changing Icons

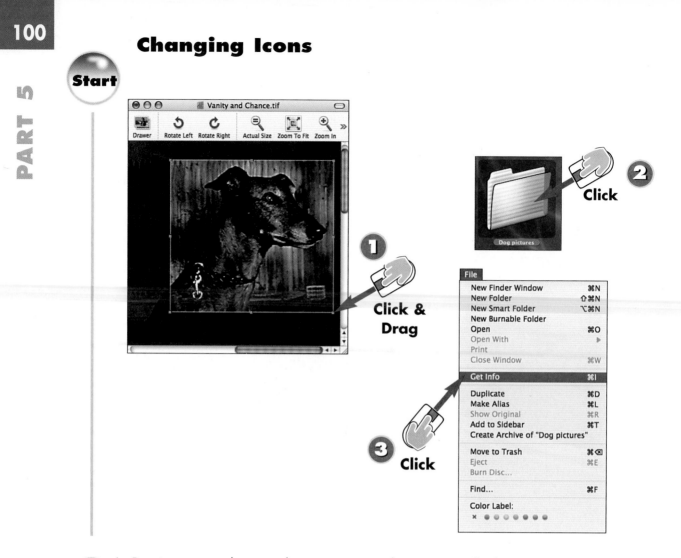

Start

Vanity and Chance.tif

Drawer Rotate Left Rotate Right Actual Size Zoom To Fit Zoom In

1 Click & Drag

2 Click

Dog pictures

File

New Finder Window	⌘N
New Folder	⇧⌘N
New Smart Folder	⌥⌘N
New Burnable Folder	
Open	⌘O
Open With	▶
Print	
Close Window	⌘W
Get Info	⌘I
Duplicate	⌘D
Make Alias	⌘L
Show Original	⌘R
Add to Sidebar	⌘T
Create Archive of "Dog pictures"	
Move to Trash	⌘⌫
Eject	⌘E
Burn Disc...	
Find...	⌘F
Color Label:	

3 Click

1. In Preview or another graphics program, select part or all of an image to be the new icon. Press ⌘-**C** to copy the selection.

2. In the Finder, click to select the file whose icon you want to change.

3. Choose **File**, **Get Info** to see the file's Info window.

Click

⌘-V

④ Click the icon shown in the Info window.

⑤ Press ⌘-**V** and the new image is pasted into the icon area.

End

TIP

For Best Results
The bigger the picture you use to create an icon, the more detailed the icon will be when it's scaled to its largest size. With that in mind, however, remember that at small sizes, simple, clear, less-detailed images are the easiest to identify.

Reading Aloud with VoiceOver

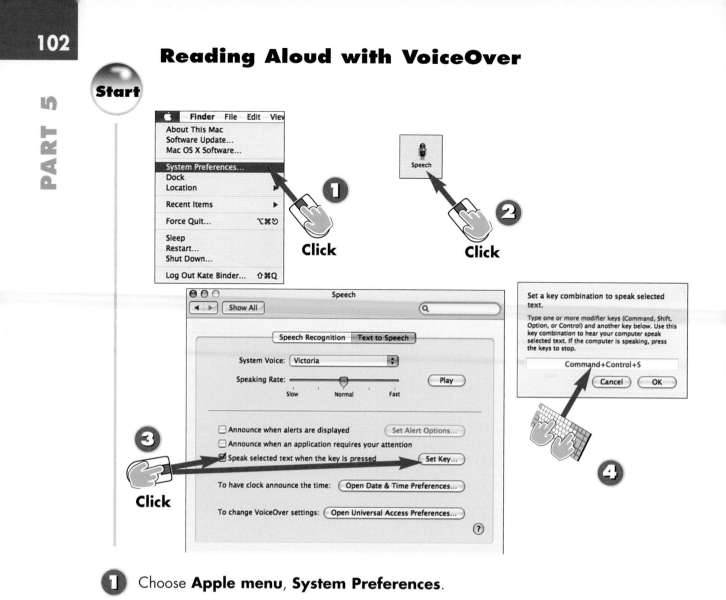

1 Choose **Apple menu**, **System Preferences**.

2 Click **Speech**.

3 In the **Text to Speech** tab, check **Speak selected text when the key is pressed**; then click **Set Key**.

4 Press the key combination you want to use, such as ⌘-**Ctrl-S**.

TIP
Guided by Voices
If you don't like the way your Mac sounds when it talks, you can return to the Speech settings in the System Preferences and change the voice and speed it uses.

HINT
Watch Those Keys
Be sure to use an unusual keyboard combination in step 4—one that isn't already in use for a function you perform often.

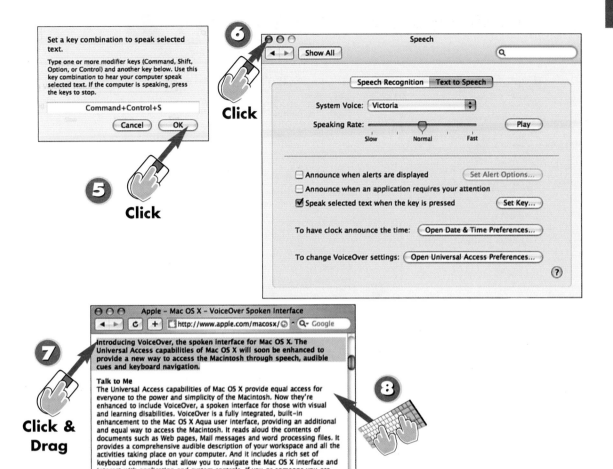

Set a key combination to speak selected text.

Type one or more modifier keys (Command, Shift, Option, or Control) and another key below. Use this key combination to hear your computer speak selected text. If the computer is speaking, press the keys to stop.

Command+Control+S

Cancel OK

5 Click

Click

Click

6

7 Click & Drag

8

5 Click **OK**.

6 Click the **Close** button to quit System Preferences.

7 Select the text you want your Mac to read.

8 Press the keyboard command you chose in step 4.

End

The Best It Can Do
HINT Remember that your Mac doesn't actually know the meaning of the text it reads and that it has to sound out names and other unfamiliar words phonetically. Don't be surprised that it doesn't sound like a human reading out loud.

Increasing Your Mac's Security

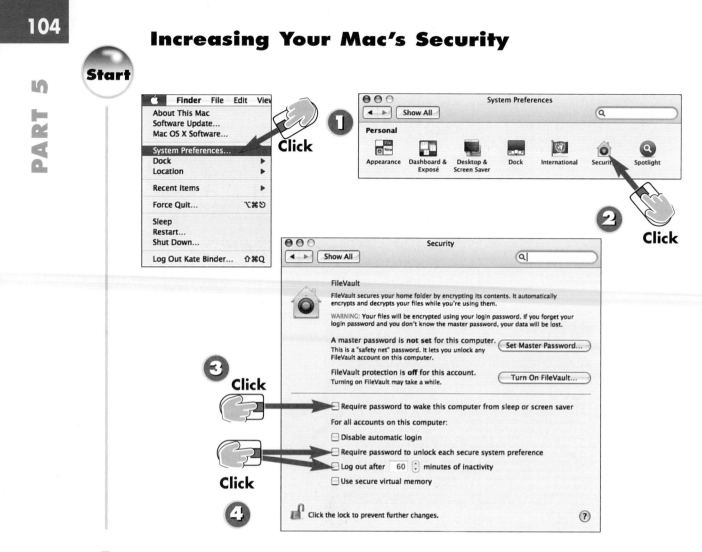

1 Choose **Apple menu**, **System Preferences**.

2 Click the **Security** icon to see your choices.

3 Click the **Require password** check box to make sure that only you can wake the computer up when it's sleeping.

4 Click the check boxes next to the other options to turn them on or off.

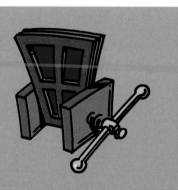

HINT

Learning to Live Together
To learn about ways to get along when you share your Mac with other users, turn to Part 11, "Sharing Your Mac with Multiple Users."

Using the Dashboard

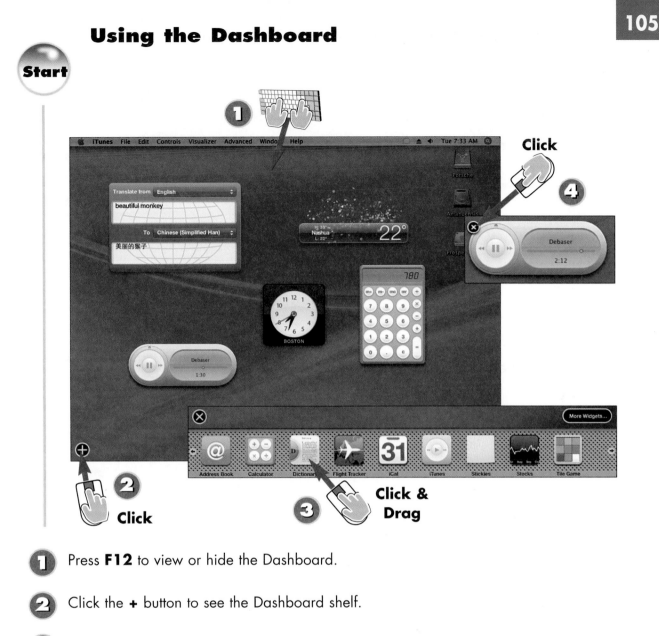

1. Press **F12** to view or hide the Dashboard.

2. Click the **+** button to see the Dashboard shelf.

3. Drag a widget out of the shelf to place it on the Dashboard.

4. Click the **Close** button in the upper-left corner of a widget to put it back on the shelf.

End

INTRODUCTION

Naturally, the Dashboard is where you keep indicators, gauges, and other useful things. New to Tiger, this feature enables you to quickly access helpful desk accessories and just as quickly sweep them out of the way when you're done using them.

TIP

Double Vision

Some widgets *can* be in two places at once—you can drag more than one sticky or calendar out of the Favorites bar. Watch out, though; if you double-click a widget, you might unintentionally end up with two copies of it.

Creating Custom Network Locations

Start

Click

Click

Click

Click

① Choose **Apple menu**, **System Preferences**.

② Click the **Network** icon to see your choices.

③ Choose **New Location** from the **Location** pop-up menu.

④ Give the location a descriptive name and click **OK**.

Network locations are groups of network settings, each saved with a descriptive name so you can switch all your settings with a single click and get online or on the local network instantly no matter where you happen to be. After you've created a location, to use it all you have to do is choose it from a pop-up menu.

A Time and a Place

You can use locations to save settings for different situations as well as different places. For example, if you have both a cable modem and a dial-up account, create a location for each so you can switch to dial-up if the cable connection goes down.

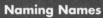

Click **5**

Click **6**

7

Click

```
⊖ ⊙ ⊙                        Network
◄ ►  Show All                          🔍

              Location:  Books 'n' Coffee shop        ▢
                 Show:  Built-in Ethernet             ▢

              TCP/IP   PPPoE   AppleTalk   Proxies   Ethernet

       Configure IPv4:  Using DHCP                    ▢
          IP Address:                        Renew DHCP Lease
         Subnet Mask:              DHCP Client ID:  _____
              Router:                              (If required)
         DNS Servers:  _____       (Optional)

     Search Domains:  _____        (Optional)
        IPv6 Address:
                       Configure IPv6...                    ?

   🔓  Click the lock to prevent further changes.   Assist me...   Apply Now
```

5 Choose the network interface you want to set up from the **Show** pop-up menu.

6 On each tab, make the appropriate settings for that network interface.

7 Click **Apply Now** to switch to the new location.

End

Organizing Your Life

Mac OS X includes several programs that work together to keep you organized: Address Book, iCal, and iSync. Address Book is a contact manager where you can store your friends', family members', and colleagues' names, addresses, and phone numbers along with their instant messaging IDs, websites, and email addresses. iCal keeps track of your appointments and a to-do list, and it can both publish and subscribe to calendars so you can share them with others. And iSync makes sure that all the data in Address Book and iCal is available to your PDA, phone, or other device so you're never without it.

In this part you'll learn how to create and organize contacts in Address Book and how to use the program to view a map of a contact's address. iCal Tasks show how to create appointments and to-do lists and how to invite Address Book contacts to events; how to search calendars; and how to publish, subscribe to, and print calendars. Finally, you'll learn how to use iSync to keep all your information straight across devices and how to find essential information on the Net with Sherlock.

Working with Contacts and Schedules

Sync PDAs, iPods, and phones with iCal and Address Book

Organize your schedule in iCal

Maintain multiple calendars

View days, weeks, or entire months

Search your calendar

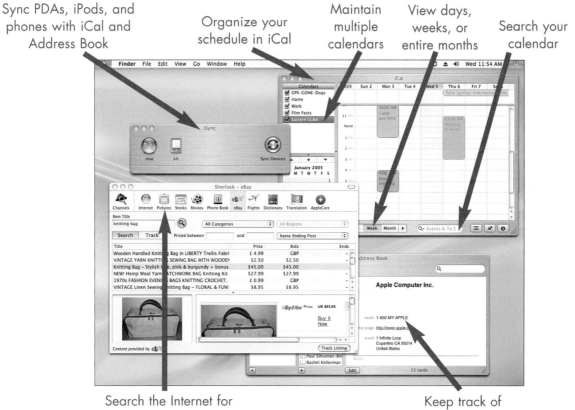

Search the Internet for pictures, addresses, web-sites, and more with Sherlock

Keep track of contacts in Address Book

Adding Contacts to Address Book

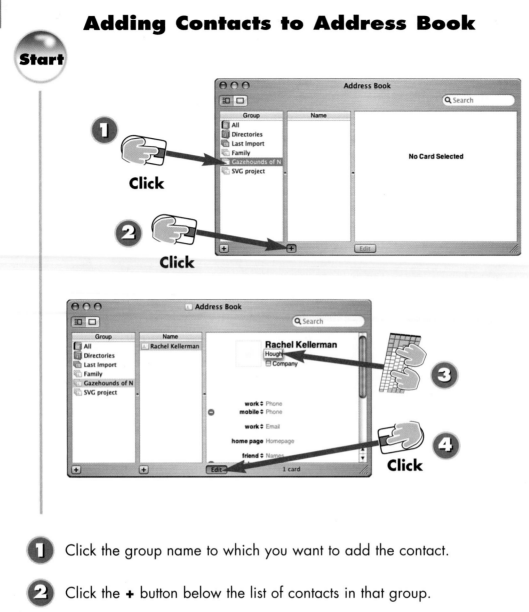

Start

Click

Click

Click

① Click the group name to which you want to add the contact.

② Click the **+** button below the list of contacts in that group.

③ Type the person or company's name and other information.

④ Click **Edit** to complete the contact.

End

INTRODUCTION

Mac OS X's Address Book is accessible systemwide, meaning its information can be used by other programs such as iChat, Mail, and even Microsoft Word. Adding contacts and sorting them into groups is easy, and Address Book has an up-to-date selection of information fields, including places to stash online messaging IDs.

TIP

Edit This
The Edit button is also where you should head (or, more specifically, click) when you want to make changes to an existing Address Book entry. To apply your changes, click **Edit** again, or you can just click another contact or group instead.

Creating Groups of Contacts

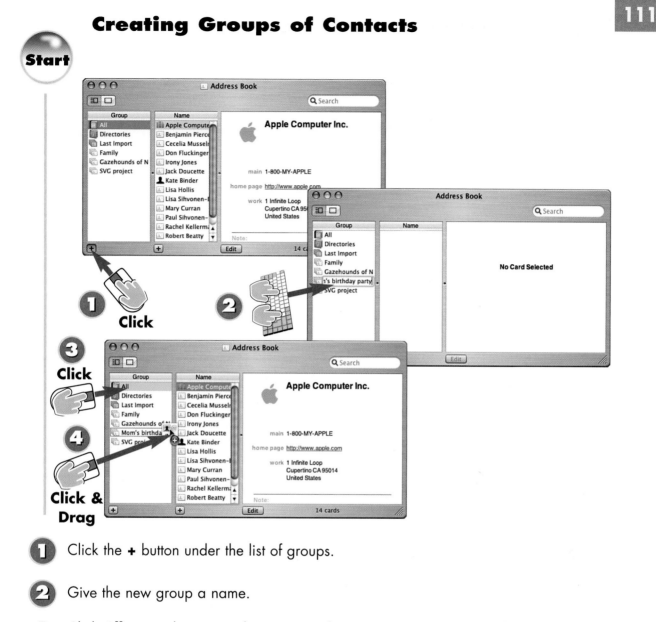

Click

Click

Click & Drag

1 Click the **+** button under the list of groups.

2 Give the new group a name.

3 Click **All** or another group that contains the contacts you want to add to the new group.

4 Drag the contacts into the new group.

INTRODUCTION

You can use Address Book's groups many ways. For example, you can create a group of people working on a current project so you can email them all at once. Or you can create a group of addresses for holiday cards so you can print address labels. Each contact can be in as many groups as you want to put it in.

TIP

A Two-Way Street
Creating a new group can work backward, too. First, ⌘-**click** to select the contacts you want to put in the group; then choose **File, New Group from Selection**.

Creating a Smart Group

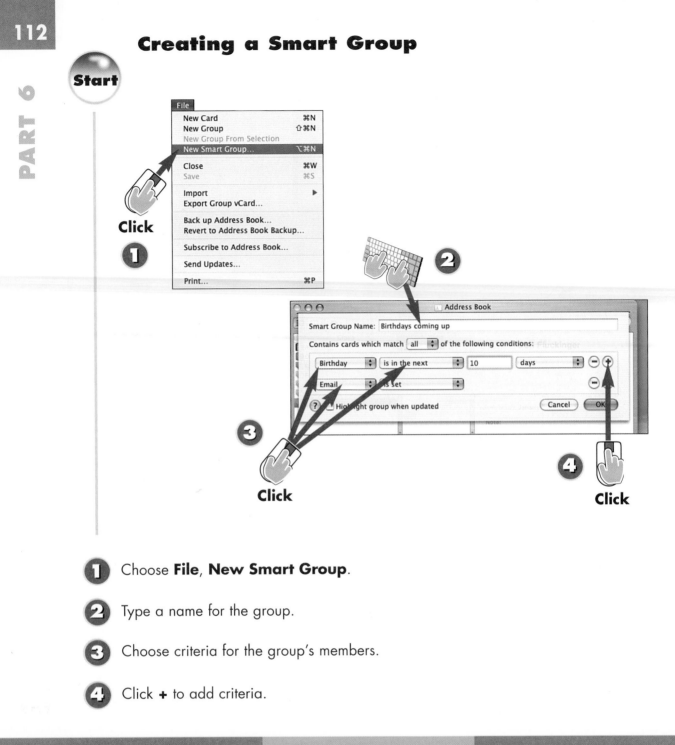

1 Choose **File**, **New Smart Group**.

2 Type a name for the group.

3 Choose criteria for the group's members.

4 Click **+** to add criteria.

○○○   Address Book

Smart Group Name: Birthdays coming up

Contains cards which match [all ▼] of the following conditions:

[Birthday ▼] [is in the next ▼] [10] [days ▼] ⊖ ⊕

[Email ▼] [is set ▼] ⊖ ⊕

☑ Highlight group when updated   (Cancel) (OK)

5 **Click**

6 **Click**

○○○   Address Book

Group   **Name**

- All
- Directories
- Last Import
- Family
- Gazehounds of New England
- SVG project
- Birthdays coming up
- Membership renewals

Jayne Daughe   **Jayne Daughe**

○○○   Address Book

Group   **Name**

- All
- Directories
- Last Import
- Family
- Gazehounds of New England
- SVG project
- Birthdays coming up
- Membership rene...

Jayne Daughe   **Jayne Daughe**

Edit Smart Group...
Export Group vCard...
Send Email to "Birthdays coming up"

work jayned@fakemail.net

January 8, 2005

Updated: 1/4/05

(+)   (Edit)   1 card

7 **Click**

8 **Control-Click**

5 Click the box labeled **Highlight Group when Updated** to have Address Book highlight the group's name when it contains new members.

6 Click **OK** to create the group.

7 Click the group's name to see its members in the **Name** column.

8 Control-click the group's name to email its members or export their contact data.

End

Setting Conditions

You're not limited to just one criterion when creating a smart group. You can set as many conditions for inclusion as you like, and you can choose whether group members must satisfy all the conditions or just a single condition.

Going Negative

Don't forget that you can set most smart group criteria to negative values—meaning you can choose to include everyone in your Address Book who *doesn't* match a particular criterion.

Exporting Contacts As vCards

Start

① **Click**

② **Click**

Address Book

Search

Group	Name
Directories	Benjamin Pierce
Last Import	Cecelia Musselma
Family	Don Fluckinger
Gazehounds of N	Irony Jones
Mom's birthday p	Jack Doucette
SVG project	Mary Curran
	Rachel Kellerman
	Robert Beatty

Benjamin Pierce

home 100 Main Street
Bangor ME 01050
USA

Note:

③ **Click & Drag**

Address Book

Search

Group	Name
All	Benjamin Pierce
Directories	Cecelia Musselma
Last Import	Don Fluckinger
Family	Irony Jones
Gazehounds of N	Jack Doucette
Mom's birthday p	Mary Curran
SVG project	Rachel Kellerman
	Robert Beatty

Benjamin Pierce

home 100 Main Street
Bangor ME 01050
USA

Note:

Edit   8 cards

④

Benjamin Pierce

① Click a name in the contacts column to select a single person, or ⌘-**click** to select more than one person.

② To create a vCard for an entire group, click the group's name in the first column.

③ Drag the group, contact, or contacts onto the desktop to create the vCard file.

④ The vCard appears on the desktop and can now be attached and sent via email. **End**

Apple has chosen the vCard as its standard method of exchanging contact information among Address Book users as well as between Address Book and other programs. vCards are very small files that you can attach to email messages. Most contact management programs can read them, so they're a good way to send contact information to just about anyone, including Windows users.

The Express Route

You can find contacts quickly in Address Book by clicking the All group and typing a name, city, or other information into the Search entry field at the upper-left corner of the Address Book window.

Importing a vCard into Address Book

Start

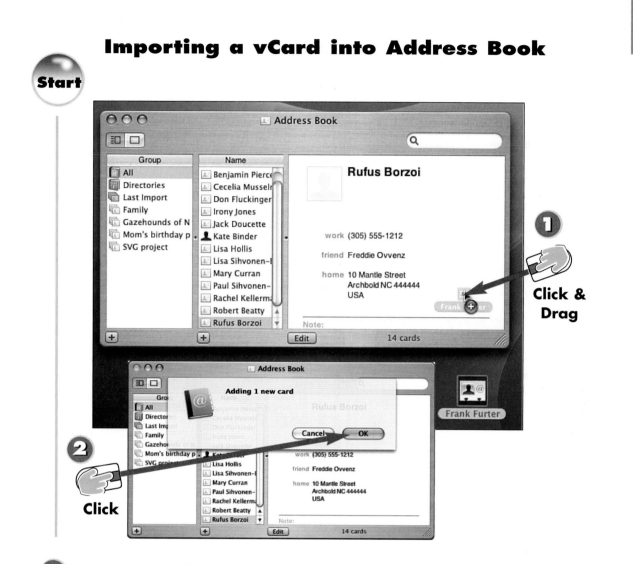

Click & Drag

Click

① Drag the vCard file from the desktop into the Address Book window.

② Click **OK** in the confirmation dialog box.

End

INTRODUCTION

Getting vCards into the Address Book is just as easy as getting them out of the Address Book. When you receive a vCard attached to an email as a sort of electronic business card, you need to locate the file in your attachments folder—you'll recognize it because of its **.vcf** filename extension.

HINT

The Case of the Missing Attachment
vCard files typically end up in your email attachments folder—the location and name can vary depending on which email program you use. To get at these files easily, try clicking their names or icons in the email window and dragging them onto the desktop.

Mapping a Contact's Address

Start

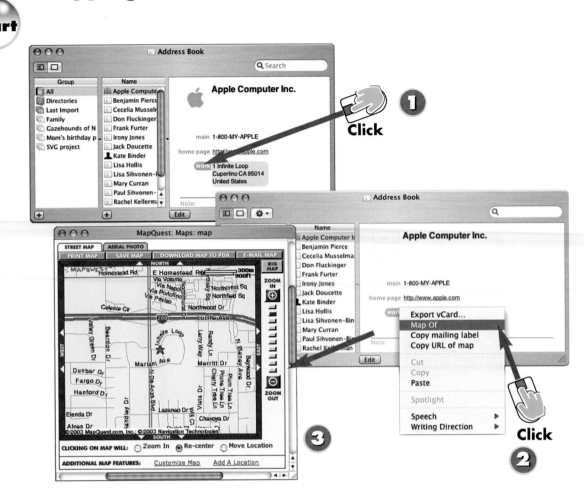

1 Click the address label next to the address to display a pop-up menu.

2 Click **Map Of**.

3 The map is displayed in your web browser.

End

If you have an instant-on or constant Internet connection, you're going to love this Address Book feature. You can view a map (and from there, driving directions) for an address in your contact list. It all starts with a simple click to a pop-up menu. Just remember, it won't work if you're not online.

Just the URL, Please

If you want to pass a map along to a friend, rather than just use it yourself, take advantage of another choice in the address pop-up menu: Copy URL of Map. After you choose this command, click in any text document or email window and press ⌘-V to paste the map's URL so the reader can click it to see the map.

Adding a To-Do in iCal

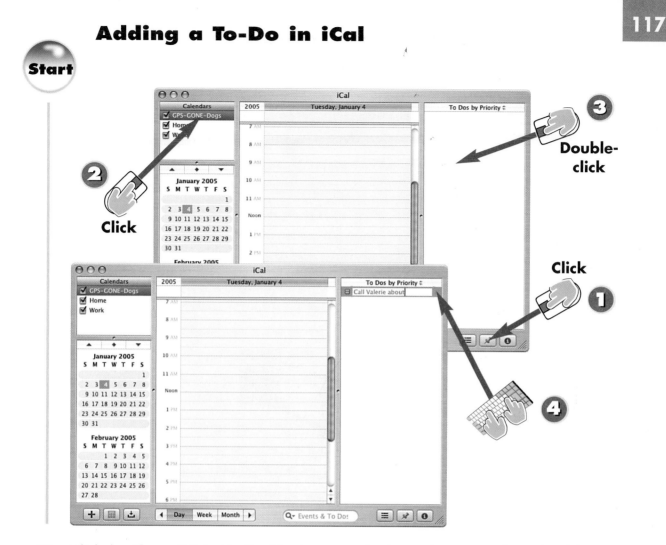

 Click the **Show/Hide To-Do List** button to display to-do items to the right of the calendar.

 Click the calendar to which you want to add the to-do item.

3 Double-click in the blank space in the **To Do items** area.

4 Enter the to-do text.

INTRODUCTION

Using a calendar to keep track of events is very important (turn to the next task to see how it works in iCal), but for many people, tracking a to-do list is an even more vital function. In iCal, you can assign each to-do item to a specific calendar, so you can distinguish among work, home, and hobby- or club-related tasks.

TIP

Making To-Do Items Disappear
Choose **iCal**, **Preferences** to change how long items stay on your calendar after they're completed and to determine how to-do items are sorted: by priority, by due date, or alphabetically.

Adding an Appointment in iCal

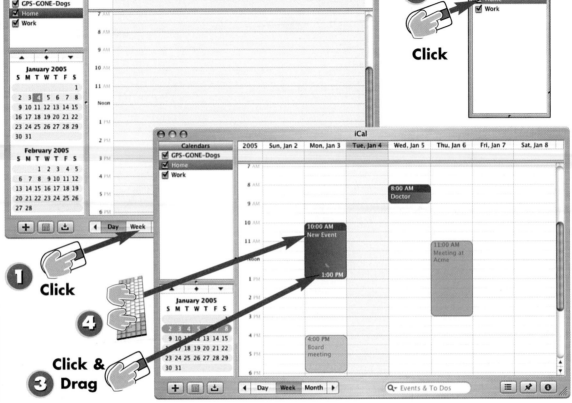

Start

Click

1 Click

2

4

3 Click & Drag

1. Click the **Day** or **Week** button to switch to Day or Week view.

2. Click the calendar to which you want to add the appointment.

3. Click and drag on the hour grid for the day of the appointment to define the time the appointment will last.

4. Type in the appointment text.

End

iCal is easy to use and compact, but don't underestimate it. This little calendar program has a surprising amount of power. Its primary purpose, of course, is keeping track of your appointments. Adding new ones couldn't be simpler, and reading iCal's neatly color-coded calendar is as easy as it gets.

TIP

Filling in the Details
To refine your appointment entry, click the **Show Info (i)** button at the bottom-right corner of the iCal window. Enter a location, add an alarm notification, set the appointment to repeat regularly, and more. You can also change the event's calendar here.

Switching Calendar Views in iCal

Start

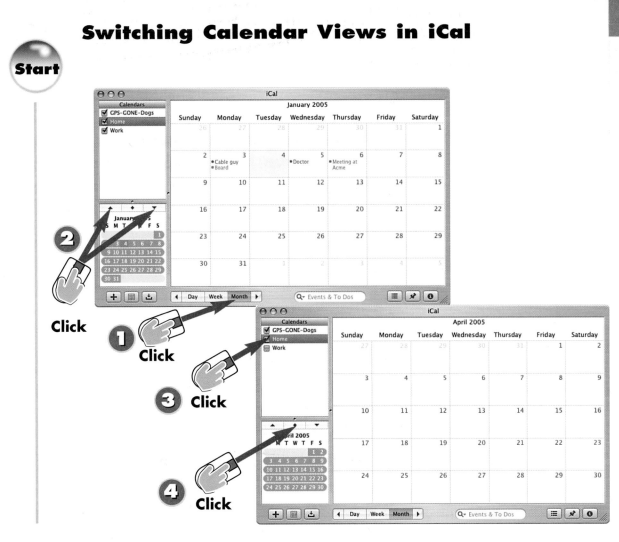

Click

Click

Click

Click

1 Click the **Day**, **Week**, or **Month** button at the bottom of the iCal window to switch views.

2 Click the up and down arrows to view different mini-months at the left side of the iCal window.

3 Click the check box next to each calendar to show or hide its appointments and to-do items.

4 Click the diamond button to return to viewing today.

End

INTRODUCTION

Whether you want to zero in on each hour of the day or back off and take in a month at a time, iCal can accommodate you. You can view your calendar by the day, week, or month. Meanwhile, mini-months off to the side enable you to keep track of the months surrounding today's date.

TIP

Customizing Day and Week Views
Choose **iCal**, **Preferences** to set the number of days displayed in Week view and choose on which day the week should start. You can also choose how many hours are shown in Day view and set start and end times for each day.

Setting Up an Alarm in iCal

Start

Click ①

Click ②

Click ③

Click ④

① Click the appointment to which you want to add an alarm.

② Click the **Show Info** button.

③ Click next to **Alarm** and choose an alarm type; then specify a sound, a file, or an email address to use, if necessary.

④ Set the time for the alarm to appear.

End

INTRODUCTION

If you want to be reminded before an appointment, you can set up an alarm that will get your attention to let you know the appointment is coming up. iCal alarms take several forms: displaying a dialog box, displaying a dialog box and playing a sound, sending an email, or opening a specified file.

TIP

Hitting the Snooze Button
iCal alarms do have a snooze button—click the small button with the circular arrow in the alarm dialog box and choose a time interval to snooze the alarm. You can snooze an alarm for as little as a minute, a couple of hours, or a day.

HINT

The Missing Drawer
If your iCal window is maximized so it takes up the entire screen, you can't see the Info drawer when it pops out. Reduce the size of the window and move it to the left to see the Info drawer on the right.

Inviting Contacts to Events in iCal

Start

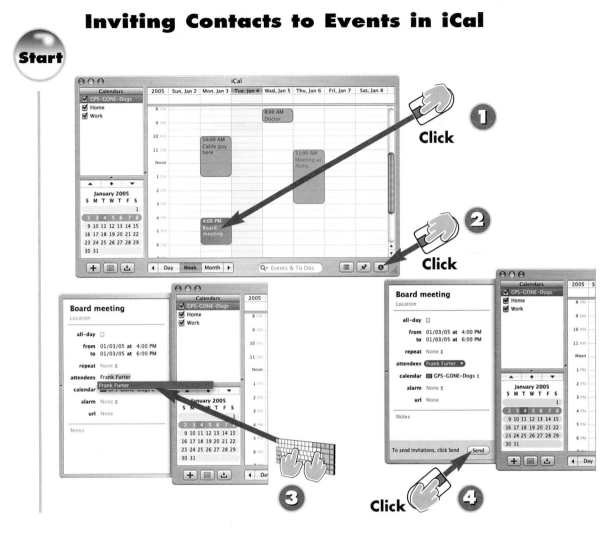

Click ①

Click ②

Click ③

Click ④

① Click the appointment to which you want to invite others.

② Click the **Show Info** button.

③ Click next to **attendees** and type the names of the people you want to invite; iCal fills the names and email addresses in from the Address Book.

④ Click **Send** to send out email invitations.

End

INTRODUCTION
Don't get too excited about this feature; it only works if you are using Apple's Mail for your email program, and you must have the email addresses of the contacts you want to invite. But if you do meet these two requirements, you can use this feature to let your contacts know about an event you've scheduled.

TIP
Getting People in the Door
Another way to add people to the attendees list for an event is to choose **Window**, **Address Panel** and drag names from the list to the event's listing in the calendar.

HINT
Separate Names
To invite more than one person to an event, type a comma after each name before you type the next name. Otherwise, iCal isn't sure where one name ends and the next begins.

Searching Calendars in iCal

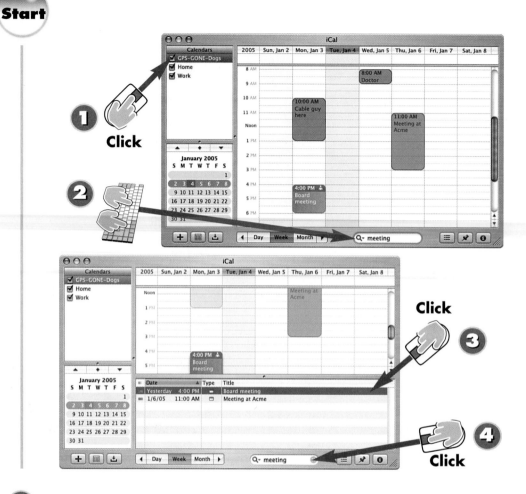

Start

Click

Click

Click

1 Click the check boxes next to the calendars you want to search.

2 Type the text you want to search for in the **search** field.

3 Click an event or to-do in the **Search Result** list to go to it.

4 To clear the search field, click the **X**.

End

Subscribing to an iCal Calendar

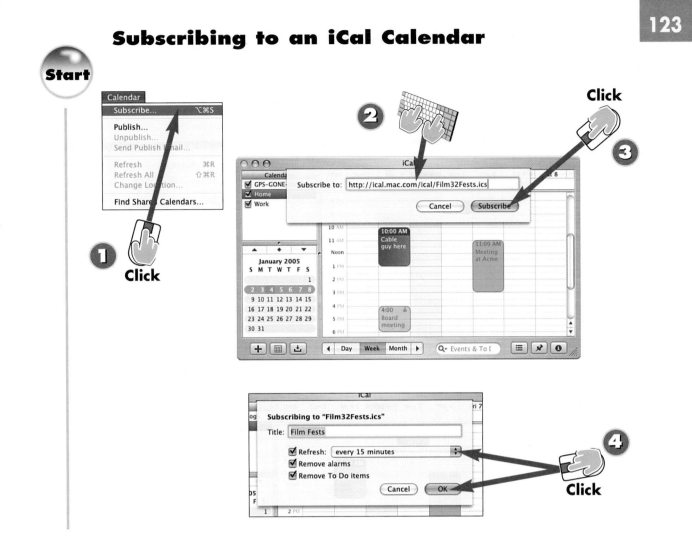

1. Choose **Calendar**, **Subscribe**.

2. Enter the URL for the calendar to which you want to subscribe. The calendar's owner provides this information.

3. Click **Subscribe**.

4. Choose a frequency in the **Refresh** pop-up menu for iCal to check the calendar for changes, and click **OK**.

End

Publishing an iCal Calendar

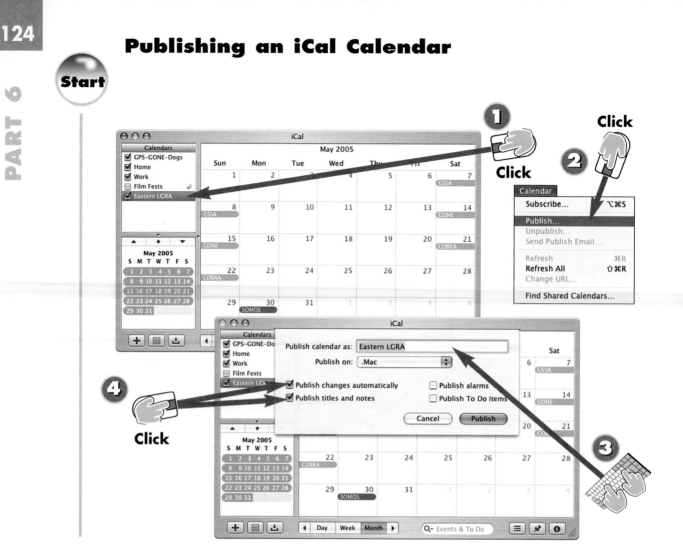

1 Click the calendar you want to publish.

2 Choose **Calendar**, **Publish**.

3 Type a name for the published calendar.

4 Click the check boxes to publish changes automatically and to publish both the title and notes for an event (rather than just its title).

What can you publish? Well, you can choose to share your home or work calendar with your family or colleagues. Or you might decide to be the keeper of the birthdays among your friends and publish a calendar showing everyone's special days. You can use your .Mac account or a free Web service to publish calendars, as you prefer.

Automatic Updates or Not?

Publishing calendar changes automatically requires a constant online connection. Don't choose this option if you use a dial-up account because you might find your computer dialing in unexpectedly.

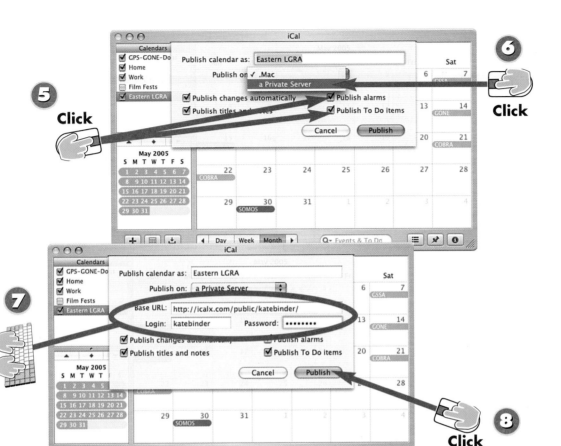

5 Click the check boxes to publish alarms and to-do items.

6 Choose an option from the **Publish on** pop-up menu for where you're publishing the calendar: using .Mac or using an independent server.

7 If you're using an independent server, enter its URL and your login name and password.

8 Click **Publish**.

End

Becoming a Publisher
If you want to publish your own calendars but don't have a .Mac account, go to iCalExchange.com (icalexchange.com). It offers free access to the WebDAV servers you need to publish calendars.

Changing Your Mind
If you decide to stop publishing a calendar, click its name in the **Calendars** list, choose **Calendar**, **Unpublish**. iCal warns you that people will no longer be able to subscribe to the calendar; just click **Unpublish** to take your calendar offline.

Putting Contacts, Bookmarks, and Calendars Online

Start

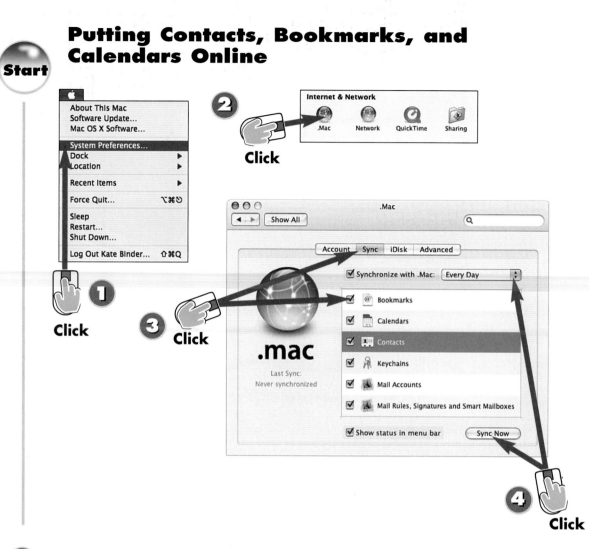

Click

Click

Click

Click

1. Choose **Apple menu**, **System Preferences**.

2. In System Preferences, click **.Mac**.

3. Click the **Sync** tab and check the boxes for the items you want to sync.

4. Select a frequency option from the pop-up menu and click **Sync Now**.

End

INTRODUCTION

If you have a .Mac membership, you can sync your contact information, Web bookmarks, calendars, and other information between two computers—or more. You can also access this information from the Web when you're using a computer that's not synced up, such as a public terminal.

TIP

In Touch Anywhere
To see your information using a web browser on any computer, go to www.mac.com and log in using your .Mac name and password. Then click one of the links on the left side of the page, such as **Address Book**, to see your data in all its glory.

HINT

Seeing Double
If you're using the same iCal calendar on two or more Macs, you'll receive duplicate event reminders. That's fine if the reminders are a simple dialog box. But if you use duplicate email reminders, it can be a bit annoying to neatniks.

Printing an iCal Calendar

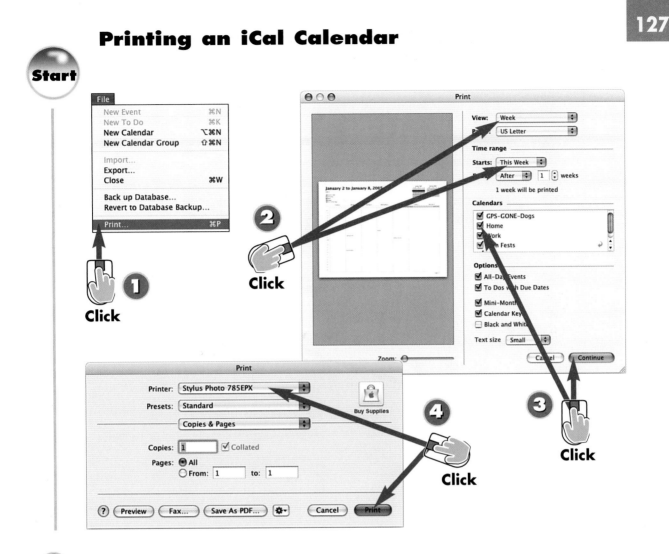

1 Choose **File**, **Print**.

2 Choose a view and a time range to print.

3 Choose which calendars should be shown on the printout and click **Continue**.

4 Choose a printer and click **Print**.

End

INTRODUCTION

Never fear, there's still a place for paper in the modern world! You can print your iCal calendars to post on the fridge or hand out at meetings. You can choose which calendars are included in a printout, as well as how it's formatted and how many days, weeks, or months it shows.

TIP

For Ancient Printers
If you're using an old printer that can't reproduce colors or gray tones (as in photographs), click **Black and White** to produce an easier-to-read printout without any grays.

Syncing a PDA, an iPod, or a Phone with Your Mac

Start

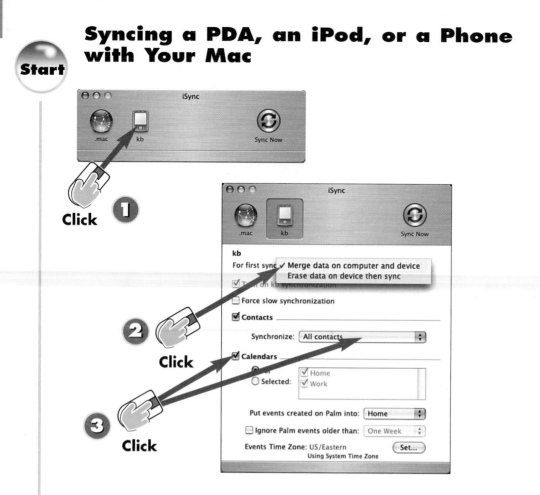

Click **1**

Click **2**

Click **3**

1 Start up iSync (located in the Applications folder) and click the icon for the device you want to sync.

2 If this is the first time you're syncing, click each device icon and choose an option from the **For first sync** pop-up menu.

3 Click the **Contacts** check box to include contacts in the sync, and choose which groups to include from the **Synchronize** pop-up menu.

Getting Hooked Up with iSync
You can download iSync at www.apple.com/isync/. To add a device to iSync, hook it up to your Mac and start iSync. Choose **Devices**, **Add Device**. Double-click the new device when it appears in the Add Device window.

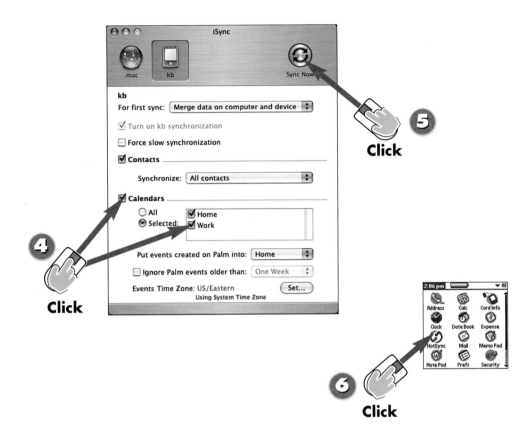

Click (4)

Click (5)

Click (6)

4. Click the **Calendars** check box to include calendars in the sync, and choose which calendars to include.

5. To sync all devices other than a Palm device, click **Sync Now** to begin the sync process.

6. To sync all devices, including a Palm PDA, start a HotSync by pushing the Palm's HotSync button.

End

Finding Almost Anything with Sherlock

Start

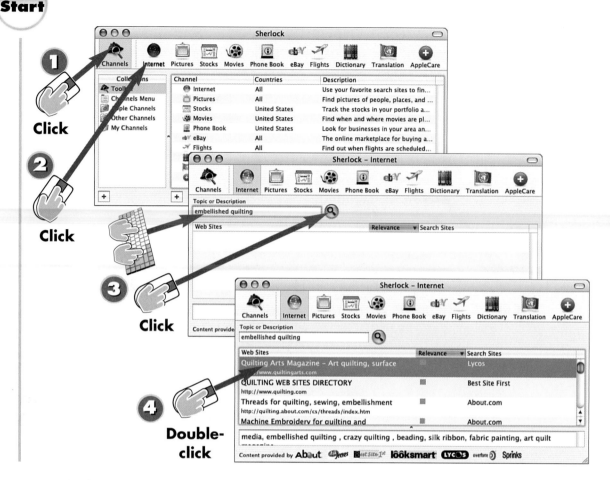

Click

Click

Click

Double-click

1. In Sherlock, click the **Channels** button to show all; then click the channel you want to use.

2. To search for websites, click **Internet**.

3. Type the search terms in the **Topic or Description** field; then click the **Search** button.

4. To go to one of the websites shown, double-click its name in the search results list.

 INTRODUCTION

Sherlock is a shortcut to some of the most-visited places on the Web. You can use it to look up everything from phone numbers to auction listings on eBay, all without even starting your web browser. After you've found what you want, a click or two in Sherlock takes you right to that location on the Web.

 TIP

Worth the Time?
When you click a website name in Sherlock's search results, you see a description of that website at the bottom of the Sherlock window. You can use this information to help you decide whether the site is worth visiting.

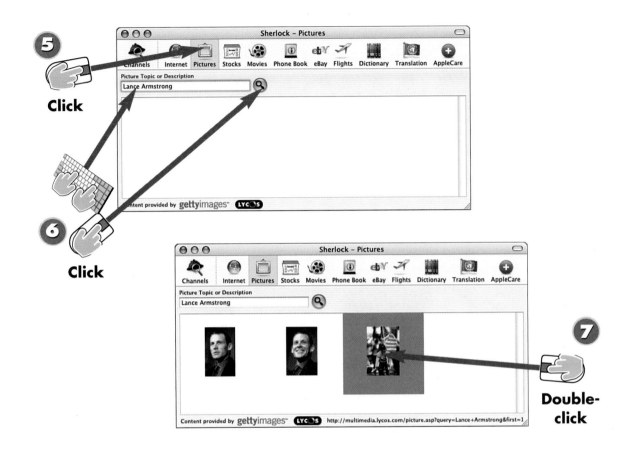

Double-click

(5) To search the Web for images, click **Pictures**.

(6) Enter the search terms in the **Picture Topic or Description** field, and then click the **Search** button.

(7) To see one of the images in its original context on the Web, double-click its thumbnail.

See next page

It's the Law
Remember that putting a picture on the Web doesn't mean its creator has relinquished ownership. Respect other people's copyright—don't redistribute their images without permission.

Good Will Searching
If you don't get enough results when you do a search, remove or change your search terms. If you get too many results and want to narrow them down, add more search terms to get a more specific set of results.

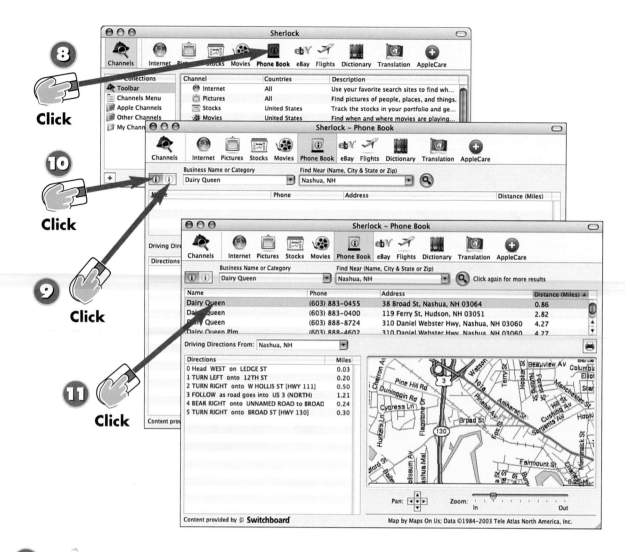

8 To search phone listings, click **Phone Book**.

9 Click the white **Info** button to search for a person; then enter the person's name and click the **Search** button.

10 Click the yellow **Info** button to search for a business; then enter the business's name or a business category and click the **Search** button.

11 Click an entry in the search results list to see a map and driving directions.

Sherlock's talents are especially useful for "quickie" searches. You can look up phone numbers, addresses, word definitions, and more at various websites, but with Sherlock all that information is in one place and getting at it is much quicker.

Getting There from Here
Driving directions need a starting point. You can type a city and a state in the **Driving Directions From** field or type a name from your Address Book. To get directions from your own house, create an Address Book entry for yourself and enter your own name.

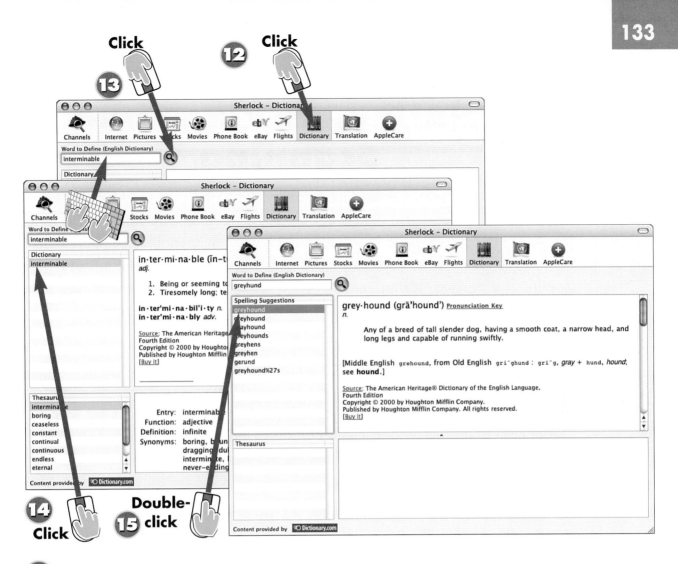

Click **Click**

Double-click **Click**

12 To look up a word, click **Dictionary**.

13 Enter the word in the **Word to Define** field, and then click the **Search** button.

14 Click the word in the **Dictionary** or **Thesaurus** area to see its definition or synonyms, respectively.

15 If the word isn't found, double-click one of the alternatives presented in the **Dictionary** area.

End

It's All Happening Online
Of course, Sherlock works only when you're online. If you don't have a constant connection to the Internet, remember that searching with Sherlock will trigger a connection attempt on the part of your Mac.

Finding More Channels
Developers and Mac hobbyists have spent time creating additional channels for Sherlock. You can find one good channel collection at Sherlockers.com (www.sherlockers.com). And try a Sherlock Internet search using the keywords "Sherlock channels" to locate more channels.

Printing, Faxing, and Scanning

After you've plugged in your printer, fax modem, and scanner, Mac OS X makes them easier to use than ever before. All three functions are built in to the system, so you don't need to worry about buggy, incompatible software that slows you down when you're trying to get things done. You have lots of options for printing, faxing, and scanning that enable you to get the most from your devices, but if you're in a hurry each function can be accomplished with just a few clicks.

Printing in Mac OS X is easier than it has ever been, with the option of using desktop printer icons for quick access to printer features and print queues. You can preview any document before printing it to make sure it looks the way you want it to, and preview documents can be saved as PDFs that you can exchange with others who don't have the software you used to create the document.

Faxing happens the same way and in the same place as printing—the Print dialog box—so you can fax any document you can print. And a small, simple, but powerful program called Image Capture takes over scanning duties—with great results.

Using Printers, Fax Modems, Scanners, and Fonts

Print and fax

Switch printers

Scan documents and pictures

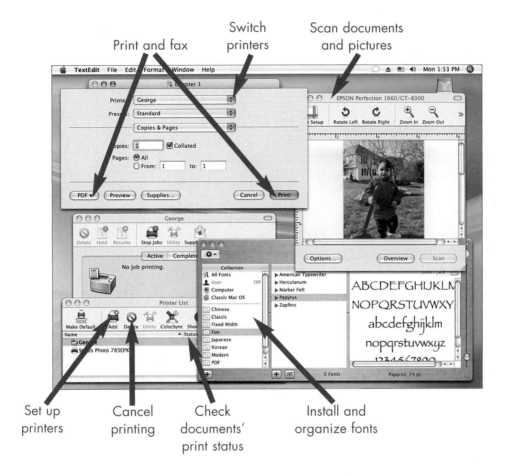

Set up printers

Cancel printing

Check documents' print status

Install and organize fonts

Setting Up a Printer

Start

Double-click

Click

Click

① Start up **Printer Setup Utility** (in the Utilities folder within the Applications folder).

② Click the **Add** button on the toolbar.

③ Select a printer from the pick list, and then click **Add**.

Before you can print, of course, you have to introduce your Mac to your printer. First, you'll need to know at least one thing about that printer: how it's connected. It might be a USB printer plugged in to the Mac itself, or it could be a network printer. When you get that figured out, the Mac's Printer Setup Utility can go out and find the printer for itself.

Two for One

If your printer doesn't have its model name and number on the front, check the manual that came with it. Sometimes multiple similar models share a driver, and in that case all the similar models should be listed in the manual.

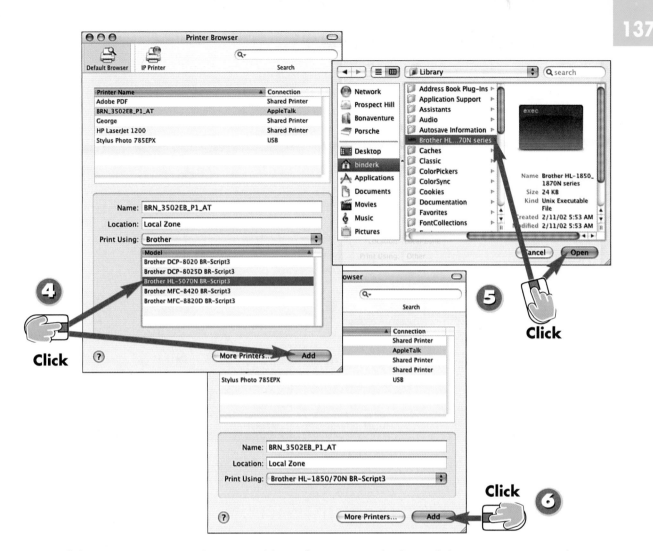

Click

Click

Click

4 If the Printer Setup Utility isn't able to figure out which model your printer is, select a make and model from the **Print Using** pop-up menu and click **Add**.

5 If you don't see your printer model in the pick list, choose **Other** from the pop-up menu; then navigate to the printer driver that came with your printer and click **Open**.

6 Click **Add**.

End

Missing Pieces
To work with your printer, the Mac has to have access to the printer drivers (the software) that came with the printer. If you don't have these, or if they're out of date, visit the printer manufacturer's Web site to download the latest drivers.

Close Enough
If you don't have the correct printer driver for your printer, you can usually get away with using one that's similar. Just choose the closest model available.

Switching Printers

Start

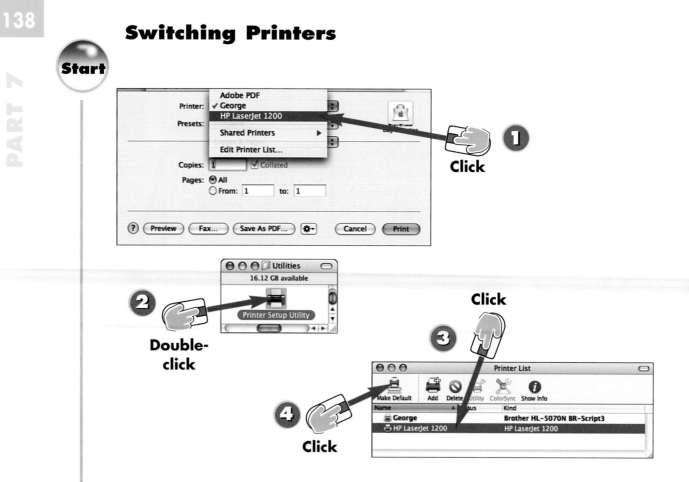

Click ①

Double-click ②

Click ③

Click ④

① To change printers on-the-fly as you prepare to print, choose a different printer from the **Printer** pop-up menu at the top of the Print dialog box.

② To change default printers ahead of time, double-click the **Printer Setup Utility** to open it.

③ Choose a printer from the pick list.

④ Click the **Make Default** button in the toolbar.

End

If you have more than one printer, you should make sure you send each document to the right printer. You can choose a printer each time you print, or you can change the default printer to ensure that the next time you click Print the desired printer will be chosen. Start by choosing **File**, **Print** in any program and then follow these steps.

Keeping Up-to-Date
If you have trouble printing, you might need new drivers to work with your updated software. In the Print dialog box, choose **Check for Printer Updates** from the Printer pop-up menu to search Apple's Web site for updated printer drivers.

Printing Success
If a friend or family member will be using your computer and you're not confident of that person's ability to select the right printer on-the-fly, set the default printer ahead of time so the right printer is preselected in the Print dialog box.

Viewing Printer Properties

Start

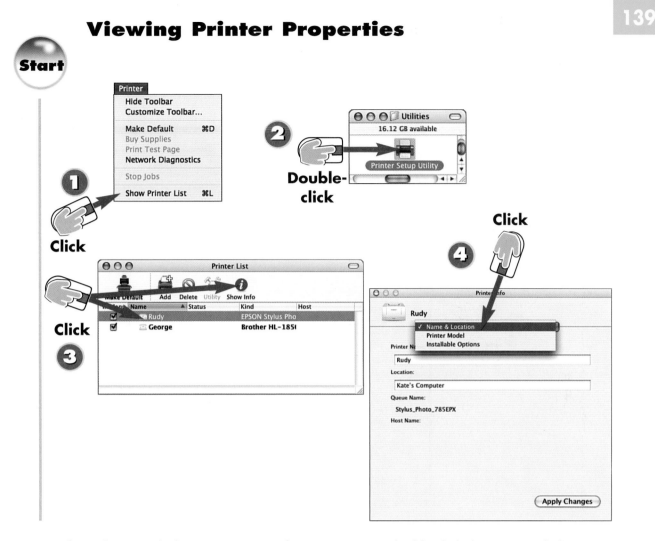

Click

Double-click

Click

Click

1. If you have a desktop printer icon for your printer, double-click the icon and choose **Printer**, **Show Printer List**.

2. If you don't have a desktop printer icon, double-click **Printer Setup Utility** (in the Utilities folder within the Applications folder).

3. Click the printer's name in the list and click the **Show Info** button.

4. Use the pop-up menu at the top of the Printer Info window to display different properties and make changes as needed.

End

INTRODUCTION

Just like any hardware device, each printer has properties that make it unique. Those characteristics include information such as its specs: What resolution can it print at? How much memory does it have? Printer properties also include the printer's name, which you can change to suit yourself.

What's in a Name?

Keep in mind that you don't have to keep the default printer name. Instead of "EPSON 785EPX," wouldn't it be more fun to call your printer "Rudy"? The name doesn't affect how the printer works, so why not let your imagination rule?

Previewing a Document Before Printing

Start

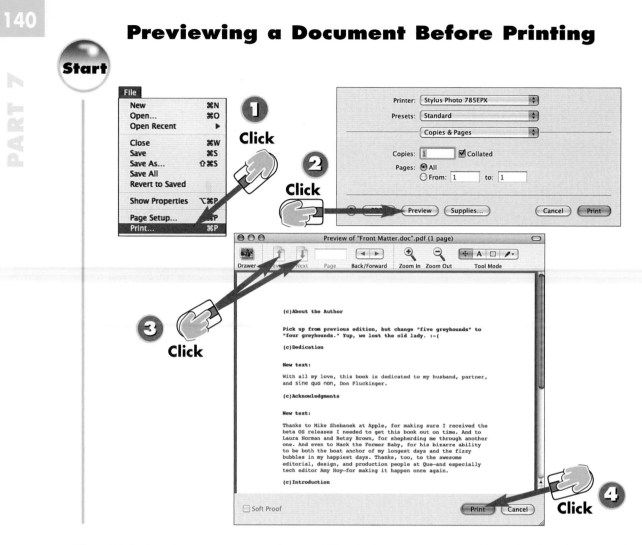

① Click

② Click

③ Click

④ Click

① With the document open, choose **File**, **Print** (or press ⌘-**P**) to display the Print dialog box.

② Click the **Preview** button; the system creates a PDF of the document and opens the PDF in the Preview program.

③ Scroll through the document in Preview using your keyboard or by clicking the **Previous** and **Next** buttons on the toolbar.

④ Click the **Cancel** button to return to the original application, or click **Print** to print the document.

End

Spreading the Wealth

When you click Preview, Mac OS X creates a new document from your original and opens it in Preview. You can save the preview document in PDF format, which also opens in Adobe Reader, to share with others who don't have the program you used to create it.

Printing a Document

Start

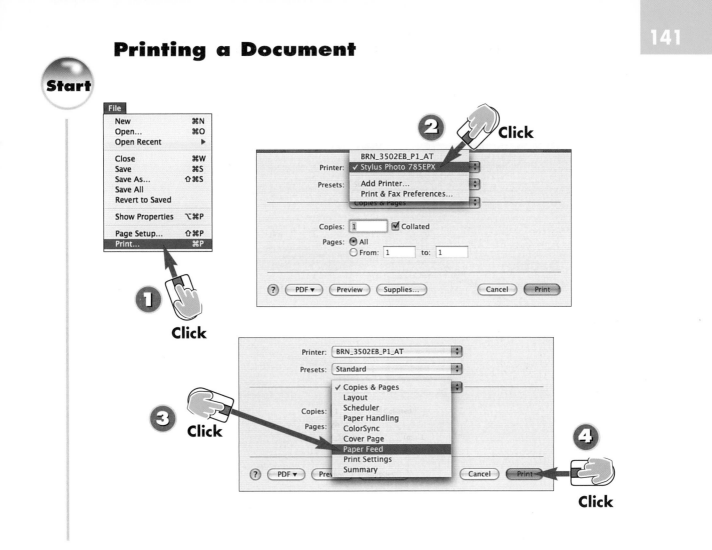

Click

Click

Click

Click

1 Choose **File**, **Print** (or press ⌘-**P**) to display the Print dialog box.

2 Choose a printer from the **Printer** pop-up menu.

3 Check the settings in each pane of the Print dialog box using the third pop-up menu and make changes as needed.

4 Click **Print**.

End

INTRODUCTION

For all practical purposes, the actual process of sending a document to the printer works the same in Mac OS X as it has in previous generations of the Mac OS. You can exert greater control if you want by inspecting each pane of the Print dialog box and adjusting the settings you find there, or you can just click Print and go.

HINT

The Print Dialog Box
The Print dialog box's panes vary according to the printer, but they always include Copies & Pages (the number of copies to print and the page range), Paper Feed (which paper tray the printer should use), and one for program-specific features.

Viewing the Print Queue

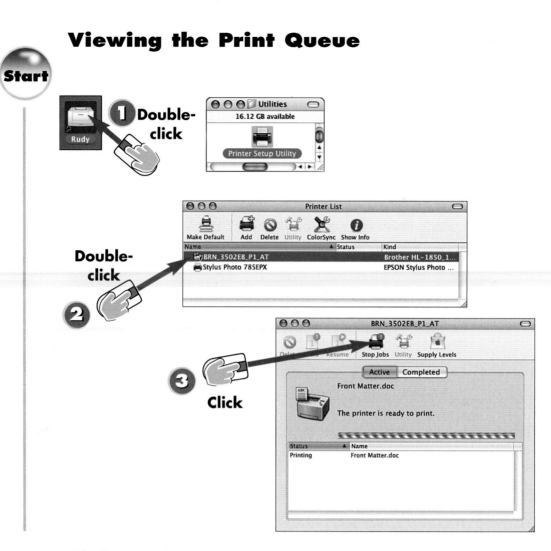

Start

1 Double-click

Utilities
16.12 GB available
Printer Setup Utility

Double-click

2

Printer List
Make Default Add Delete Utility ColorSync Show Info
Name | Status | Kind
BRN_3502EB_P1_AT | | Brother HL-1850_1...
Stylus Photo 785EPX | | EPSON Stylus Photo ...

3

Click

BRN_3502EB_P1_AT
Delete Hold Resume Stop Jobs Utility Supply Levels
Active Completed
Front Matter.doc
The printer is ready to print.
Status | Name
Printing | Front Matter.doc

1 Double-click your desktop printer icon, or start the **Printer Setup Utility** (in the Utilities folder within the Applications folder) to see the queue for that printer.

2 In the pick list, double-click a printer name to see its queue.

3 Click **Stop Jobs** to pause the print queue; click **Start Jobs** to restart the queue.

End

Printing has a twist, though, that would certainly come in handy in real life: the ability to send a document to the front of the line by giving it a higher priority when you print it so that it jumps to the head of the printing queue.

Sort List By...
When you're looking at a print queue, you can click the Status or Name column head to re-sort the current print jobs. This doesn't change the order in which they'll print, just the order in which you can read them.

Line Jumping
Choose **Scheduler** from the Print dialog box's third pop-up menu to set the time you want the document to print and choose a priority for it. If the document's priority is higher than other jobs queued for the same printer, it's printed before them.

Canceling a Print Job

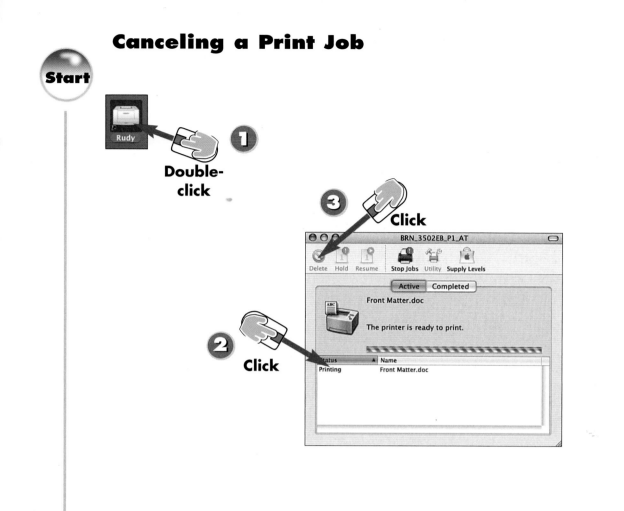

Start

Double-click

1

3 **Click**

2 **Click**

BRN_3502EB_P1_AT

Delete Hold Resume Stop Jobs Utility Supply Levels

Active Completed

Front Matter.doc

The printer is ready to print.

Status ▲ Name
Printing Front Matter.doc

1 View the printer's print queue, either by double-clicking the desktop printer icon or by starting up Printer Setup Utility.

2 Click the job you want to cancel.

3 Click the **Delete** button in the toolbar.

End

It happens to the best of us: You send a received fax or a rough draft of your term paper to the printer, only to realize that you're printing the document on $1/page glossy photo paper. Cancel that print job—now! Here's how.

Not Now, But Later

If you want to stop a job from printing now but you plan on allowing it to print later, don't delete it from the queue. Instead, click the **Hold** button in the print queue's toolbar to put all the documents that are currently printing on hold. When you're ready to restart printing, click **Resume**.

Sending a Fax

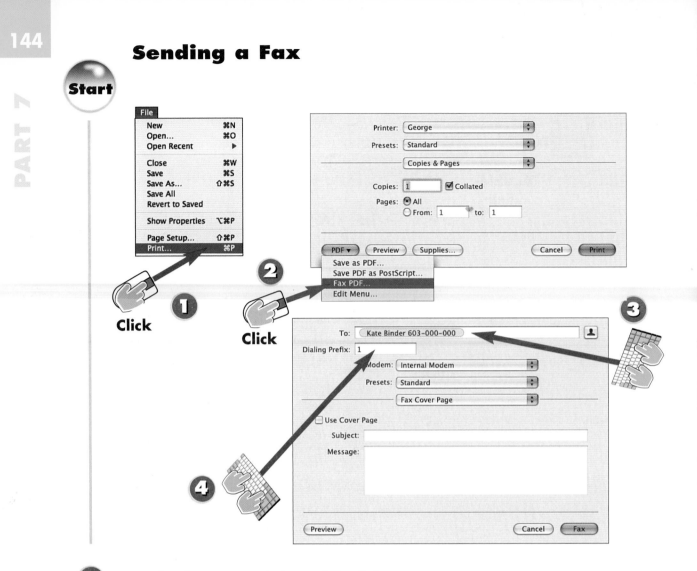

Start

Click

Click

1 Open the document and choose **File**, **Print**.

2 Choose **PDF**, **Fax PDF**.

3 Type the name and fax number of the person you want to fax. If the fax recipient's name is in the Address Book, the fax number is filled in automatically.

4 Type a dialing prefix (such as 1 for long distance or a long distance access code).

If you have a fax modem, you've probably spent some time wrestling with third-party fax software, which never seems to work right with either the system software or all the programs from which you want to fax. Those days are over; fax sending capability is built in to Mac OS X, and it's as close as the Print command.

Choosing Fax Recipients
To select fax recipients from your Address Book, click the **Address Book** button to the right of the To field. A small dialog box appears in which you can click to select a single person or ⌘-click to select multiple people.

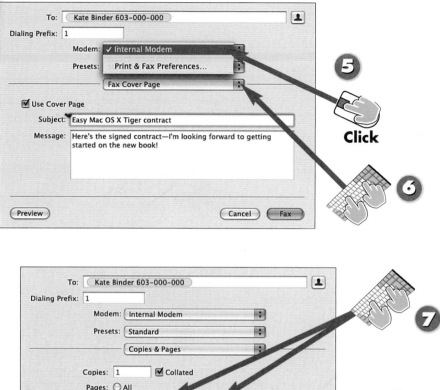

5 Choose your fax modem from the **Modem** pop-up menu.

6 Choose **Fax Cover Page** from the third pop-up menu and select a type of cover page. Click **Use Cover Page** and enter a subject and message for the fax's cover page.

7 Choose **Copies & Pages** from the third pop-up menu, and then type the range of pages you want to include in the fax.

8 Click **Fax**.

End

What Goes Out Can Come In, Too
To receive faxes on your Mac, choose **Apple menu, System Preferences**; then click **Print & Fax**. Click the **Faxing** tab and click the check box labeled **Receive faxes on this computer**. Then type your fax number and set options for what your Mac is to do when a fax is received.

Using a Scanner

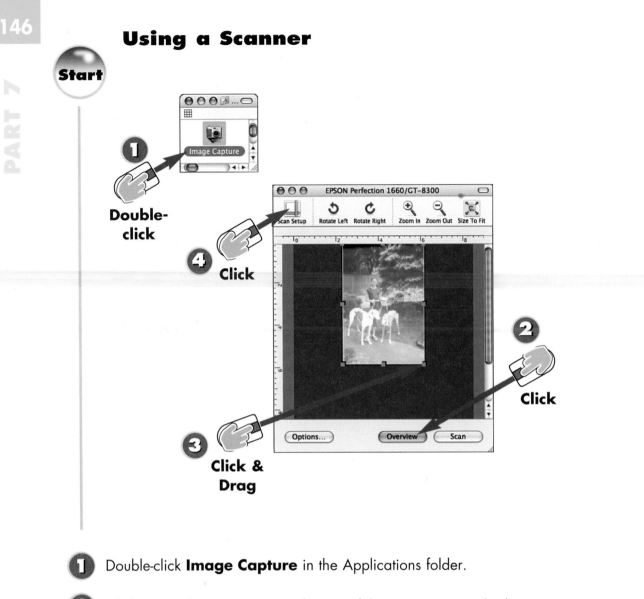

Start

1 Double-click

4 Click

2 Click

3 Click & Drag

---

1 Double-click **Image Capture** in the Applications folder.

2 Click **Overview** to see a quick scan of the entire scanner bed.

3 Click and drag in the window to select the portion of the image you want to scan.

4 Click the **Scan Setup** button to open the Scan Setup Drawer.

Your scanner is the way to get pictures inside your Mac, whether you need to copy a document, email a photo, or produce a Web image of a flat item you're selling at auction online. First, install the scanner and its software according to the instructions that came with it. Then you're ready to get scanning.

Sticking to the Safe Side
You should be conservative in selecting the scan area. If you scan a larger area than you need, you can trim it when you edit the image in Adobe Photoshop or another program. If you don't scan enough, you'll have to rescan the image.

Click

5

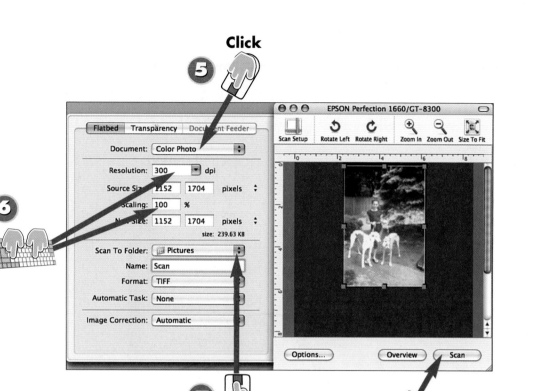

6

7
Click

8
Click

5 Click a tab to choose a source type, such as **Flatbed**, and select a document type from the **Document** pop-up menu.

6 Set the **Resolution** and the **Scaling** percentage.

7 Choose a location for the image file.

8 Click **Scan**. The image opens in the selected program and is saved in the selected folder.

Making It Better
If you don't plan to edit your scanned image in an image editor such as Photoshop, you can adjust its brightness, tint, hue, and saturation right in Image Capture before scanning. Select **Manual** from the **Image Correction** pop-up menu to see the controls you can use.

More Scanner Options
Click **Options** to change some of the scanner's global settings, such as the resolution at which it makes overview scans and which programs start up when you press the buttons on the front of the scanner.

Adding Fonts

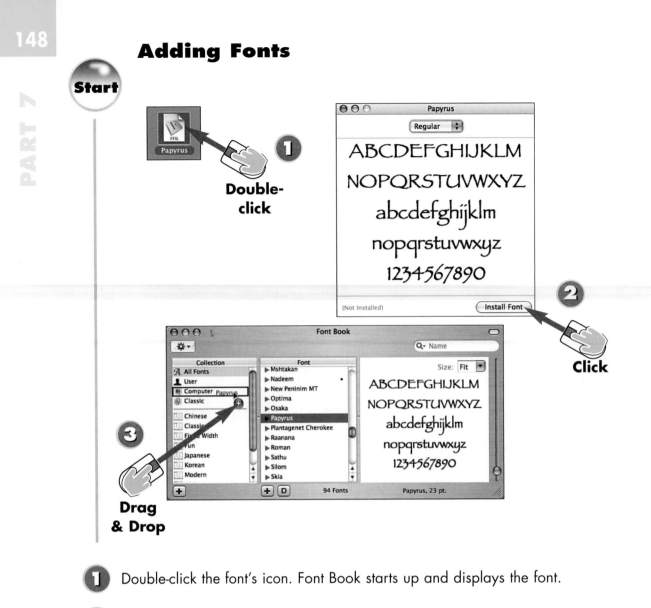

Start

Double-click

①

② Click

③ Drag & Drop

① Double-click the font's icon. Font Book starts up and displays the font.

② Click **Install Font**. The font is installed in your home folder's Library folder.

③ To install the font so that all your Mac's users can use it, drag the font to the **Computer** folder in the **Collection** column.

End

TIP

Shopping Time
Where do fonts come from? One place to start is Apple's Macintosh Products Guide (www.guide.apple.com). Click **Productivity & Utilities** in the left navigation bar on the Web page and click the **Fonts** radio button; then click **Find Products** in the subsequent page.

Organizing Fonts

Start

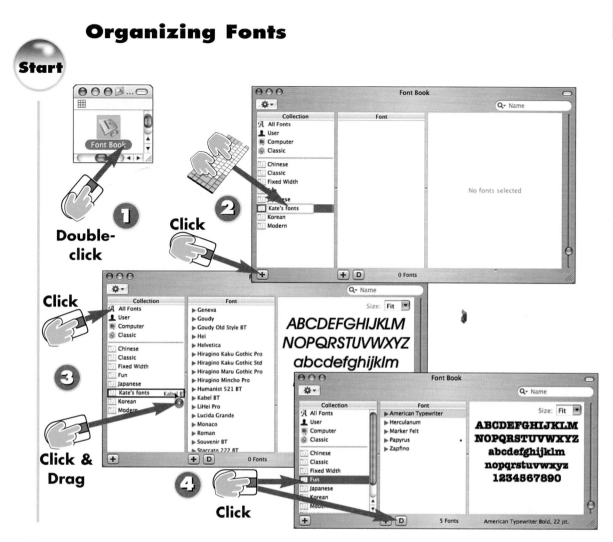

Double-click

Click

Click

Click & Drag

Click

1 Double-click **Font Book** in the Applications folder.

2 Click the **+** button below the Collection column to create a new collection; then type in a name.

3 Click **All Fonts** in the Collection column and drag a font from the Font column into the new collection.

4 Click a collection name or a font name and click **Disable** to remove that font from the Font panel. If you see a confirmation dialog box, click **Disable** again.

End

INTRODUCTION

If your font collection has been growing, you'll love the ability to group the installed fonts into collections. Collections keep your fonts organized so you can quickly apply the fonts you're using for a given project. Mac OS X comes with a few predefined collections, but feel free to create as many collections as you want.

TIP

Putting Fonts Back on the Menu
Disabling a font doesn't delete it—you can always return to Font Book, select the font from the All Fonts collection, and click Enable to make the font available again.

Getting Online

Before you can do anything online, you have to actually get online. Fortunately, with Mac OS X getting online couldn't be easier. In fact, your Mac might have completed some of these tasks for you already based on the information you gave it when you first started up Mac OS X. If not, don't worry—nothing here will take you more than a couple of minutes to complete, and then you'll be ready to go.

In this part you learn how to set up an Internet connection and how to get online using those settings. Although the details vary somewhat depending on your connection type, the setup process is similar no matter how you connect. Don't be intimidated by the techie terminology—after you have your settings in place, you won't need to worry about any of the details again. You might need to get some information from your Internet service provider, but if that's the case, you'll receive this information when you sign up with the provider.

You'll also learn about Mail accounts: how to set them up and use them to send and receive email. And you'll learn ways to keep your email spam-free, organized, and easy to deal with—no matter how much email you receive each day. You can even automate some organizational tasks so Mail takes care of them for you, such as filing your email in the proper mailboxes according to sender, recipient, or subject; this part shows you how.

Setting Up an Internet Connection and Your Email

Configure your
Mac to get
online

Sort and filter
email messages

Connect to
your ISP

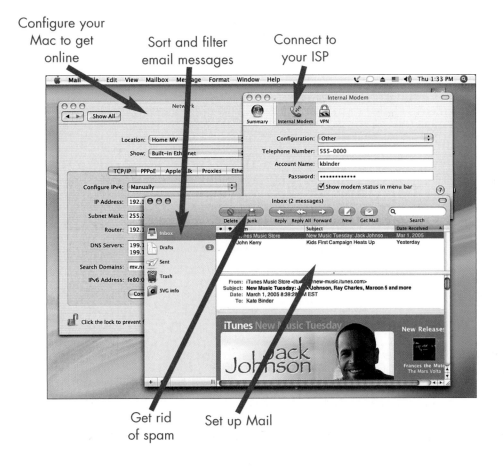

Get rid
of spam

Set up Mail

Setting Up Your Connection

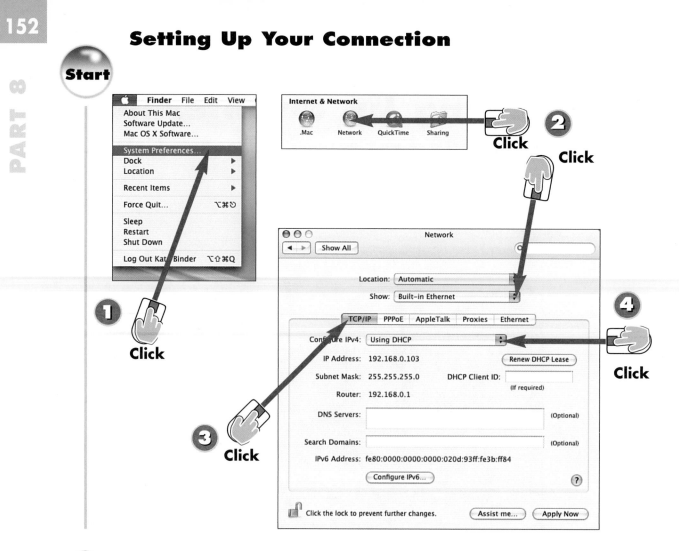

1 Choose **Apple menu**, **System Preferences**.

2 Click the **Network** icon to see your connection settings and choose your connection type from the **Show** pop-up menu.

3 Click the **TCP/IP** tab if it's not visible.

4 Choose your ISP's configuration method from the **Configure IPv4** pop-up menu: usually **Using PPP** for phone modems, **Manually** for LAN connections, or **Using DHCP** for cable and DSL modems.

To set up your Internet connection, you'll need to find out a few things from your Internet service provider (ISP): your login name and password, possibly the ISP's DNS server addresses, and definitely the preferred configuration method.

Talk to Me

The Transmission Control Protocol/Internet Protocol (TCP/IP) is the language in which your Mac communicates with the other computers on the Internet. The choices in the Configure IPv4 menu are different ways of setting up a TCP/IP connection. PPP (Point-to-Point Protocol) is used for phone line connections, and DHCP (Dynamic Host Configuration Protocol) is used for broadband connections and internal networks. With DHCP, your ISP's server makes most of your TCP/IP settings for you. If your ISP doesn't use DHCP, you need to make those settings manually.

5. If your configuration method is Manually, enter your IP address, the subnet mask, and the router address for your network.

6. Enter your ISP's DNS server in the **DNS Servers** field.

7. If your configuration method is Using DHCP and your ISP requires it, enter your DHCP Client ID.

See next page

Getting Help When You Need It

If any of these settings don't make sense to you, get in touch with your ISP's tech support people. It's their job to help you make the connection, so stick with it until you have what you need.

Don't Worry, Be Happy

You might notice different tabs in the Network preferences pane as you switch interfaces, but don't worry—that's normal. For example, when you're configuring Ethernet, you see a PPPoE pane that doesn't appear when you're configuring a phone modem because phone modem connections don't use PPPoE.

Click 8

Click 9

Click 10

8 If you have DSL and your ISP uses PPPoE, click **PPPoE**, choose **Connect using PPPoE**, and enter your account name and password.

9 If you're connecting via phone modem using PPP, click **PPP** and enter your account name, password, and your ISP's dial-up access number.

10 Click **Apply Now**.

End

Status Quo
After your network settings are in place, you shouldn't need to change them unless you buy new hardware (such as a router for Internet connection sharing) or your service provider changes the way its service is set up.

If Your Mac Is a PowerBook
If you connect using different methods in different places, you should definitely look into creating custom locations so you don't have to change all these settings every time you switch connections (see Part 5, "Customizing the Mac").

Connecting to Your ISP

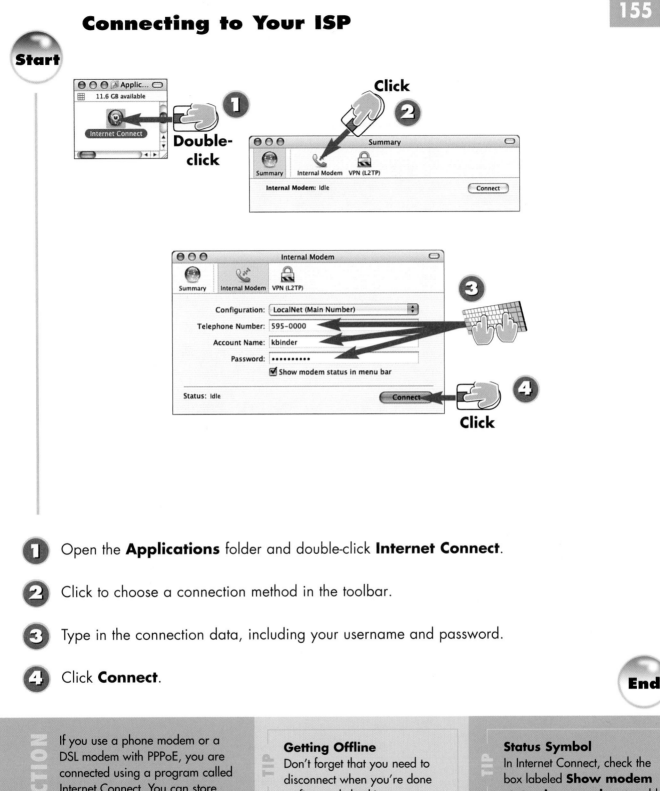

Start

Click

Double-click

Click

1 Open the **Applications** folder and double-click **Internet Connect**.

2 Click to choose a connection method in the toolbar.

3 Type in the connection data, including your username and password.

4 Click **Connect**.

End

If you use a phone modem or a DSL modem with PPPoE, you are connected using a program called Internet Connect. You can store more than one configuration, in case you connect in different ways at home, at work, and on the road. Internet Connect always remembers the last connection you made.

Getting Offline
Don't forget that you need to disconnect when you're done surfing and checking your email. Go back to Internet Connect and you'll find that the Connect button has changed to a Disconnect button. Click that and you're offline again.

Status Symbol
In Internet Connect, check the box labeled **Show modem status in menu bar** to add a Modem Status menu to your menu bar. And in the Modem Status menu, choose **Show time connected** to display how long you've been online.

Setting Up Email Accounts

Start

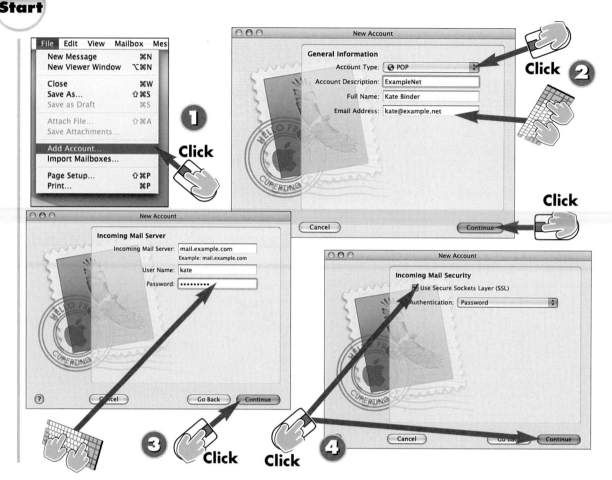

 Choose **File**, **Add Account**. (If you're starting Mail for the first time, you're taken directly to this series of dialog boxes.)

Choose an account type and name and fill in your name and email address. Then click **Continue**.

Type your incoming mail server's address, your username, and your password; then click **Continue**.

Check **Use Secure Sockets Layer (SSL)** and then click **Continue**.

INTRODUCTION

Setting up new email accounts works the same way whether you're using Mail for the first time or adding an umpteenth different email address for yourself. You'll go through a series of dialog boxes that ask you for your user-name, password, server names, and other information.

TIP

Different, But the Same

If you choose .Mac from the Account Type pop-up menu in the first dialog box, your choices will be slightly different. Mail knows how .Mac is config-ured, including the server addresses, so it fills in a lot of information itself.

HINT

More Fun with Mail Accounts

You can set up as many Mail accounts as you have email addresses. Mail automatically filters your incoming email into a separate mailbox for each address, so you can keep your messages organized.

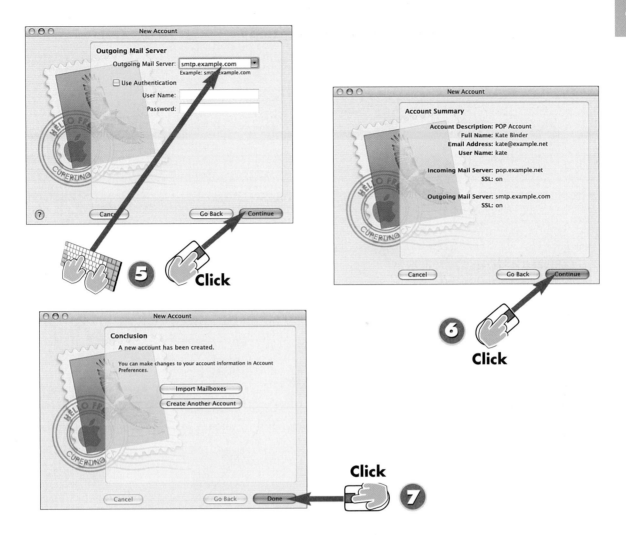

Click

5 Type your outgoing mail server's address and (if necessary) your username and password; then click **Continue**.

6 Double-check the settings you made; click **Go Back** to change them or **Continue** to accept them.

7 Click **Done**.

End

Pop Goes the Email!
POP and IMAP, the two Account Type choices that you are most likely to use, refer to the way your email is handled on the server, the computer that receives your email over the Internet and forwards it to your Mac. Most commercial ISPs use POP, but university systems, for example, often use IMAP. If you're not sure which account type your email uses, check with your network administrator or technical support department.

Sending Email with Mail

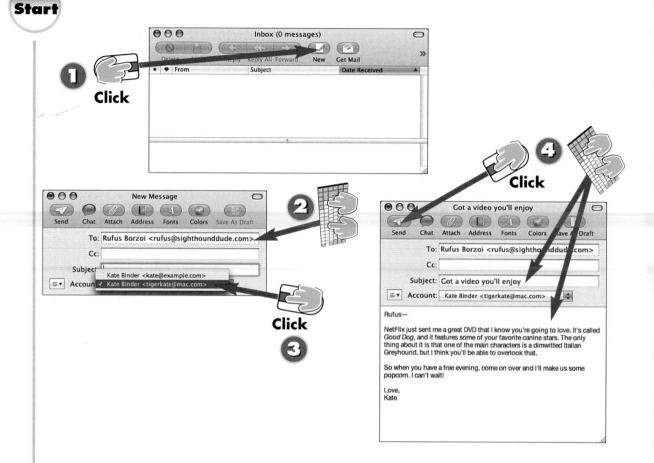

Start

Click

Click

Click

1 Click the **New** button in the toolbar.

2 Type the name of the person you want to email. If the email address doesn't appear automatically, type the email address in angle brackets after the name.

3 If you've set up multiple email accounts, choose the one from which you want to send in the **Account** pop-up menu.

4 Type a subject in the **Subject** line and your message in the message area. Click **Send**.

End

Sending email works the same whether you're composing a new message or forwarding or replying to a received message. The steps given here assume you want to start from scratch with a new message. If you click a received message in one of your mailboxes, you'll see toolbar buttons for replying and forwarding.

Jazzing Up Your Emails
To attach a file, click the **Attach** button in the toolbar and navigate to the file you want to attach. To make your email text colored, click the **Colors** button and choose a color in the Colors panel.

It's Better to Receive
To see email others have sent you, select **Mailbox, Get All New Mail**. Or, you can schedule automatic mail pickups by choosing **Mail, Preferences**. Click **General** and choose an option from the **Check for new mail menu**.

Receiving Mail with Mail

Start

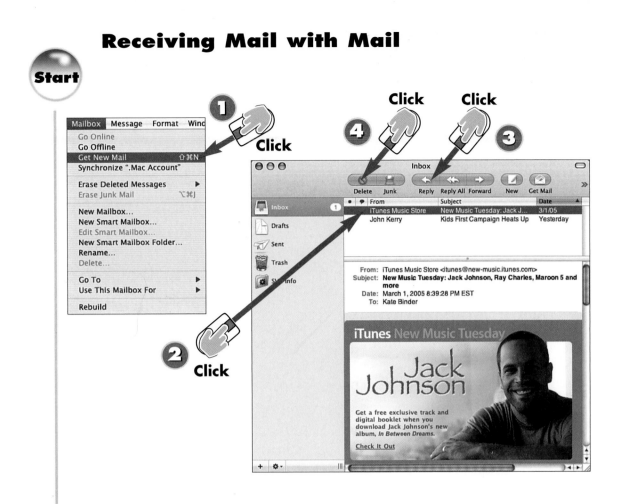

Click

Click **Click**

Click

Click

1. Choose **Mailbox**, **Get New Mail**.

2. Click a message listing in the In Box to see the message's contents.

3. Click **Reply** to answer the current message.

4. Click **Delete** if you want to send the message to the Trash.

End

There's nothing quite like that friendly chime (or beep, or other sound) from your computer indicating that you, yes you, have email. By default, Mail drops all your new, unread email into your In Box each time you check for new messages.

I've Got Mail?
Mail can retrieve your email messages automatically on a schedule you determine. Choose **Mail**, **Preferences** and click **General**. Choose a time interval from the **Check for New Mail** pop-up menu.

More Ways to Reply
When you want to answer an email message, click **Reply** to send your answer to just the original sender. Click **Reply All** to send it to the sender and to everyone who received the email. And click **Forward** to send it to another recipient.

Organizing Mailboxes

Start

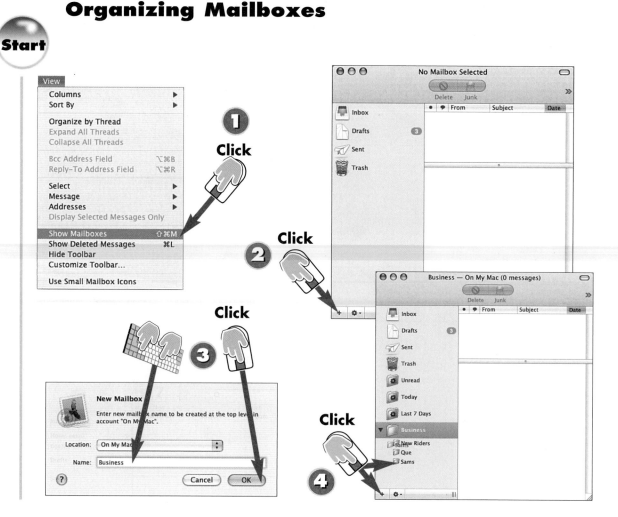

① Click

② Click

③ Click

④ Click

① In Mail, select **View**, **Show Mailboxes** if mailboxes are not visible.

② Click the **+** button at the bottom of the drawer to create a new mailbox.

③ Enter a name for the mailbox and click **OK**.

④ To create a mailbox inside another mailbox, click a mailbox name and then click the + button.

If you get a lot of email, you'll quickly find your In box filling up. Creating a system of mailboxes in which you can file all that email will save you time in the long run because it makes finding what you want when you need it easier. You can nest mailboxes within other mailboxes to set up as complex a system as you need.

Like Parent, Like Child
If a mailbox is selected when you click the + button you type the name of an existing mailbox, then a slash, and then the new name. The new mailbox is created as a child of the selected mailbox—in other words, it is within the selected one.

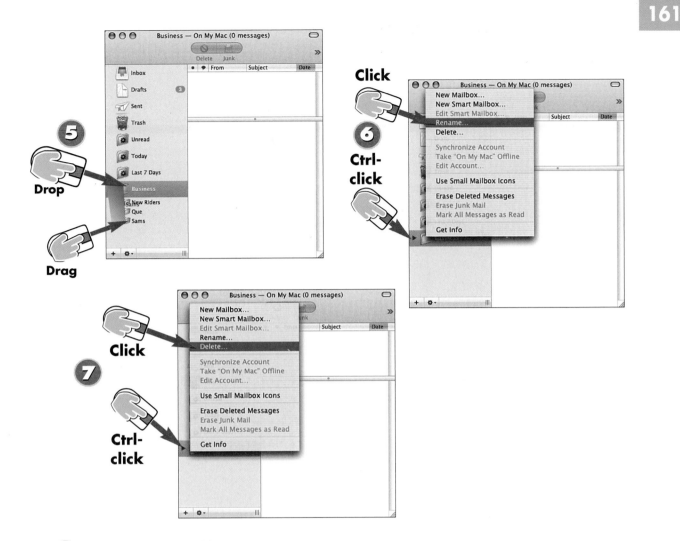

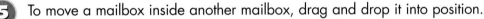

5 To move a mailbox inside another mailbox, drag and drop it into position.

6 **Ctrl-click** a mailbox and choose **Rename** from the contextual menu to change its name.

7 **Ctrl-click** a mailbox and choose **Delete** from the contextual menu to remove it.

End

Another Way to Get There
The same commands you see in the contextual menu are available in the Action menu at the bottom of the Mailbox drawer—click the button next to the + button to see the menu.

You Can't Go There
You can't add mailboxes inside the default mailboxes (In, Out, Drafts, and Sent). However, Mail automatically creates mailboxes within your In box to segregate mail received at different email addresses.

Creating a Smart Mailbox

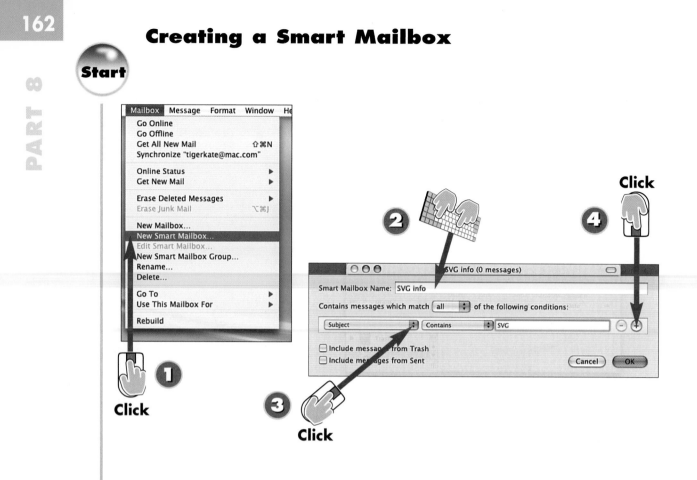

Start

Click

Click

Click

Click

1. Select **Mailbox**, **New Smart Mailbox**.

2. Type a name for the mailbox.

3. Choose criteria for which messages should be sorted into the mailbox.

4. Click **+** to add criteria.

Like smart groups in Address Book, smart mailboxes in Mail are maintained by your Mac. After you determine the criteria for a message's inclusion in a smart mailbox, the Mac takes over to sort messages into that mailbox as you receive new mail. Because messages can exist in both a regular mailbox and a smart mailbox, smart mailboxes don't interfere with your usual filing scheme.

What's It Good For?

Use smart mailboxes to track messages related to a particular project or from people who share a company or ISP. For example, you can have Mail sort all messages about your upcoming Flamingo Party into a smart mailbox.

Smart Mailbox Name: SVG info

Contains messages which match ✓ all / any of the following conditions:

| Subject | Contains | SVG |
| Sender is Member of Group | SVG project |

☐ Include messages from Trash
☐ Include messages from Sent

Cancel | OK

Click **5**

Click **6**

Inbox (0 messages)

Smart Mailbox Name: SVG info

Contains messages which match [any] of the following conditions:

| Subject | Contains | SVG |
| Sender is Member of Group | SVG project |

☑ Include messages from Trash
☑ Include messages from Sent

Cancel | OK

7 **Click**

8 **Click**

---

5 Select **All** or **Any** from the pop-up menu to determine whether messages must meet all the criteria or any single criterion.

6 Click the box labeled **Include Messages from Trash** to file messages that are currently in the Trash folder.

7 Click the box labeled **Include Messages from Sent** to file messages you send along with ones you receive.

8 Click **OK** to create the smart mailbox.

End

Any or All

TIP

Use Any to collect messages that fulfill one criterion *or* another (if the subject contains "Paris" or "Grand Canyon," file it under Vacation Plans). Use All to collect messages that fulfill both criteria (if the message sender's name is "Claus" and the email address contains "northpole.com," file it under Christmas).

Filtering Email in Mail

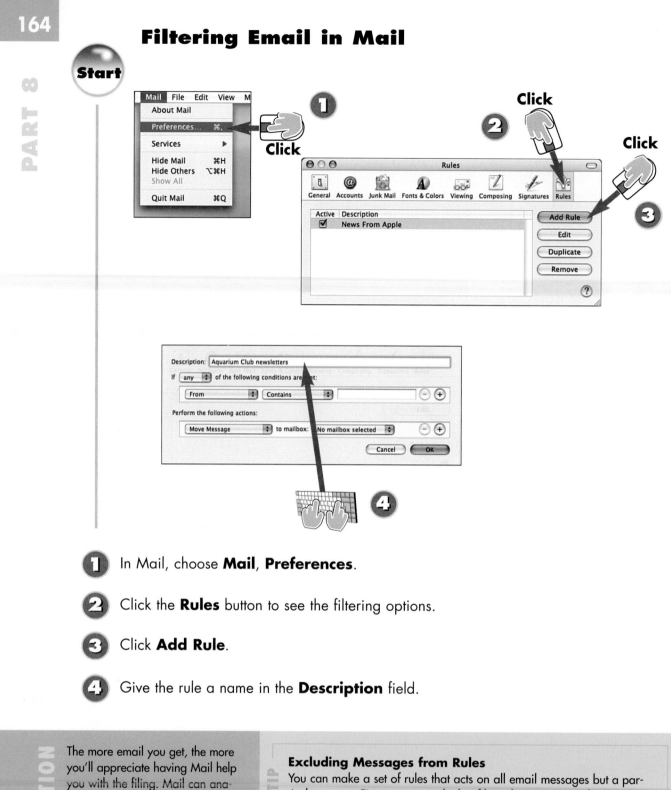

1 In Mail, choose **Mail**, **Preferences**.

2 Click the **Rules** button to see the filtering options.

3 Click **Add Rule**.

4 Give the rule a name in the **Description** field.

The more email you get, the more you'll appreciate having Mail help you with the filing. Mail can analyze each message you receive based on who sent it, where it was addressed, what it says, or several other criteria, and it can file that message in the appropriate mailbox. Mailboxes with unread messages are shown in bold type.

Excluding Messages from Rules
You can make a set of rules that acts on all email messages but a particular group. First, create a rule that filters the group you don't want to act on into the Trash or a mailbox. Then create another rule to apply your action to Every Message; this rule acts on all the messages remaining after the first rule is executed.

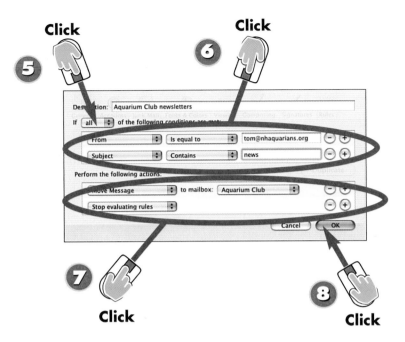

Click ⑤   **Click** ⑥

Click ⑦   **Click** ⑧

⑤ Choose **any** or **all** from the pop-up menu; with any, the rule is activated if one or more condition is met, and with all it's activated only if they're all met.

⑥ Set up the condition you want to filter on; click the **+** button to add more conditions.

⑦ Set up the action to be invoked if the conditions are met; click the **+** button to add more actions.

⑧ Click **OK**.

End

Intercepting Spam in Mail

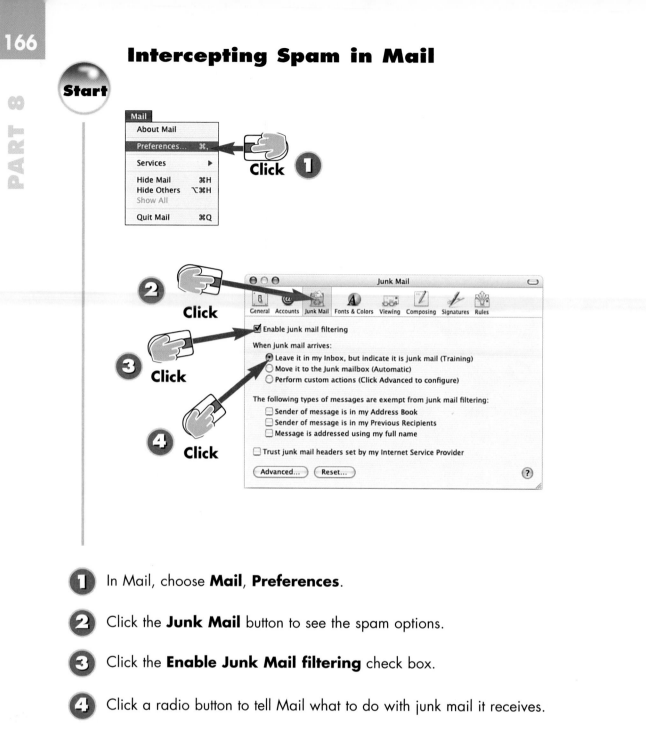

Start

Click **1**

Click **2**

Click **3**

Click **4**

1 In Mail, choose **Mail**, **Preferences**.

2 Click the **Junk Mail** button to see the spam options.

3 Click the **Enable Junk Mail filtering** check box.

4 Click a radio button to tell Mail what to do with junk mail it receives.

Spam (or junk mail, or unsolicited commercial email) is everywhere, and it's increasing by the moment. Email users are constantly looking for new ways to deal with the deluge, and Apple has done its part by including a built-in, smart junk mail filter in Mail. With your help, the filter learns to better recognize spam day by day.

How Does It Work?
Mail recognizes junk mail using what Apple calls "latent adaptive semantic analysis." The program scans email messages for certain word patterns—not typical spam keywords such as "make money," but speech patterns spammers tend to use.

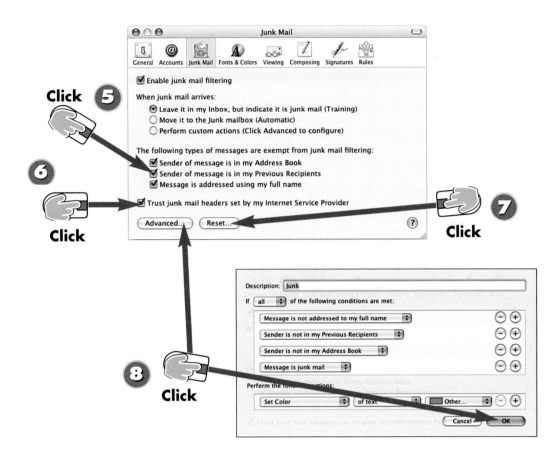

Click **5**

6

Click

7 **Click**

8 **Click**

5 Click the check boxes to indicate which types of email shouldn't be considered spam.

6 Click the check box to take advantage of junk mail prefiltering done by your ISP.

7 Click **Reset** to make Mail forget the list of known junk mail senders and subjects it has compiled.

8 Click **Advanced** to create your own junk mail filter (see the task "Filtering Email in Mail" for more information); then click **OK** when you're done creating the filter.

End

Teaching Mail More About Spam

TIP

Mail marks junk mail with a brown label. If a message is brown but isn't spam, click it and choose **Message, Mark As Not Junk Mail**. If you get spam that's not labeled brown, choose **Message, Mark As Junk Mail**. This trains Mail to recognize spam better.

Where to Put Spam

TIP

To put all your junk mail in a special mailbox, choose **Mail, Preferences** and click **Junk Mail**. Click **Move it to the Junk mailbox (Automatic)**. You can get rid of all the spam you've received by choosing **Mailbox, Erase Junk Mail**.

Living Online

So much of modern life happens online. Despite some people's complaints that community is disappearing, it's thriving on the Internet. That's what the World Wide Web is all about—a network of people sharing a network of information—and Safari is your passport to that network. Instant messaging, too, is a great way to keep in touch with others, and iChat brings it right to your Mac OS X menu bar.

In this part you learn how to set up iChat and begin exchanging messages with others. iChat works with AOL, .Mac, and Jabber screen names, but if you don't have a screen name already you'll learn how to create one for free. With iChat, you can set up your own chat rooms in which multiple people can exchange messages; in this part you learn how to create a chat room and how to take advantage of iChat's video and audio chat features to actually talk with your buddies or even see them over a video feed. For those features, of course, your Mac must have a microphone and a webcam (a small digital video camera).

Other tasks introduce you to surfing the Web with Apple's very own web browser, Safari—a fast, compact browser that you'll quickly learn to love. You'll learn how to create bookmarks and use the History so you can return to your favorite sites, as well as how to keep those bookmarks organized and accessible. And you'll see how to download files, view RSS feeds, save a Safari web page, and enable Safari to automatically fill out web forms for you—a great time-saving feature if you do a lot of online shopping.

Hanging Out on the Net

Organize your
bookmarks

Save
bookmarks

Chat online
with iChat

Edit your
buddy list

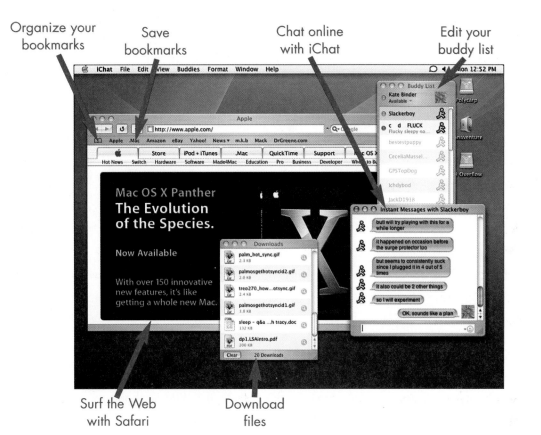

Surf the Web
with Safari

Download
files

Setting Up an iChat Account

Start

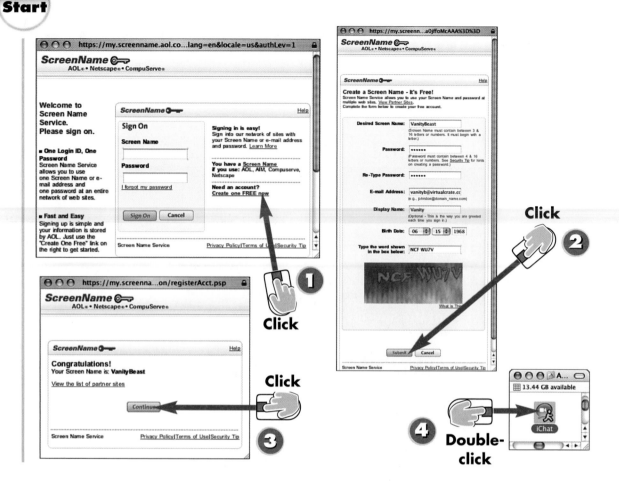

Click

Click

Click

Double-click

1 If you need to get an AIM screen name, go to the AIM website (my.screenname.aol.com). Click the **Create one FREE now** link.

2 Enter the requested information and click **Submit**.

3 Click **Continue** in the confirmation screen (or, if you're told that the screen name you chose isn't available, go back and try another one).

4 Open the Applications folder and double-click **iChat**.

INTRODUCTION

iChat works with either your .Mac username or an America Online Instant Messenger (AIM) screen name. If you don't have either, use the AIM screen name—it's free. The steps below walk you through getting a screen name and then entering your name and password in iChat so you can get online and start chatting.

HINT

What's in a Name?
When choosing a screen name, think about how you want to appear. If you'll be using iChat with clients and colleagues, you probably don't want to choose "FluffyBunny." And if you'll be chatting mainly with friends, "AcmeInc" isn't the best choice.

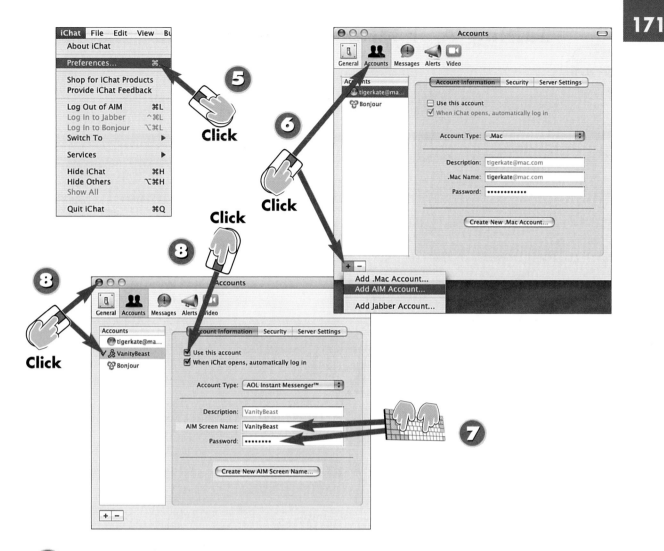

5 Choose **iChat**, **Preferences**.

6 Click the **Accounts** button, click the **Add** button, and choose **Add AIM Account**.

7 Enter your AIM screen name and password.

8 Click **Use This Account**, and then click the **Close** button to save your changes.

End

First Time for Everything
If it's the first time iChat has been started on your Mac, you'll see a series of dialog boxes in which you can enter your screen name and password.

Chatting on the Menu
Choose **iChat**, **Preferences** and click the **General** button to enter global iChat settings. The most useful one is Show status in menu bar, which enables you to start a chat with an online member of your buddy list without even starting up iChat first.

Chat This
iChat's not just for chatting—you can use iChat to transfer files as well. Click a person in your buddy list and choose **Buddies**, **Send File** to open a dialog box where you can choose the file.

Editing Your iChat Buddy List

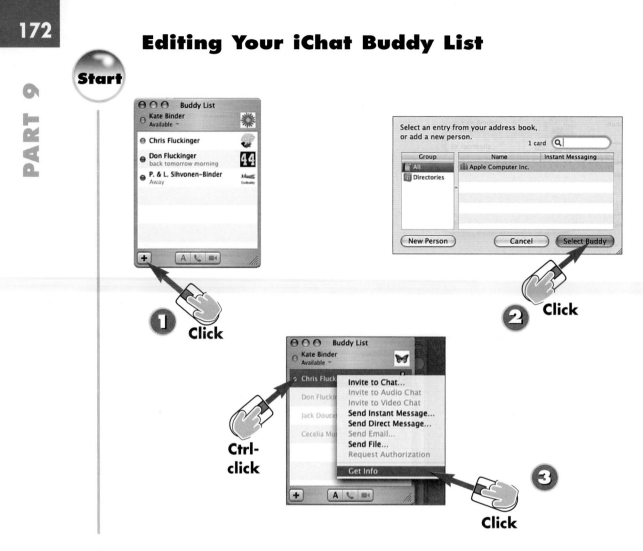

Start

1 Click

2 Click

Ctrl-click

3 Click

1 To add a buddy in iChat, choose **Window**, **Buddy List** and click the **+** button.

2 Choose a listing from your Address Book and click **Select Buddy**, or click **New Person** to add someone who's not in your Address Book.

3 To change a buddy's screen name or other information, **Ctrl-click** the name and choose **Get Info** from the contextual menu.

PART 9

INTRODUCTION

If iChat finds your buddies' screen names in your Address Book, it can attach their real names to them and display those in the Buddy List window. The most convenient thing you can do with the buddy list is set it to show only buddies who are online at the moment.

TIP

Nice to Meet You
If you're adding a completely new person to your buddy list, you must enter the screen name. If you want, you can also add the person's first and last name and email address. When you're done, click **+**.

TIP

Bye-Bye
To remove a buddy, click to select the name and choose **Buddies, Remove Buddy**.

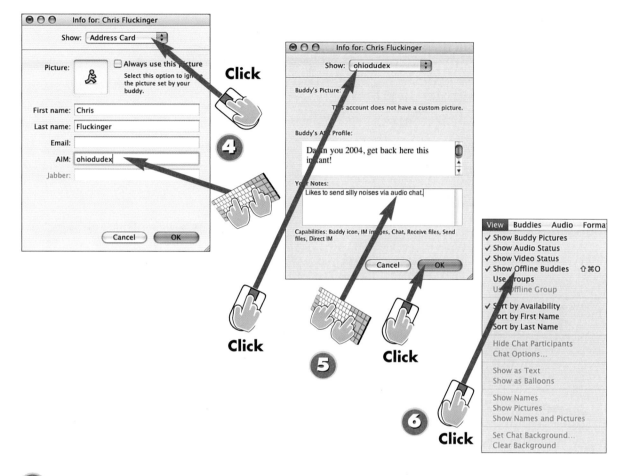

Click

Click

Click

Click

4 Choose **Address Card** from the **Show** pop-up menu and make your changes.

5 To make notes about the person, choose the screen name from the pop-up menu and enter the information in the **Your Notes** field; then click **OK**.

6 To show only buddies who are currently online, choose **View, Show Offline Buddies** to remove the check mark next to it.

End

TIP

Everything's in Order
You're also in control of the order in which your buddies are displayed in the Buddy List window. Choose a sorting option from the View menu: Sort by Availability, Sort by First Name, or Sort by Last Name.

Messaging with iChat

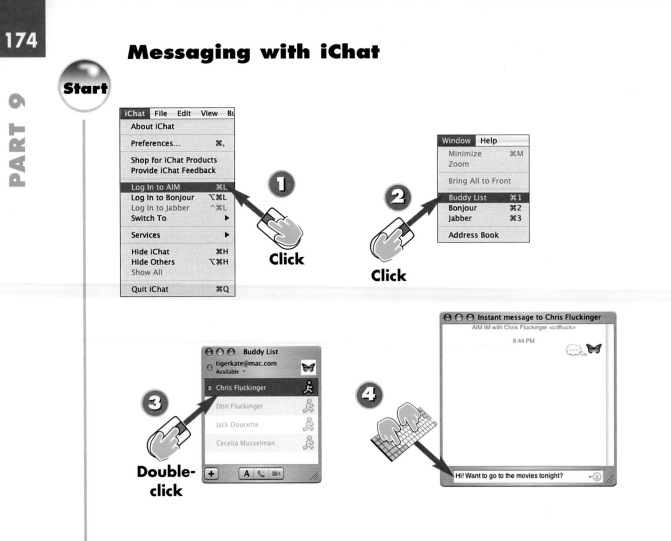

1. Open iChat from the Applications folder and (if not already logged in) choose **iChat**, **Log In to AIM**.

2. Choose **Window**, **Buddy List** if your buddy list isn't visible.

3. Double-click the name or screen name of the person to whom you want to send an instant message.

4. Type your message at the bottom of the message window and press **Return** to send the message.

End

Chatting with iChat requires two things: You must sign on to AIM with iChat and know the screen name of the person you want to reach. Conveniently enough, your buddy list is stored on AOL's servers, so it follows you around— you'll always see your own buddy list even if you log in on a computer other than your own.

TIP

On the Record
You can save transcripts of iChat conversations: Choose **iChat**, **Preferences** and click the **Messages** button. Click **Automatically save chat transcripts**. Click the **Open Folder** button to go to the folder of saved transcripts.

HINT

A Two-Way Street
You don't have to be an AOL member to use iChat. Whether you use an AOL screen name or a .Mac one, iChat works the same. However, you can use an AOL screen name with AOL Instant Messenger, but you can't use a .Mac name with AIM.

Talking over the Internet in iChat

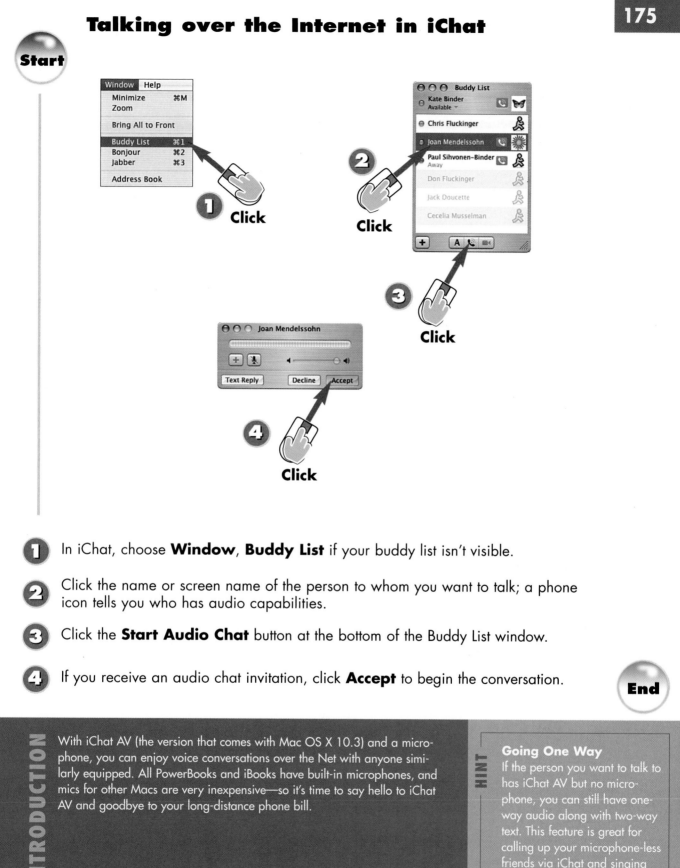

Start

1 In iChat, choose **Window**, **Buddy List** if your buddy list isn't visible.

2 Click the name or screen name of the person to whom you want to talk; a phone icon tells you who has audio capabilities.

3 Click the **Start Audio Chat** button at the bottom of the Buddy List window.

4 If you receive an audio chat invitation, click **Accept** to begin the conversation.

End

INTRODUCTION

With iChat AV (the version that comes with Mac OS X 10.3) and a microphone, you can enjoy voice conversations over the Net with anyone similarly equipped. All PowerBooks and iBooks have built-in microphones, and mics for other Macs are very inexpensive—so it's time to say hello to iChat AV and goodbye to your long-distance phone bill.

HINT

Going One Way
If the person you want to talk to has iChat AV but no microphone, you can still have one-way audio along with two-way text. This feature is great for calling up your microphone-less friends via iChat and singing "Happy Birthday" to them.

Holding a Videoconference

Start

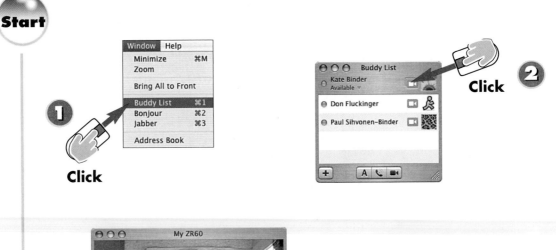

① **Click**

② **Click**

③

④ **Click**

① In iChat, choose **Window**, **Buddy List** if your buddy list isn't visible.

② Click the **camera** button next to your own icon.

③ Looking at the preview window, adjust your camera angle and height until you're happy with your appearance.

④ Click the name or screen name of the person to whom you want to talk.

INTRODUCTION

Who needs a videophone? You don't—you have your Mac. If you also have a high-speed Internet connection and a FireWire webcam, you're good to go. First, make sure your camera is plugged in to your Mac and working correctly. Then check your iChat preferences to ensure that iChat realizes the camera is there.

TIP

In a Rush?
A quicker way to begin a videoconference is to click the camera button next to the name of the person with whom you want to chat. You can start an audio chat session quickly by clicking the microphone button next to a buddy's name.

TIP

Let's Have a Party
To conference with multiple people, ⌘+click to select their names in the Buddy List window; then click the **Start Video Chat** button. To add a participant during a chat, click the + button in the chat window.

Click 5

Click 7

Click 8

5 Click the **Start Video Chat** button at the bottom of the Buddy List window.

6 The video window opens and you can see yourself; when your buddy answers, you can see both your buddy and yourself in the window.

7 Click the **Full Screen** button to expand the window to fill your screen.

8 Click the **Mute** button to freeze the video and mute the audio of yourself.

End

Setting Up a .Mac Account

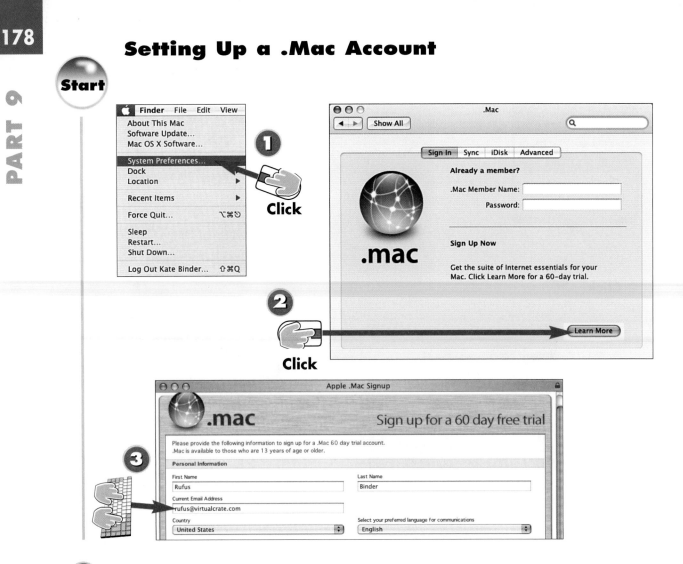

1 Choose **Apple menu**, **System Preferences**, and click the **.Mac** icon.

2 Click **Learn More** to go to the .Mac web page.

3 Click the **Free Trial** button to see the sign-up page. Enter the requested information and click **Continue**.

.Mac is Apple's own set of web services, including email, a custom website, online storage space (iDisk), e-cards, and more. It costs $99 per year, but the first two months are free—so why not give it a try? Many .Mac services are accessible directly from your Mac desktop—such as file storage on your iDisk—and others are based on the .Mac website.

What's an iDisk?

An iDisk is your hard drive on the Internet. It's storage space on an Apple server that belongs just to you. You can use it to store pictures for your .Mac web page, for backing up your important files, or to hold anything you want.

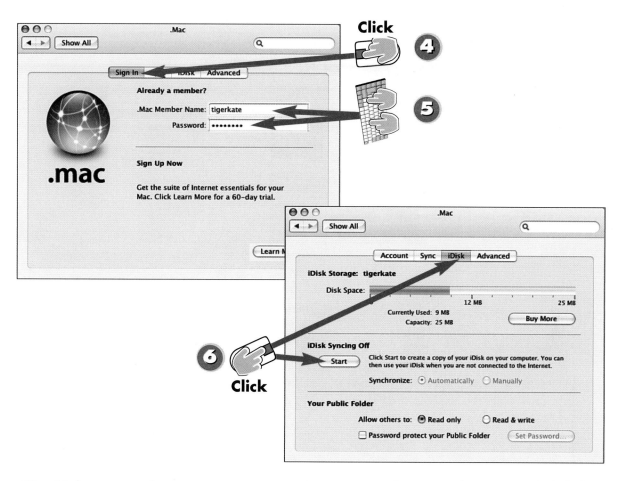

Click

Click

4. Make a note of your account settings; then return to System Preferences and click the **Sign In** tab in .Mac preferences.

5. Enter your new .Mac username and password.

6. Click the **iDisk** tab, and then click **Start** to create a copy of your iDisk on your hard drive.

End

HINT

Why a Local Copy?
If you don't feel like waiting around on your online iDisk, you can rearrange a local copy of your iDisk instead; then your Mac updates the real iDisk later. If you're short on disk space, turn off this option.

TIP

I Just Don't Remember
If you've forgotten your .Mac password, go to the .Mac website (www.mac.com) and click **Log In**. On the login page, click **Forget your password** and follow the directions to get your password back.

Surfing in Safari

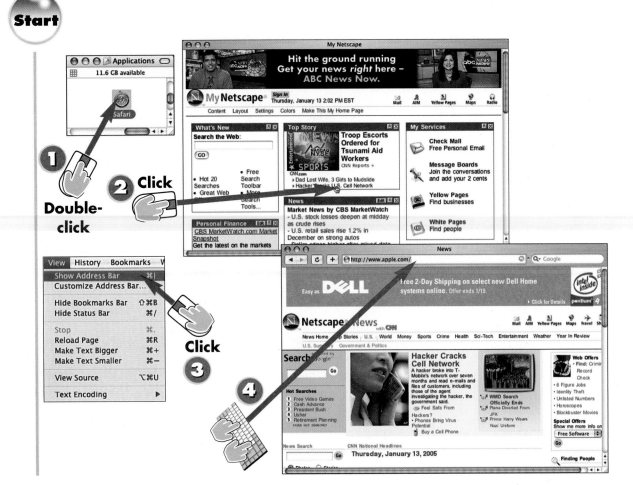

Start

1 Double-click

2 Click

3 Click

4

View menu:
History Bookmarks
Show Address Bar ⌘|
Customize Address Bar...
Hide Bookmarks Bar ⇧⌘B
Hide Status Bar ⌘/
Stop ⌘.
Reload Page ⌘R
Make Text Bigger ⌘+
Make Text Smaller ⌘—
View Source ⌥⌘U
Text Encoding ▶

1 Start up Safari (in the Applications folder).

2 Click a link on your home page to go to another page.

3 Choose **View**, **Show Address Bar** if the address bar isn't already visible.

4 Type the URL in the address bar for the site you want to visit.

TIP

Two for the Price of One
If you want to view a new web page without getting rid of the one you're looking at now, press ⌘-**N** or choose **File**, **New Window** to begin surfing in a new window while leaving the current window open in the background.

5 Click

6 Click

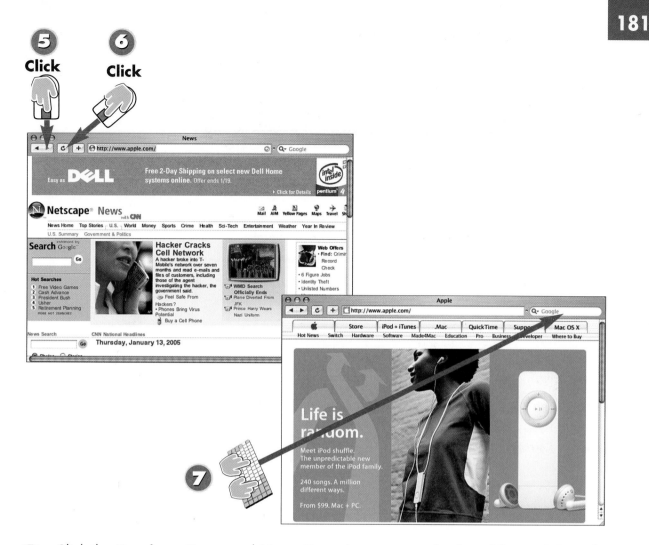

7

5 Click the **Previous Page** and **Next Page** buttons to go back and forward through the web pages you've visited.

6 Click **Reload** to have Safari redisplay the page from scratch; this is how you can update pages that change every few minutes, such as online auction listings.

7 Type search terms in the **Google Search** field and press **Return** to go to the Google site and initiate the search.

End

TIP

Browsing with Tabs
You can view different web pages in a single window, switching views by clicking a tab showing the page's name. Choose **Safari, Preferences** and click the **Tabs** button; then click to check the box marked **Enable Tabbed Browsing**.

TIP

Successful Surfing
To go back or forward, respectively, press ⌘-**[** or ⌘-**]**. To reload a page, press ⌘-**R**. And to see your bookmarks, press ⌘-**Option-B**.

TIP

Checking Your Status
Safari's Status bar shows you when it's contacting a web server, and it shows you the address behind any link you hold the mouse cursor over. To see the Status bar, choose **View, Show Status Bar**.

PART 9

Making a Bookmark in Safari

Start

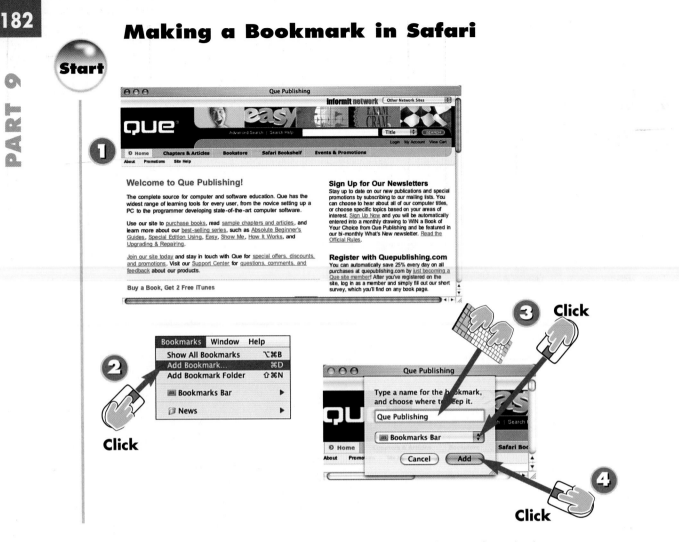

1 Click

2 Click

3 Click

4 Click

1 Open Safari (in the Applications folder) and go to the site for which you want to create a bookmark.

2 Choose **Bookmarks, Add Bookmark** (or press ⌘-**D**).

3 Enter a name for the bookmark (the page title is inserted by default) and choose a location for it.

4 Click **Add**.

End

INTRODUCTION

Whether you're used to calling them *bookmarks* or *favorites*, they mean the same thing: Your web browser notes a website's address so it can get you there again the next time you ask for that page. Bookmarks have two components: the web address (called a *URL*) and a name.

TIP

Bookmarks Here, There, and Over There
Safari stores bookmarks in three places: the Bookmarks menu, the Bookmarks bar, and its main Bookmarks collection. If you create a bookmark but don't put it in the Bookmarks menu or bar, go to your Bookmarks collection to find the bookmark. To see your Bookmarks collection, click the **Bookmarks** button on the Bookmarks bar or choose **Bookmarks, Show All Bookmarks**.

Viewing an RSS Feed

Start

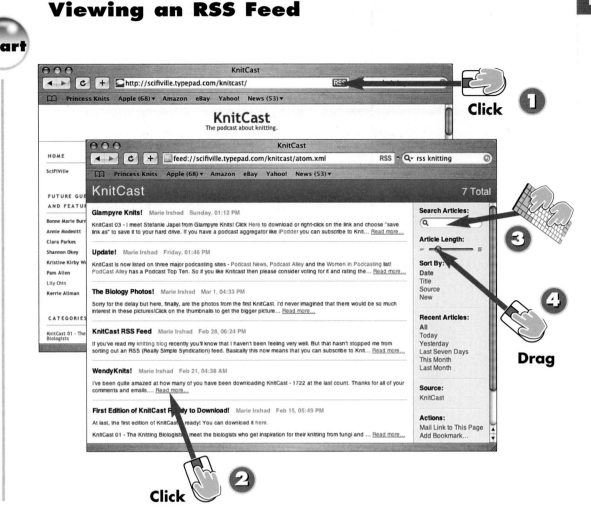

Click **1**

Click **2**

3

4

Drag

1 Click the **RSS** button to see the site's RSS feed.

2 Click **Read More** to see the rest of an article if it's not all visible.

3 Type words in the **Search Articles** field to search for those terms in the site's RSS articles.

4 Drag the slider to determine how much of each article shows in the window.

End

INTRODUCTION

RSS stands for *really simple syndication*, and it's an easy way for news organizations, bloggers, and others to offer a constantly updated stream of content. With Tiger, Safari has been renamed Safari RSS and can display RSS feeds for any website that offers one[md]you can tell by the RSS button next to the site's web address.

TIP

That's the Way I Like It
You can further customize your RSS display by choosing a different Sort By option (**Date** is the default) and by choosing which articles to view (**All** is the default).

TIP

Time and Again
When you have a feed's settings just the way you like them—including article length and sort order—you can bookmark it so that when you return, the display will be just the same. Click **Add Bookmark** under **Actions**.

Organizing Bookmarks

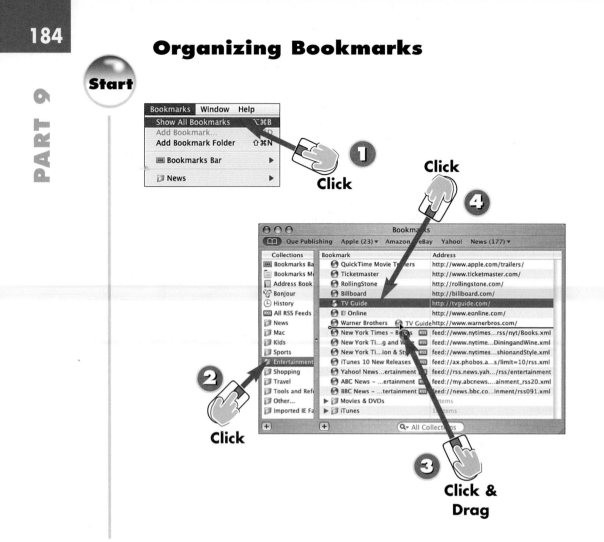

Start

Click

Click

Click

Click & Drag

1. Choose **Bookmarks**, **Show All Bookmarks** (or click the **Bookmarks** button in the Bookmarks bar).

2. Click a collection in the **Collections** column to see the bookmarks it contains.

3. Drag bookmarks up or down to change their order.

4. Click a bookmark and press **Delete** to remove it.

INTRODUCTION

Some people never bookmark anything. Others are sensible enough to bookmark only sites they know they'll need again. And still others—naming no names here—bookmark just about everything. If you're in that third group, chances are you could stand to spend some time organizing your bookmarks.

HINT

More Bookmarks
You can fit a lot more bookmarks in the Bookmarks bar by using submenus. Create a folder for each bookmark category, and then drop your bookmarks inside. Back in the main window, click a category name to see the submenu of bookmarks.

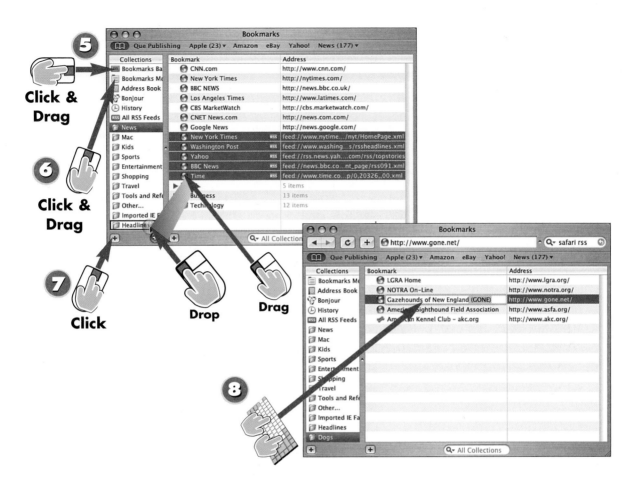

5. To add a bookmark to the Bookmarks bar, drag it into the **Bookmarks Bar** collection.

6. To add a bookmark to the Bookmarks menu, drag it into the **Bookmarks Menu** collection.

7. To add a submenu to the Bookmarks menu, add a folder by clicking the **Add** button, give it a name, and then drag bookmarks into the folder.

8. To change the name of a bookmark or folder, click it again, type the new name, and press **Return**.

End

More Address Book Integration

If you keep your contacts' URLs in the Address Book, you can add them to the Bookmarks bar or menu automatically. Choose **Safari**, **Preferences** and click the **Bookmarks** button; then click the appropriate check box to add Address Book items.

Using the History in Safari

Start

History	Bookmarks	Window	Help
Back			⌘[
Forward			⌘]
Home			⇧⌘H
Mark Page for SnapBack			⌥⌘K
Page SnapBack			⌥⌘P
Search Results SnapBack			⌥⌘S

- 🌐 Que Publishing
- 🌐 Welcome to the Virtual Crate
- eBay – The World's Online Marketplace
- 🌐 LGRA Home
- 🌐 PayPal – Welcome
- Amazon.com: Welcome
- CNN.com
- 🌐 Richard Binder – Fountain Pens
- Upromise – The Way to Save for College
- iGive.com – Change Online Shopping for Good

Earlier Today
Tuesday, August 26 ▸
Monday, August 25 ▸
Friday, August 22 ▸

Clear History

Click ① ② **Click**

History	Bookmarks	Window	Help
Back			⌘[
Forward			⌘]
Home			⇧⌘H
Mark Page for SnapBack			⌥⌘K
Page SnapBack			⌥⌘P
Search Results SnapBack			

- Upromise – The Way to Save for College
- 🌐 Que Publishing
- 🌐 Welcome to the Virtual Crate
- eBay – The World's Online Marketplace
- 🌐 LGRA Home
- 🌐 PayPal – Welcome
- Amazon.com: Welcome
- CNN.com
- 🌐 Richard Bind
- iGive.com –

Earlier Today
Tuesday, Augus
Monday, Augus
Friday, August

Clear History

③ **Click**

History	Bookmarks	Window	Help
Back			⌘[
Forward			⌘]
Home			⇧⌘H
Mark Page for SnapBack			⌥⌘K
Page SnapBack			⌥⌘P
Search Results SnapBack			⌥⌘S

- The Apple Store (U.S.)
- CNN.com
- Upromise – The Way to Save for College
- 🌐 Que Publishing
- 🌐 Welcome to the Virtual Crate
- eBay – The World's Online Marketplace
- 🌐 LGRA Home
- 🌐 PayPal – Welcome
- Amazon.com: Welcome
- 🌐 Richard Binder – Fountain Pens

Earlier Today ▸
Tuesday, August 26 ▸
Monday, August 25 ▸
Friday, August 22 ▸

Clear History

④ **Click**

① To return to one of the last 10 pages you've visited, click the **History** menu in Safari and choose the page's name.

② To go back to an earlier page, click the **History** menu and choose the appropriate submenu; then choose the page's name.

③ To mark a specific page you know you'll want to return to, choose **History**, **Mark Page for SnapBack**.

④ To return to a marked page, choose **History**, **Page SnapBack**.

End

TIP

A Fresh Start for History
If you've been surfing a lot and you're finding the History list a bit too crowded to let you find what you want, choose **History, Clear History** to start over with a blank History.

TIP

Automatic SnapBack
When you use Safari's Google search field, search results are automatically marked for SnapBack. When you click to view a page in the results, click the orange **SnapBack** button in the search field to return to that page.

Downloading Files

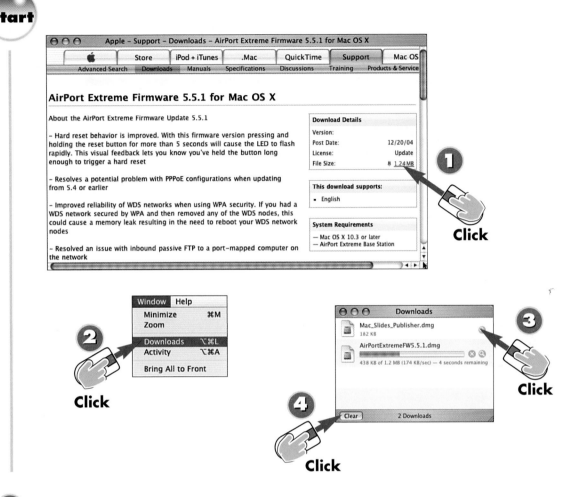

1 Click a web page link to download a file.

2 To watch the download's progress, choose **Window**, **Downloads**.

3 To go to a previously downloaded file, locate it in the Downloads window and click the **Show in Finder** button next to its name.

4 Click the **Clear** button to remove all downloaded files from the Downloads window. This deletes Safari's record of the download, not the file itself.

Download with Care

TIP

Virus scanning software is a good investment if you transfer files from other computers. Check out Norton AntiVirus (www.symantec.com), Sophos Anti-Virus (www.sophos.com), Virex (www.drsolomons.com), and VirusBarrier X (www.intego.com).

Saving a Web Page in Safari

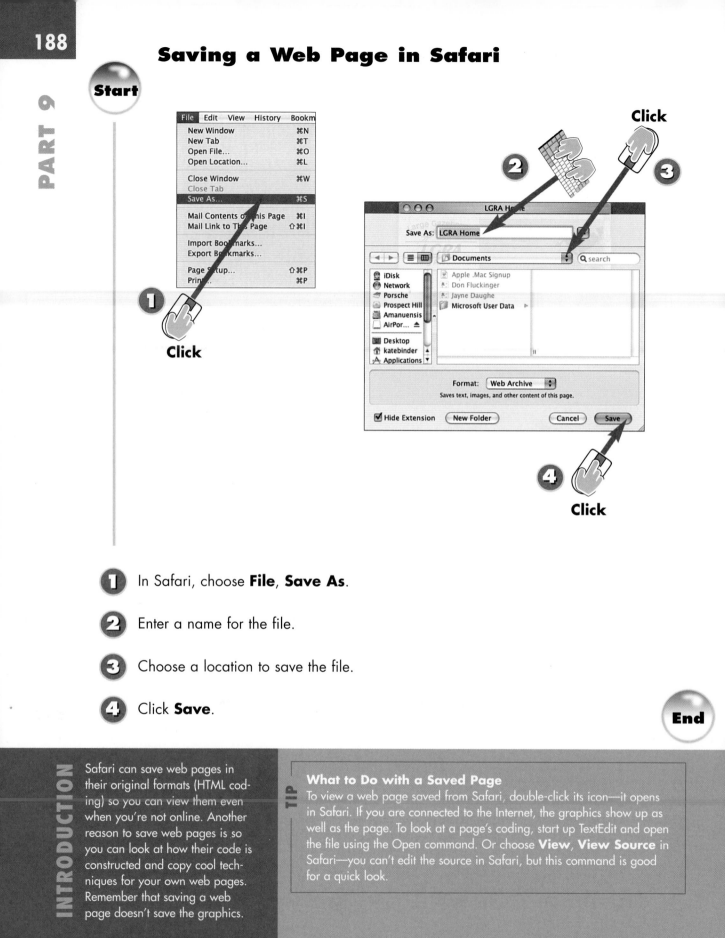

Start

Click

2

3

Click

1

4

Click

1 In Safari, choose **File**, **Save As**.

2 Enter a name for the file.

3 Choose a location to save the file.

4 Click **Save**.

End

Safari can save web pages in their original formats (HTML coding) so you can view them even when you're not online. Another reason to save web pages is so you can look at how their code is constructed and copy cool techniques for your own web pages. Remember that saving a web page doesn't save the graphics.

TIP

What to Do with a Saved Page
To view a web page saved from Safari, double-click its icon—it opens in Safari. If you are connected to the Internet, the graphics show up as well as the page. To look at a page's coding, start up TextEdit and open the file using the Open command. Or choose **View**, **View Source** in Safari—you can't edit the source in Safari, but this command is good for a quick look.

Automatically Filling Out Forms

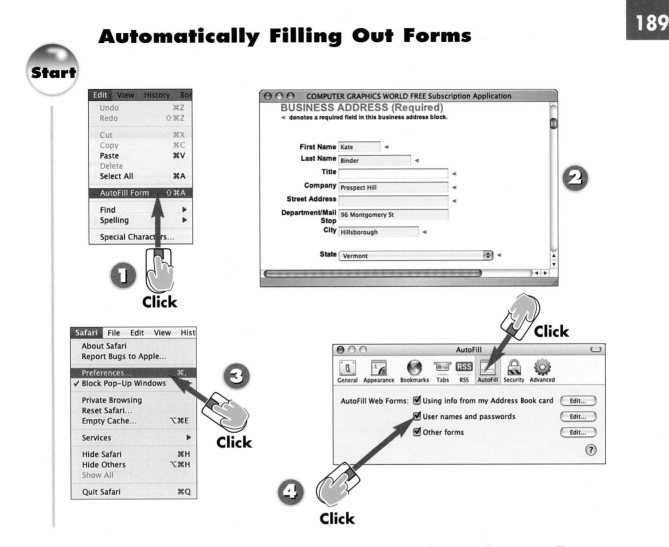

Start

Click

Click

Click

1 On a page with a form that requires this information, choose **Edit**, **AutoFill Form** (or press ⌘-**Shift-A**).

2 The information is automatically filled in.

3 To enable AutoFill to work with other types of forms, choose **Safari**, **Preferences**.

4 Click the **AutoFill** button and check **User names and passwords** and **Other forms**.

End

INTRODUCTION
Every time you buy something from a web store, create a new account with a website, or sign up to receive some service from a website, you have to input the same information. Wouldn't it be nice if Safari could remember that information and type it in for you? Guess what? It can.

TIP
When Safari Gets It Wrong
Safari tints the fields yellow where it's inserted information. If Safari guesses wrong and inserts incorrect data, just click in the field and type the correct information to fix it.

HINT
First Things First
Before using AutoFill, make sure your address, phone numbers, fax number, and other information are correct in your Address Book (which you'll find in the Applications folder).

Backing Up to Your iDisk

Start

①

Backup

Double-click

Click

②

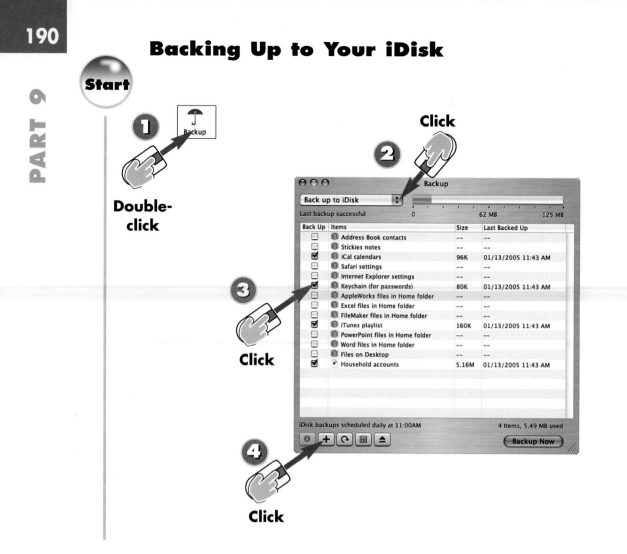

Backup

Back up to iDisk

Last backup successful   0   62 MB   125 MB

Back Up	Items	Size	Last Backed Up
☐	Address Book contacts	--	--
☐	Stickies notes	--	--
☑	iCal calendars	96K	01/13/2005 11:43 AM
☐	Safari settings	--	--
☐	Internet Explorer settings	--	--
☑	Keychain (for passwords)	80K	01/13/2005 11:43 AM
☐	AppleWorks files in Home folder	--	--
☐	Excel files in Home folder	--	--
☐	FileMaker files in Home folder	--	--
☑	iTunes playlist	160K	01/13/2005 11:43 AM
☐	PowerPoint files in Home folder	--	--
☐	Word files in Home folder	--	--
☐	Files on Desktop	--	--
☑	Household accounts	5.16M	01/13/2005 11:43 AM

iDisk backups scheduled daily at 11:00AM   4 Items, 5.49 MB used

Backup Now

③

Click

④

Click

① Copy Backup from the Software folder in your iDisk to your Applications folder and double-click it to open it.

② Choose **Back up to iDisk** from the pop-up menu.

③ Click check boxes to select the files you want to back up. The total size of those files appears at the bottom of the window.

④ Click the **Add** button to include other files in the backup.

HINT

When to Upgrade

Backup is great for home users or very small businesses that don't need to back up a lot of data. If you need to back up your entire hard drive daily, however, you should look into an industrial-strength backup program such as Retrospect (www.dantz.com).

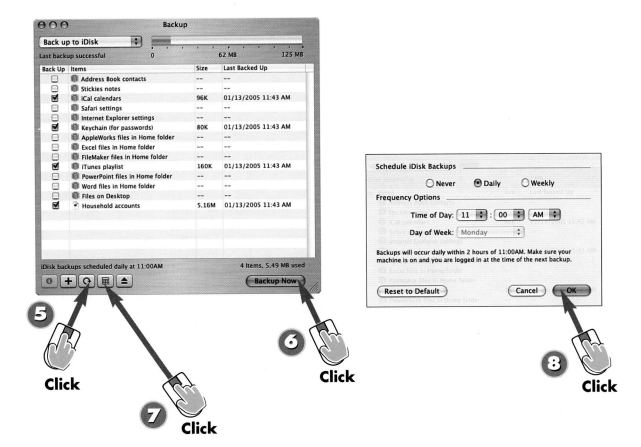

Click (5)

Click (7)

Click (6)

Click (8)

(5) Click the **Update** button if you've made changes to your files since you started Backup.

(6) Click **Backup Now** to begin moving files to the iDisk.

(7) Click the **Schedule** button to set a schedule for automatic backups.

(8) Select a frequency, time, and day and click **OK**. Backup starts automatically at that time and backs up the files currently selected.

End

Creating a .Mac Home Page

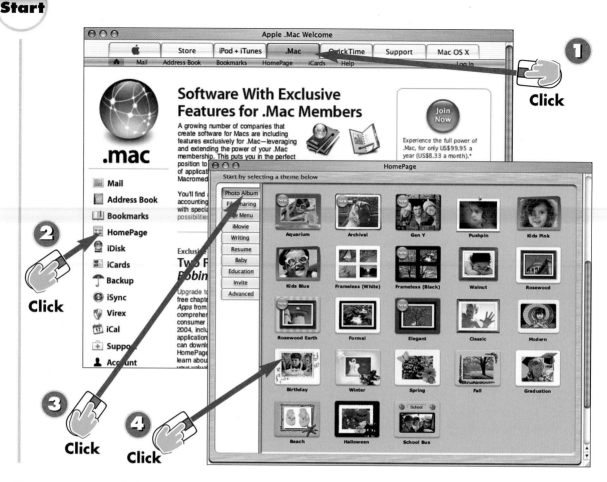

Start

Click **1**

2 Click

3 Click

4 Click

1 Use your web browser to go to Apple's website; then click the **.Mac** tab and sign in.

2 Click **HomePage** in the column on the left side of the page.

3 Click a page category on the left side of the page.

4 Click the right side of the page to choose a page from the category.

INTRODUCTION

HomePage features built-in templates for photo albums, file sharing, iMovies, résumés, new baby announcements, invitations, and more—each category comes with anywhere from a few to a couple dozen page templates you can customize to suit your needs.

TIP

Rolling Your Own
If you're already a web wizard, you can create your own web pages in any program. Just drop them into the Sites folder on your iDisk and make sure the main page is called **index.html**; your pages will be published just like ones created in HomePage.

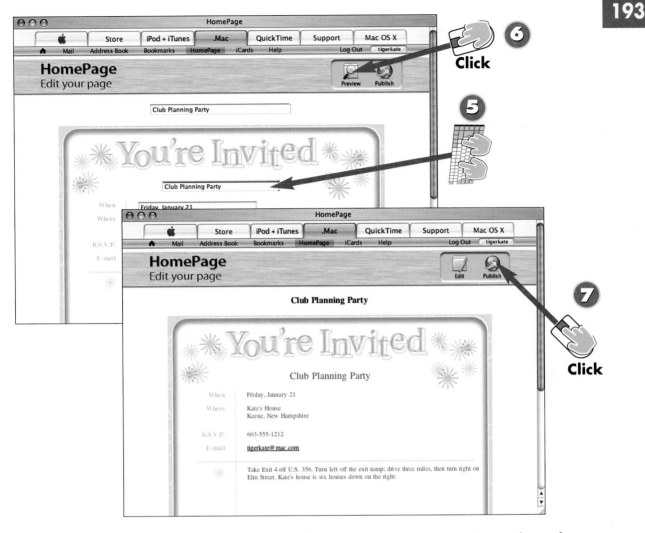

5 Type your changes in the text entry fields and click the buttons to insert photos from the Pictures folder on your iDisk or add web links.

6 Click **Preview** to see how the page looks.

7 Click **Edit** if you want to make more changes, or click **Publish** if you're satisfied.

End

Letting the World Know

TIP

If you want to let your friends know about your new website, click the **Announce Site** button at the top of the page that appears after you click Publish. You'll be guided through creating an e-card that will be emailed to your friends to publicize your new home on the Web.

Getting an iLife

iLife is Apple's name for its collection of five "digital hub" *i* programs: iPhoto, iTunes, iMovie, Garageband, and iDVD. This software represents the company's effort to empower Mac users to create and control their own entertainment media. With iLife, you can manage and share your digital photos; acquire and mix music; make your own music; produce digital movies; and create professional-looking DVDs that combine movies, music, still images, and more.

In this part you'll learn how to get your pictures into iPhoto and organize them into albums. When you have albums, you can print your photos, share them on the Web, and design real coffee-table-style books of photos. You'll also learn how to import music from your CD collection into iTunes, create custom mixes called *playlists*, and burn your own CDs. With a visit to the iTunes Music Store, you'll pick and choose from the latest tunes on the market—at 99¢ a pop. And you'll have a chance to discover your inner Mozart—or your inner Jimi Hendrix—by using GarageBand to put together your own tuneful masterpieces.

With iMovie, you'll learn how to import video from your camcorder, add scene transitions and fun special effects, and save the final result so you can share it with your friends and family. Finally, you'll be introduced to iDVD; with this program, you'll create a new DVD project, add video and other elements to it, preview it to make sure it's just the way you want it, and then burn it to a DVD disc so you can play it in your DVD player.

Managing Photos, Video, and Music

Compose original music

Organize songs in playlists

Turn playlists into CDs

Rip CDs to your hard drive

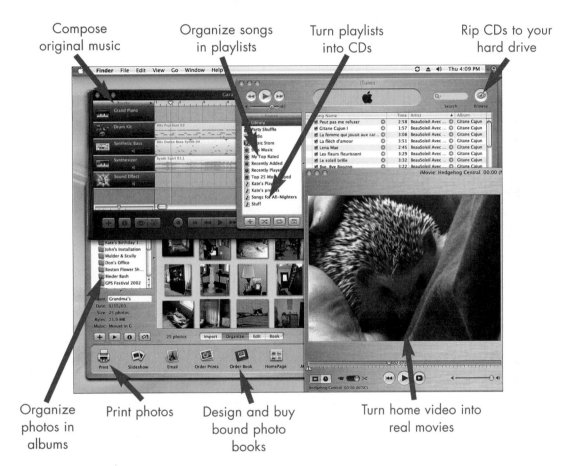

Organize photos in albums

Print photos

Design and buy bound photo books

Turn home video into real movies

Importing Photos into iPhoto

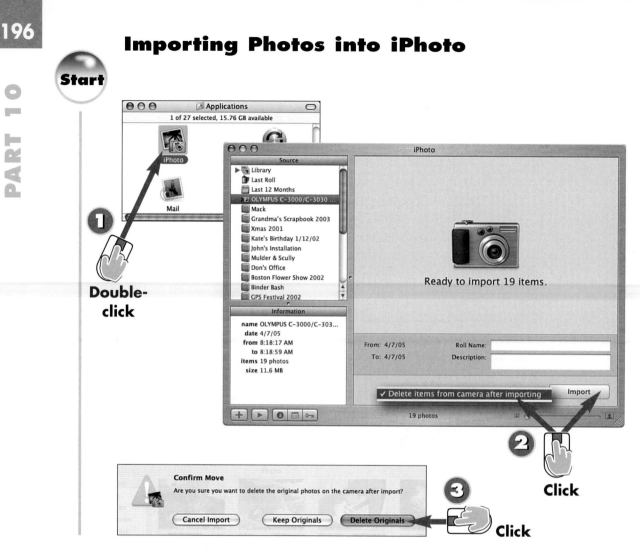

Start

Double-click

Applications
1 of 27 selected, 15.76 GB available

iPhoto

Mail

iPhoto

Source
▶ Library
  Last Roll
  Last 12 Months
  OLYMPUS C-3000/C-3030 ...
  Mack
  Grandma's Scrapbook 2003
  Xmas 2001
  Kate's Birthday 1/12/02
  John's Installation
  Mulder & Scully
  Don's Office
  Boston Flower Show 2002
  Binder Bash
  GPS Festival 2002

Information
name OLYMPUS C-3000/C-303...
date 4/7/05
from 8:18:17 AM
to 8:18:59 AM
items 19 photos
size 11.6 MB

Ready to import 19 items.

From: 4/7/05   Roll Name:
To: 4/7/05   Description:

✓ Delete items from camera after importing   Import

19 photos

2 Click

Confirm Move
Are you sure you want to delete the original photos on the camera after import?

Cancel Import   Keep Originals   Delete Originals

3 Click

1 Plug your camera in to your Mac's USB port, turn it on, and start up iPhoto (in the Applications folder). iPhoto switches into Import mode.

2 In the pop-up menu, choose the **Delete items from camera after importing** box to erase the camera's storage media; then click **Import**.

3 Click **Delete Originals** if you're deleting the original images from the camera. iPhoto imports the photos and switches to the Organize tab to display them.

End

INTRODUCTION

iPhoto can do a lot of things, but its most important function is simply providing a place to keep all your digital photos. Think of it as a super-duper photo album, or maybe a filing cabinet for your photos (if you take a lot of them). So, the first step in doing anything with iPhoto is getting your photos into its database.

TIP

You Can Get There From Here
To import image files from your hard drive, a removable disk, or camera media you've mounted on the Desktop, drag and drop the files directly onto the Photo Library entry in the Albums list.

HINT

Found, Not Lost
If you can't find the latest photos you brought into iPhoto, check out the Last Import album. That's where the most recent group of images you imported is always stored.

Creating iPhoto Albums

Start

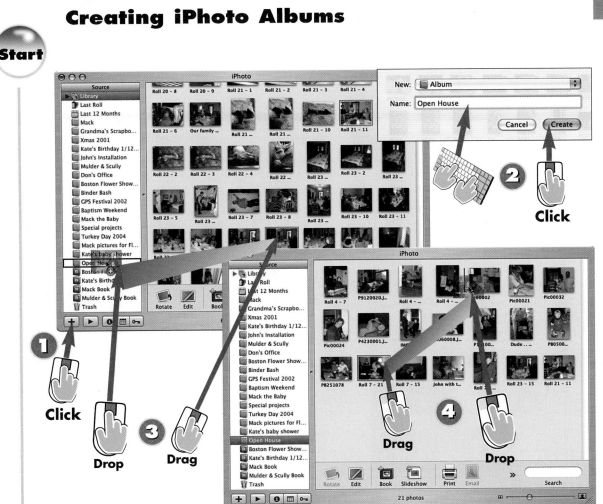

1 Click

2 Click

3 Drag / **Drop**

4 Drag / **Drop**

1 In iPhoto, click the **Create New Album** button.

2 Type a name for the new album and click **Create**.

3 Add photos to the new album by dragging and dropping them from the preview area to the album's name.

4 Click the album's name and drag and drop the album's photos in the preview area to change their order.

End

Rather than being exactly parallel to a real-word photo album, an iPhoto album is really just a way to group photos together so iPhoto knows which photos you want to print, display, or export. Albums are the way you organize your photos so you can find the ones you want. Creating an album is also the first step in creating a book or web page.

Information Please
You can add descriptive information to the photos in your albums. Click the **Show Info (i)** button below the Album column to display Title, Comments, and Date fields that you can fill out.

Printing Photos

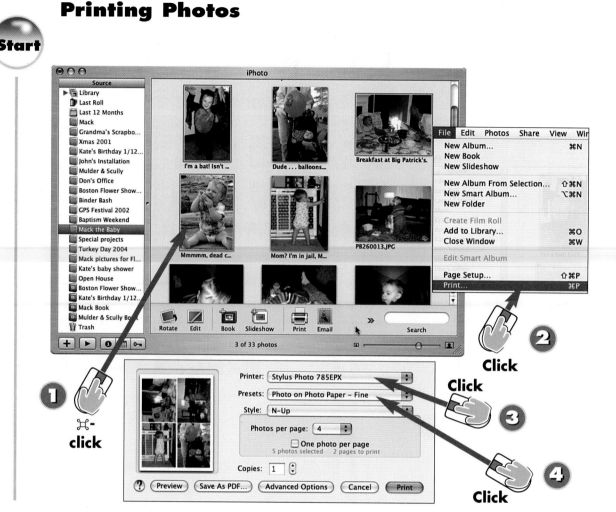

1 Click an album to print all its photos, or ⌘-click in the preview area to select individual photos.

2 Choose **File**, **Print**.

3 Choose a printer from the **Printer** pop-up menu.

4 If available, choose an option from the **Presets** pop-up menu to set the output type.

INTRODUCTION
It's not a paperless world yet, so you're bound to want to print your photos at some point. iPhoto offers several printing layouts so you can create standard prints, picture packages like the ones photo studios offer, or just plain printouts in your choice of size and number.

TIP
Fine-Tuning Print Settings
Although your printer driver probably includes presets for photo and plain paper, you'll need to fine-tune the settings for your printer. Click **Advanced Options** to get to a Print dialog box with the usual options, including color and media.

TIP
Cutting Paper Costs
If you're printing the Contact Sheet layout, check the **Save Paper** box to put the photos closer together; depending on the number of photos in your selection, this could save one or more sheets of paper.

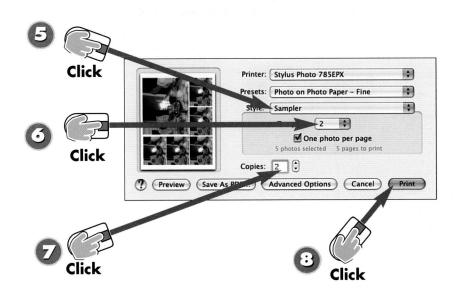

5 Click

6 Click

7 Click

8 Click

5 Choose a **Style** option.

6 Make the style's settings, such as the number of prints per page.

7 Enter the number of copies you want to print.

8 Click **Print**.

End

Proxy Preview

The proxy preview area in iPhoto's Print dialog box shows you how your printouts will look with the selected printer's paper size and the selected Style option. The proxy preview updates on-the-fly as you change the settings for the selected style.

Printing Mini-Pictures

If you want to print several copies of a photo and the exact size of each print isn't important, choose **N-Up** from the Style pop-up menu. Choose the number of prints you want on each page; then, click the check box labeled **One photo per page**.

Sharing Photos on the Web

Start

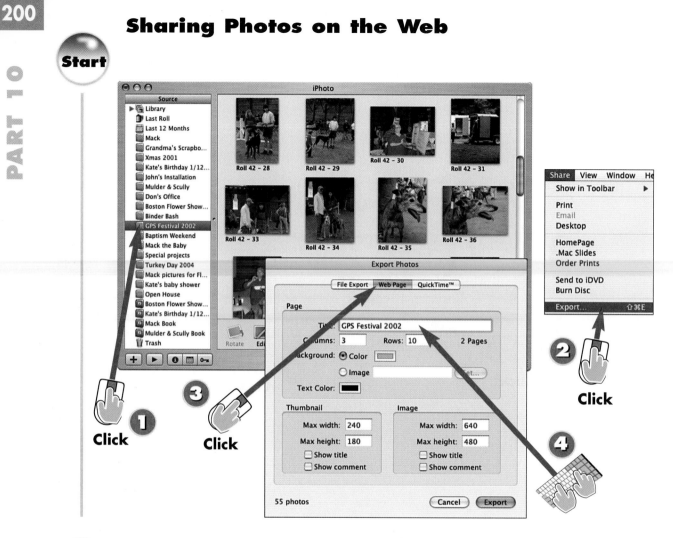

Click

1

Click

3

2

Click

4

1 Click the album you want to share on a web page.

2 Choose **Share**, **Export**.

3 Click the **Web Page** tab in the Export dialog box.

4 Type a name for the web page and specify options for the page's layout.

INTRODUCTION

The best way to share your photos with friends and family all over the country or the world is to put them on the Web. iPhoto makes creating a web picture gallery easy. To share pictures, all you have to do is put the files that iPhoto generates on your .Mac home page or any other web space available and let everyone know the URL.

HINT

Color Sense
You might be tempted to get creative with the photo gallery's background and text colors, but be sure to pick a contrasting pair. White on black, black on white, or similar high-contrast colors are much easier to read than, say, light blue on soft gray.

HINT

What's in a Name?
iPhoto inserts the album's name in the Title field, but you can change the page title to anything you want. Because it's visible at the top of the document window, you have a little more room to work with than in the Album list in iPhoto's window.

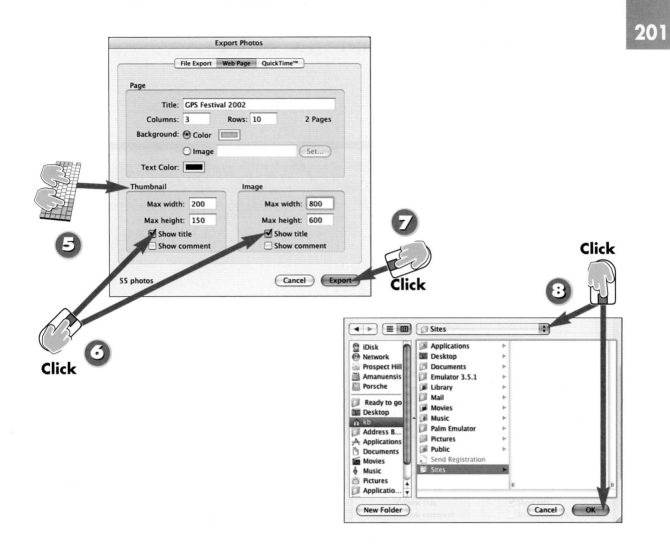

5 Type the dimensions in pixels for thumbnail and full-sized images.

6 Click **Show Title** or **Show Comment** in the Thumbnail and Image areas to display text with the images.

7 Click **Export**.

8 Navigate to the location where you want to save the files; then click **OK**.

Big and Little
iPhoto creates all the full-size and thumbnail images your web album needs, but you must specify sizes. Thumbnail images are small versions of the photos on which viewers can click to see the full-size versions.

Taking Your Photos Home
If you have a .Mac account (see "Setting Up a .Mac Account" in Part 9, "Living Online"), you can publish your photos on your .Mac HomePage website. Click the **HomePage** button at the bottom of the **Organize** pane and follow the prompts.

Measuring in Pixels
Pixels—the dots of light that make up the picture on your Mac's screen—are the unit in which onscreen objects are measured. Most monitors have 72 pixels to the inch, which means that a 640 pixel by 480 pixel photo measures 8.9"×6.7".

Creating and Mixing a Song in GarageBand

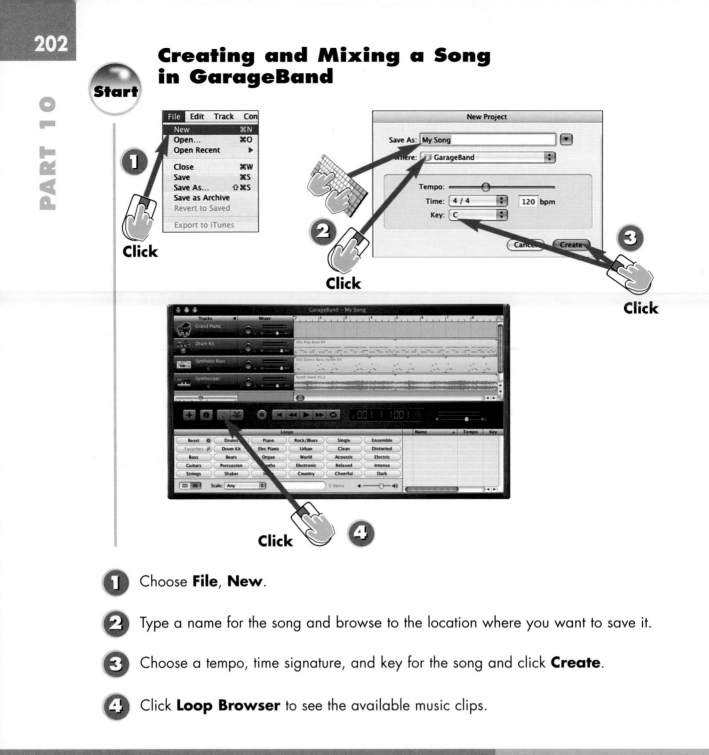

Start

Click

Click

Click

Click

1. Choose **File**, **New**.

2. Type a name for the song and browse to the location where you want to save it.

3. Choose a tempo, time signature, and key for the song and click **Create**.

4. Click **Loop Browser** to see the available music clips.

INTRODUCTION

GarageBand is pure fun—and pure genius. With this snazzy music-mixing program, you can create your own music, from pop ditties to atmospheric riffs. GarageBand compositions can be entirely synthesized, or you can record your own instruments. Use your tuneful creations to back up your latest movies and DVDs, or share your genius with the world on sites like iCompositions.com.

TIP

Froot Loops
Don't think you're stuck with just the loops that ship with GarageBand. Try typing **GarageBand loops** into Google's search field (www.google.com) and you'll find more downloadable loops than you can shake a mouse at.

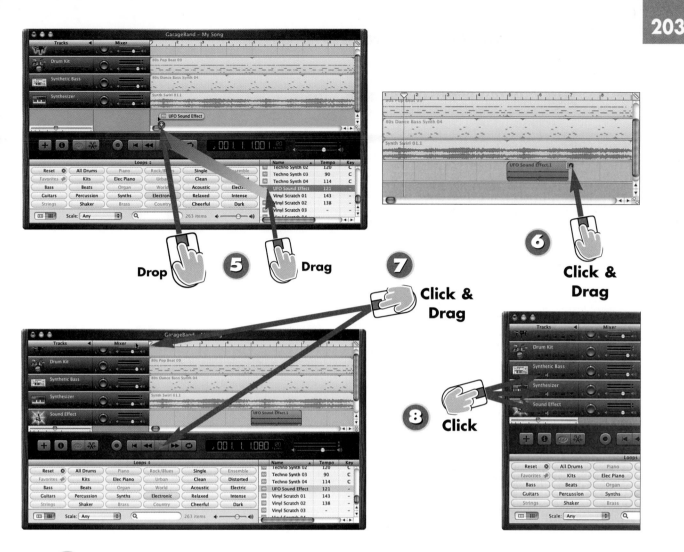

Drop **5** **Drag**

7 **Click & Drag**

6 **Click & Drag**

8 **Click**

 5 Drag loops from the Loop Browser and drop them into the **Timeline**.

6 Drag each loop to the measure where you want it and stretch its top corner edge to loop it (play it repeatedly).

7 Drag the playhead to the beginning of the song and click **Play** to preview the song.

8 Click **Mute** to turn off a track so you can listen to the song without hearing that track.

 End

It's Just the Beginning
GarageBand can do a lot—lots more, in fact, than this book can explain. If you've caught the music-making bug, check out http://www.tidbits. com/takecontrol/ garageband-recording.html.

Mixing It Up
To change the way an instrument sounds, double-click the header at the left end of the track (in the Tracks pane) to open the Track Info window. You can choose a different sound or choose a completely different kind of instrument.

Recording Your Instruments

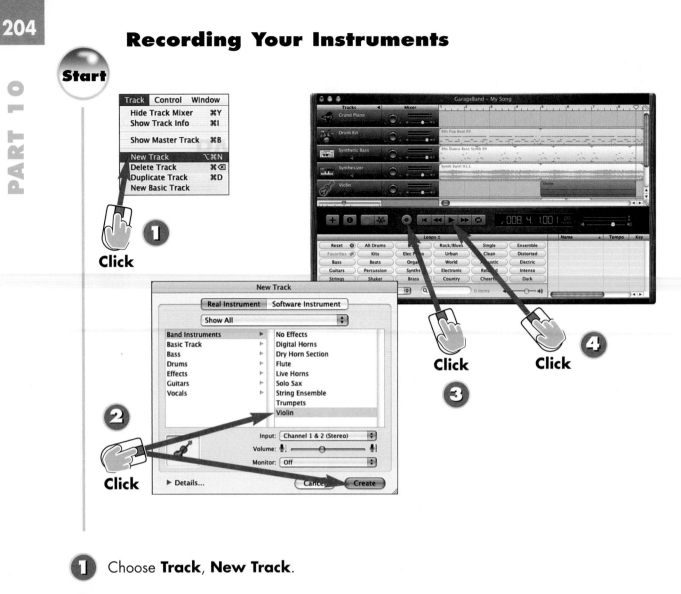

Start

Click ①

Click ③

Click ④

Click ②

① Choose **Track**, **New Track**.

② Choose an instrument and click **Create**.

③ Click **Record** and play your instrument.

④ Click **Stop** to stop recording.

End

INTRODUCTION

If you're a musician, GarageBand is more than a music box—it's a mini recording studio. Now you can record your own vocals or instruments and combine them with all the backing tracks you need to fully realize your music. Start by connecting your instrument or a microphone to your Mac; then follow the steps in this task.

TIP

Amping It Up

If you're recording an electric guitar, you can simulate the sound of various real-life amplifiers. Click a track to select it and then double-click its header to open the **Track Info** window. Click the **Details** triangle and choose **Amp Simulation** from one of the **Effect** pop-up menus. Then choose a preset sound from the **Preset** pop-up menu to the right. If you really want to get down and dirty, you can adjust the amp presets by clicking the **Edit** button (it has a pencil icon) next to the Preset pop-up menu.

Exporting GarageBand Songs to iTunes

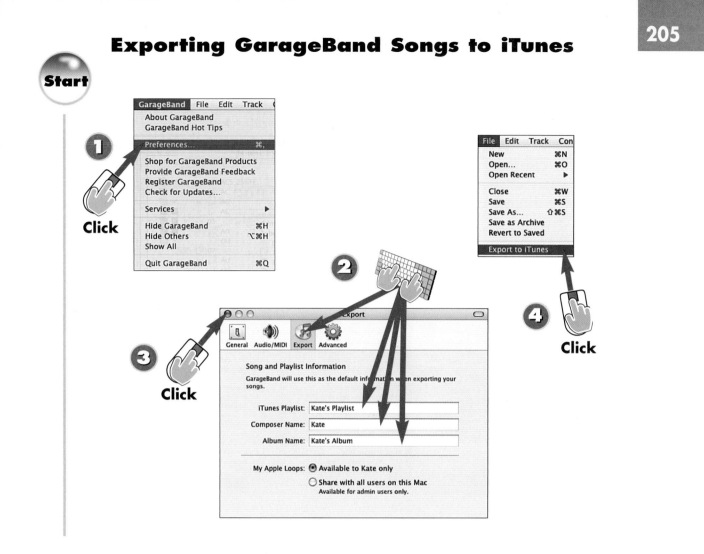

1 Choose **GarageBand**, **Preferences**.

2 Click the **Export** button, and then enter a playlist name and the composer name and album title that you want iTunes to display for your songs.

3 Click to close the Preferences window.

4 Choose **File**, **Export to iTunes**.

Ripping Songs from a CD

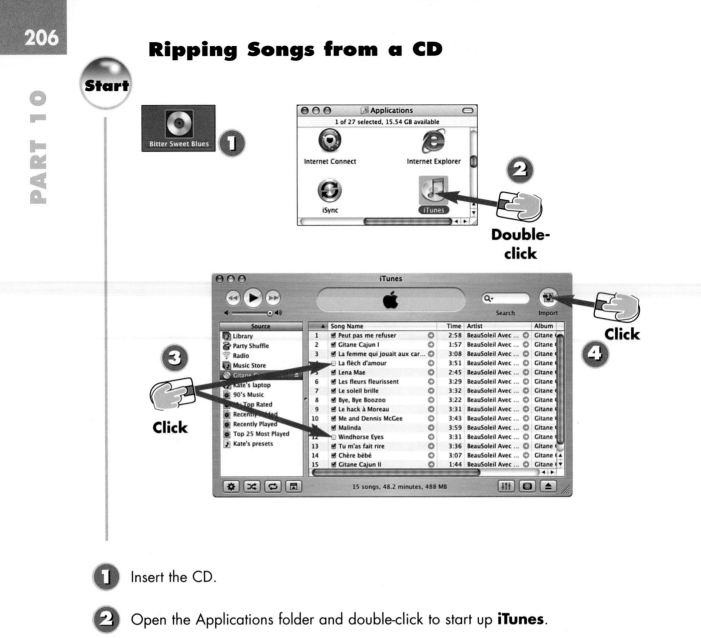

Start

Bitter Sweet Blues ①

Applications
1 of 27 selected, 15.54 GB available

Internet Connect   Internet Explorer

iSync   iTunes ②

Double-click

iTunes

Search   Import

Click ④

	Song Name		Time	Artist	Album
1	☑ Peut pas me refuser	○	2:58	BeauSoleil Avec ... ○	Gitane
2	☑ Gitane Cajun I	○	1:57	BeauSoleil Avec ... ○	Gitane
3	☑ La femme qui jouait aux car...	○	3:08	BeauSoleil Avec ... ○	Gitane
	☐ La flèch d'amour	○	3:51	BeauSoleil Avec ... ○	Gitane
5	☑ Lena Mae	○	2:45	BeauSoleil Avec ... ○	Gitane
6	☑ Les fleurs fleurissent	○	3:29	BeauSoleil Avec ... ○	Gitane
7	☑ Le soleil brille	○	3:32	BeauSoleil Avec ... ○	Gitane
8	☑ Bye, Bye Boozoo	○	3:22	BeauSoleil Avec ... ○	Gitane
9	☑ Le hack à Moreau	○	3:31	BeauSoleil Avec ... ○	Gitane
10	☑ Me and Dennis McGee	○	3:43	BeauSoleil Avec ... ○	Gitane
11	☑ Malinda	○	3:59	BeauSoleil Avec ... ○	Gitane
12	☐ Windhorse Eyes	○	3:31	BeauSoleil Avec ... ○	Gitane
13	☑ Tu m'as fait rire	○	3:36	BeauSoleil Avec ... ○	Gitane
14	☑ Chère bébé	○	3:07	BeauSoleil Avec ... ○	Gitane
15	☑ Gitane Cajun II	○	1:44	BeauSoleil Avec ... ○	Gitane

Source
Library
Party Shuffle
Radio
Music Store
Gitane C...
Kate's laptop
90's Music
Top Rated
Recently ...ded
Recently Played
Top 25 Most Played
Kate's presets

③ ← **Click**

15 songs, 48.2 minutes, 488 MB

① Insert the CD.

② Open the Applications folder and double-click to start up **iTunes**.

③ Click to remove the check marks next to any songs you don't want to add to your library.

④ Click **Import**.

End

You'll be amazed at how much more use you get from your CD collection after you get the music off CDs and into iTunes. The songs on CDs are already digital files; *ripping* them consists of transferring them to your hard drive and resaving them in MP3 format.

TIP
The Sounds of Silence
iTunes plays songs while it's importing them, but if you don't want to listen to them, you can click Pause to stop the playback. iTunes continues importing the songs.

TIP
Mind the Gap
If you want consecutive songs to play with no pause between them, choose **Advanced**, **Join CD Tracks** before clicking Import.

Making a New Playlist

Start

Click

Click

Drag

Drop

1 In iTunes, click the **Create Playlist** button.

2 Type a name for the playlist.

3 Click the **Library** entry in the **Source** column to see all your songs, or click the name of another playlist.

4 Drag songs from the **Song Name** column and drop them into the new playlist.

End

INTRODUCTION

Playlists are simply groups of songs, containing just one song or hundreds. You can use them to create party mixes, plan mix CDs, or categorize your music by genre or any other criterion. Building playlists is a simple drag-and-drop operation.

TIP

Finding What You Want
To locate a specific song in the Library or in a playlist, click in the **Search** field and type part of the song name. As you type, the list of songs shortens to include only the songs that match your search term.

TIP

Changing Your Mind
To remove a song from a playlist (but not from your Library), click to select it and press **Delete**.

Burning a Music CD

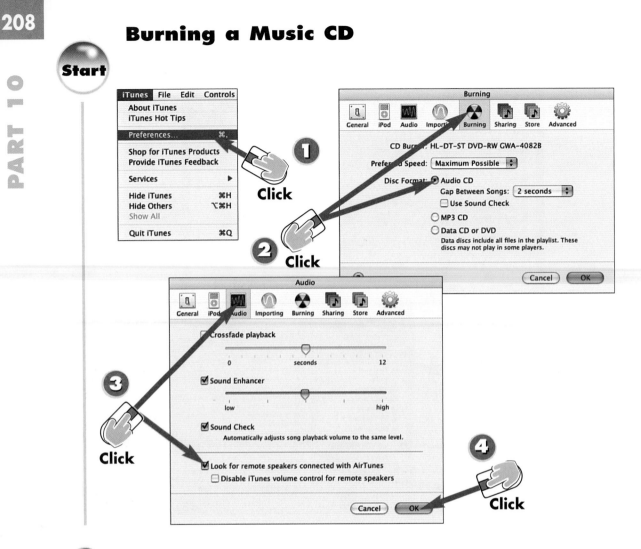

1 In iTunes, choose **iTunes**, **Preferences**.

2 Click the **Burning** button at the top of the window; then choose **Audio CD** as the Disc Format.

3 Click the **Audio** button and click the check box to turn on **Sound Check**.

4 Click **OK**.

Picture This
TIP
Any song you buy from the iTunes Music Store (see the next task) comes with cover artwork. When you burn a compilation, iTunes creates a custom mosaic of the songs' cover art and drops that into a template to create an insert for the CD case.

The Right Media
TIP
Make sure you use CD-R media, rather than CD-RW media, if you plan to play your CD in a regular CD player (meaning, on your stereo) rather than in a computer CD drive.

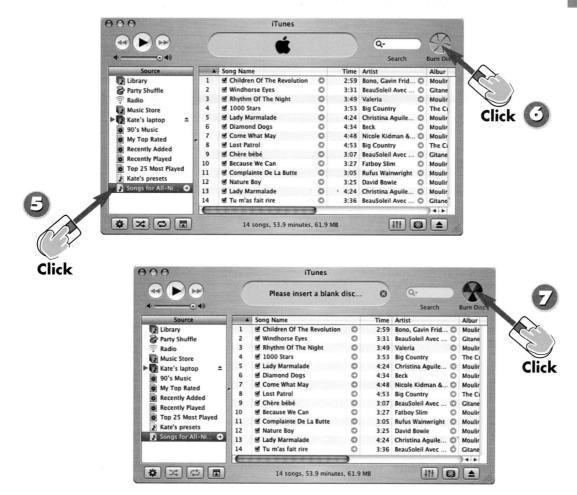

5 Click to select the playlist you want to make into a CD.

6 Click the **Burn Disc** button.

7 Insert a blank CD-R disc and click **Burn Disc** again.

CD Limits
If you include too many songs in the playlist to fit on the CD, iTunes lets you know that they won't all fit. You'll have the option of burning the songs to an MP3 CD instead or creating a disc that contains as many songs as will fit.

Stop Right There
To stop the CD burner after you click Burn Disc, click the **X** next to the progress bar. You can use your CD drive again immediately, but the CD you canceled is no longer usable.

Avoiding a Small Annoyance
If you insert a blank CD before clicking Burn Disc in the iTunes window, your Mac asks you what you want it to do with the CD. Clicking Burn Disc before putting the CD-R in the drive bypasses this dialog box.

Buying New Songs Through iTunes

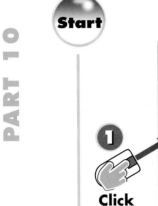

Start

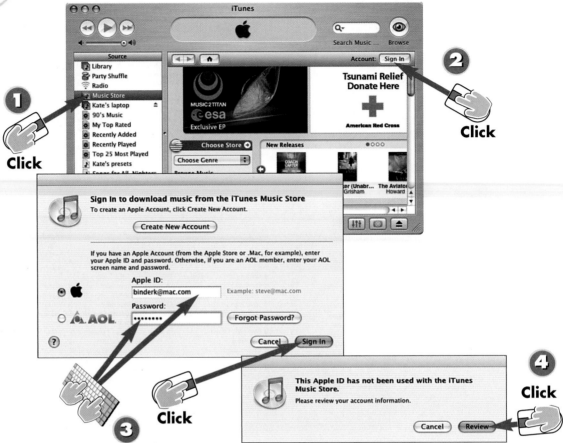

1. In iTunes, click **Music Store** in the Source column.

2. Click **Sign In**.

3. Type your Apple ID and password and click **Sign In**.

4. If you haven't bought songs before, a dialog box tells you that this ID hasn't been used with the Music Store; click **Review**.

The iTunes Music Store offers thousands of tunes in all genres at very reasonable prices. You can download entire albums or one song at a time. Your purchases are charged to your credit card, and the songs are downloaded directly into iTunes, where you can play them on your computer, transfer to them to an iPod, or burn them to a CD.

TIP

Getting an iTunes Account

If you already have an Apple ID, you're all set—just enter that username and password to sign in to the iTunes Music Store. If you have a paid subscription to .Mac, use that username and password for the Music Store. If you don't have either, follow the Music Store's prompts to create a new ID and supply your credit card information for purchases.

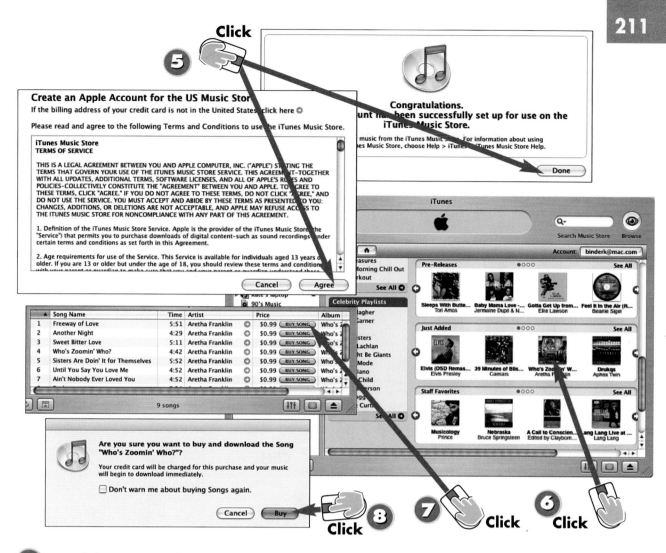

Click

Create an Apple Account for the US Music Store
If the billing address of your credit card is not in the United States, click here ⊙

Please read and agree to the following Terms and Conditions to use the iTunes Music Store.

iTunes Music Store
TERMS OF SERVICE

THIS IS A LEGAL AGREEMENT BETWEEN YOU AND APPLE COMPUTER, INC. ("APPLE") STATING THE
TERMS THAT GOVERN YOUR USE OF THE ITUNES MUSIC STORE SERVICE. THIS AGREEMENT-TOGETHER
WITH ALL UPDATES, ADDITIONAL TERMS, SOFTWARE LICENSES, AND ALL OF APPLE'S RULES AND
POLICIES-COLLECTIVELY CONSTITUTE THE "AGREEMENT" BETWEEN YOU AND APPLE. TO AGREE TO
THESE TERMS, CLICK "AGREE." IF YOU DO NOT AGREE TO THESE TERMS, DO NOT CLICK "AGREE," AND
DO NOT USE THE SERVICE. YOU MUST ACCEPT AND ABIDE BY THESE TERMS AS PRESENTED TO YOU:
CHANGES, ADDITIONS, OR DELETIONS ARE NOT ACCEPTABLE, AND APPLE MAY REFUSE ACCESS TO
THE ITUNES MUSIC STORE FOR NONCOMPLIANCE WITH ANY PART OF THIS AGREEMENT.

1. Definition of the iTunes Music Store Service. Apple is the provider of the iTunes Music Store (the
"Service") that permits you to purchase downloads of digital content-such as sound recordings-under
certain terms and conditions as set forth in this Agreement.

2. Age requirements for use of the Service. This Service is available for individuals aged 13 years or
older. If you are 13 or older but under the age of 18, you should review these terms and conditions

Cancel   Agree

Congratulations.
...unt has been successfully set up for use on the
iTunes Music Store.

...music from the iTunes Music Store. For information about using
...es Music Store, choose Help > iTunes ...Tunes Music Store Help.

Done

	Song Name	Time	Artist		Price		Album
1	Freeway of Love	5:51	Aretha Franklin	⊙	$0.99	BUY SONG	Who's Z
2	Another Night	4:29	Aretha Franklin	⊙	$0.99	BUY SONG	Who's Z
3	Sweet Bitter Love	5:11	Aretha Franklin	⊙	$0.99	BUY SONG	o's Z
4	Who's Zoomin' Who?	4:42	Aretha Franklin	⊙	$0.99	BUY SONG	Who's Z
5	Sisters Are Doin' It for Themselves	5:52	Aretha Franklin	⊙	$0.99	BUY SONG	Who's
6	Until You Say You Love Me	4:52	Aretha Franklin	⊙	$0.99	BUY SONG	Who's Z
7	Ain't Nobody Ever Loved You	4:52	Aretha Franklin	⊙	$0.99	BUY SONG	Who's Z

9 songs

Are you sure you want to buy and download the Song
"Who's Zoomin' Who?"?

Your credit card will be charged for this purchase and your music
will begin to download immediately.

☐ Don't warn me about buying Songs again.

Cancel   Buy

Click 8   7   Click   6 Click

Search Music Store   Browse
Account: binderk@mac.com

Pre-Releases   ●○○○   See All
Sleeps With Butte... Baby Mama Love -... Gotta Get Up from... Feel It In the Air (R...
Tori Amos   Jermaine Dupri & N... Elle Lawson   Beanie Sigel

Just Added   ●○○○   See All
Elvis (DSD Remas... 39 Minutes of Bliss... Who's Zoomin' W... Drukqs
Elvis Presley   Caesars   Aretha Franklin   Aphex Twin

Staff Favorites   ●○○○   See All
Musicology   Nebraska   A Call to Conscien... Lang Lang Live at ...
Prince   Bruce Springsteen   Edited by Clayborn... Lang Lang

⑤ Read the Terms and Conditions and click **Agree**; then click **Done**.

⑥ Click a song or album title to see more information about it.

⑦ Click **Buy Song** or **Buy Album** to purchase music.

⑧ Click **Buy**. The song downloads into iTunes and appears in a new playlist called
Purchased Music.

End

Importing Video Footage into iMovie

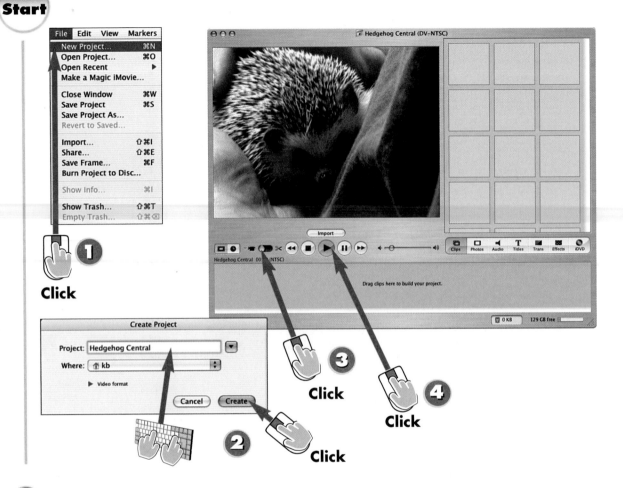

1 In iMovie, choose **File**, **New Project**.

2 Type a name for your new movie and click **Create**.

3 With your camera connected to the Mac and turned on, click iMovie's **Camera** switch so that it is in Camera mode.

4 Click **Play** below the monitor area to begin viewing the tape in the camera.

With iMovie, your home movies will reach new heights. You can add titles and credits, special effects, music and sound effects, and more. Then you can save your finished creations as small QuickTime files for emailing, high-quality DVD movies, or anything in between. The first step is to bring video from your video camera into iMovie. iMovie can control your camcorder so you can get to the right place on the tape to locate the footage you want. The playback controls work just like the buttons on the camera itself or on your VCR. When iMovie is in camera mode, you can use the controls to play, pause, stop, rewind, and fast-forward the tape in the video camera.

Trouble in iMovie Paradise

Can't seem to get the camera to respond to iMovie's controls? Check to make sure the camera is in playback mode (VTR or VCR mode) rather than recording mode.

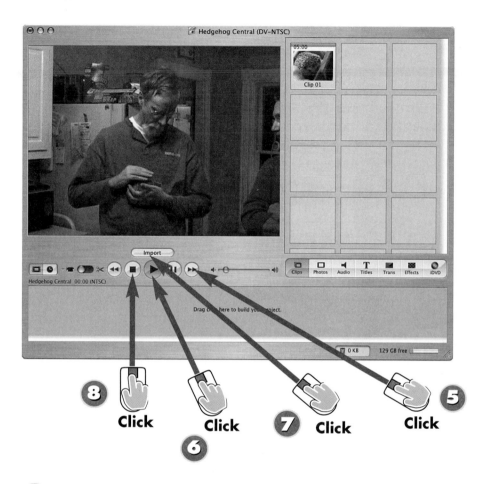

5 Click **Fast Forward** to move the tape to the section you want to import.

6 Click **Play** again to begin viewing the footage you want to import.

7 Click **Import** to start importing footage.

8 Click **Stop** when you've imported the footage you want. The video is added to the Clip Shelf.

End

On the Safe Side

HINT

Be conservative when importing video—always import a bit extra on either end of the section you want. You can trim extra footage in iMovie to end up with just the right scene, but if you cut off the scene you'll need to import it again.

Camera Tips

TIP

Here are a few words of wisdom regarding your camera. First, if you have a power adapter, use it while importing video to your Mac, rather than running down your batteries. And second, be sure to turn off the camera while connecting its FireWire cable.

Sound and Vision

TIP

Drag the slider next to the playback controls to adjust the volume level of the tape's audio while you watch it import. Doing this doesn't affect the recording level on the tape or in the final movie.

Inserting Transitions and Effects

Start

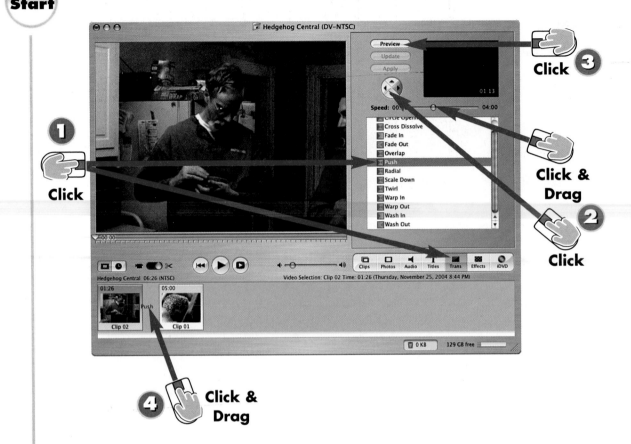

1. To add a transition between two clips, click **Trans** and choose a transition style.

2. Set the duration and direction of the transition.

3. Click **Preview** to play the transition.

4. Drag the transition to the Clip Viewer and drop it into the point in the movie where you want it.

After you've assembled your movie's raw footage by dragging clips from the Clip Shelf into the Clip Viewer, you can spice up the production by adding *transitions* between clips and applying special effects.

Controlling Transitions

Most transitions have just one control: Speed, or the amount of time the transition takes. Push, in which the new scene slides in from one side of the screen, also has a direction control that enables you to determine which way the scene moves.

The Story Continues...

There's not nearly enough room to show you all the wonders of iMovie in this book! If you want to learn more about how to use iMovie, check out the iMovie chapter in *Special Edition Using Mac OS X Panther*.

5 To apply a special effect, ⌘-click to select the clips you want to apply it to.

6 Click **Effects** and choose an effect; then set the effect's options.

7 Click **Preview** to see how the effect looks.

8 Click **Apply**.

Creative Transitioning
HINT
You're not restricted to using one transition between each pair of clips—you can combine as many transitions as you like to create the effect you're looking for. You can also use transitions before and after titles, photos, and other elements.

Moving Pictures
TIP
For that zippy public television documentary look, drop in some still photos (click **Photos** to see the contents of your iPhoto Library) and apply the Ken Burns Effect. This effect zooms and pans on a photo, giving the impression of motion.

Transition Timing
HINT
As you drag the Speed slider, the total time the transition occupies is displayed in the lower-right corner of the transition thumbnail preview. Keep an eye on that time; quick transitions are okay, but 5-minute ones are a bad idea.

Saving a Movie

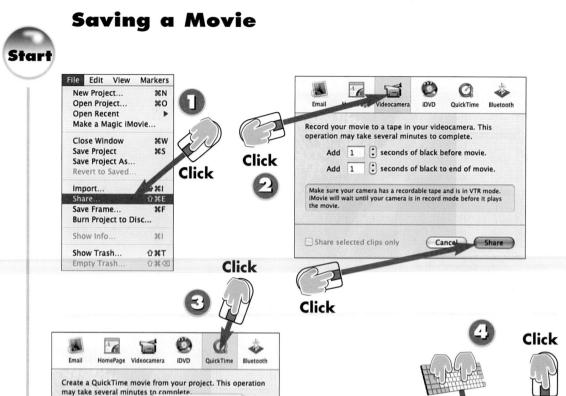

Start

Click

Click

1

2

Click

Click

3

Click

4

Click

Click

1 Choose **File**, **Share**

2 To save the movie to a videotape, choose **Videocamera**; then enter the appropriate time settings to accommodate the camera and click **Share**.

3 To save the movie to a QuickTime document, click **QuickTime**. Choose an option from the **Compress Movie For** pop-up menu and click **Share**.

4 Choose a location to save the file, enter a name, and click **Save**.

End

TIP

Doing a DVD
To turn your movie into a DVD, rather than a video, choose **File**, **Export** and then choose **To iDVD** from the pop-up menu. Then click **Export**. iDVD opens immediately, with the movie already incorporated into an iDVD project.

TIP

Saving Your Work
Choose **File**, **Save Project** to save your movie as an iMovie project—in other words, a work in progress. You don't need to export the movie until you're done working on it.

Creating a New iDVD Project

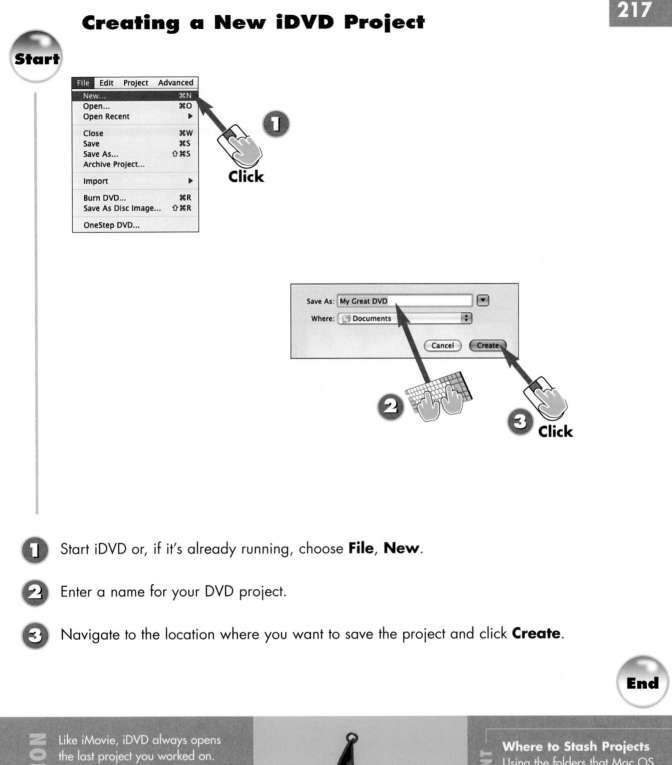

Start

File	Edit	Project	Advanced
New...			⌘N
Open...			⌘O
Open Recent			▶
Close			⌘W
Save			⌘S
Save As...			⇧⌘S
Archive Project...			
Import			▶
Burn DVD...			⌘R
Save As Disc Image...			⇧⌘R
OneStep DVD...			

1 **Click**

Save As: My Great DVD
Where: 📁 Documents

Cancel Create

2

3 **Click**

1 Start iDVD or, if it's already running, choose **File**, **New**.

2 Enter a name for your DVD project.

3 Navigate to the location where you want to save the project and click **Create**.

End

INTRODUCTION

Like iMovie, iDVD always opens the last project you worked on. You can open another project by choosing File, Open, or you can begin a new project from scratch. Here's how to do that.

HINT

Where to Stash Projects
Using the folders that Mac OS X creates for certain purposes makes remembering where you put things much easier. In the case of iDVD, the default folder in which to save your projects is the Documents folder within your home folder.

Adding Elements to a DVD

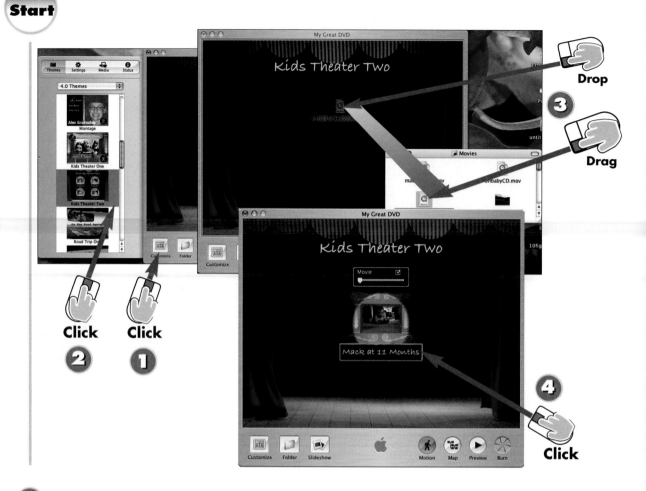

Start

Drop

Drag

Click   Click
  2   1

Click

1 In iDVD, click **Customize** to open the drawer at the side of the window.

2 Choose a theme from the list.

3 Click and drag a movie file into the preview area that shows the main menu of your DVD. iDVD creates a button for that movie.

4 Click the button's name to change the text.

DVDs have three types of elements: content, in the form of movies, photos, or other documents; navigation, in the form of folders that open to reveal menu screens; and interface, in the form of background images, sound effects, and the like. Adding these elements is incredibly easy in iDVD.

More Theme Choices
If iDVD's built-in themes aren't to your liking, you can purchase more themes online. A good place to start is www.idvdthemepak.com, where you'll find a selection of very cool iDVD ThemePAKs.

Supersizing Your DVDs
If your content won't fit on a 60-minute DVD, you can tell iDVD to create a 90-minute DVD instead. But to see this option, you have to add all your content at once so iDVD sees that it won't fit in 60 minutes.

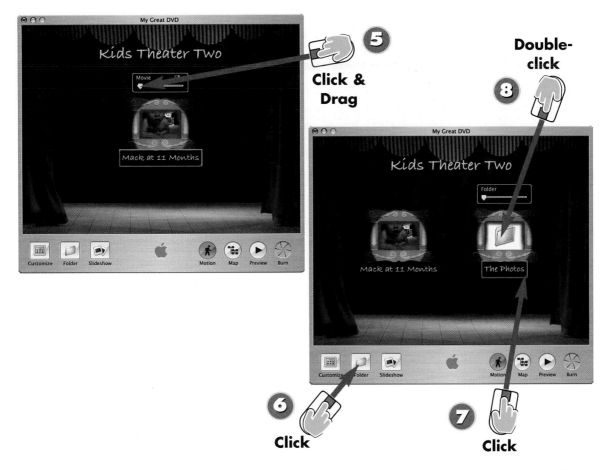

Click & Drag ⑤

Double-click ⑧

Click ⑥

Click ⑦

⑤ If the current theme includes video buttons, click and drag the slider above the button to change the video frame that appears on the button.

⑥ Click **Folder** to add a folder.

⑦ Click the folder's name to change the text.

⑧ Double-click the folder's icon to view the submenu it represents.

 End

HINT
The theme you choose for your DVD project determines the placement of buttons and whether they're text buttons or video buttons. You can experiment with applying different themes at any point during the creation process.

TIP
iDVD Assistance
Apple's free helper program, iDVD Companion, is a useful tool for iDVD users. With it you can move quickly to menus and slideshows, place buttons and titles precisely, and change menu layouts. Learn more at www.apple.com/applescript/idvd/idvd_companion/.

Previewing a DVD

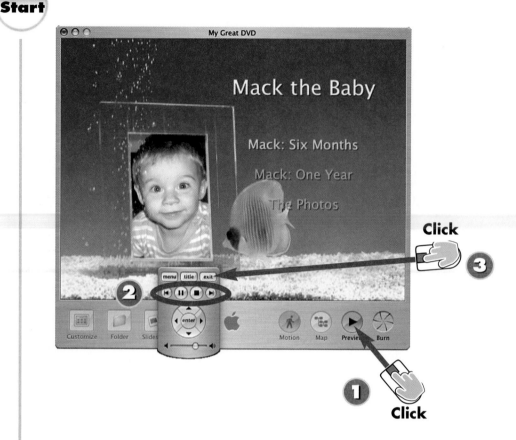

Start

Click

Click

1. Click **Preview** to play the DVD.

2. Click buttons on the remote control to test the way the DVD will work on a TV.

3. Click **Exit** to leave preview mode.

End

It's a well-known fact that creative projects don't always turn out the way they're envisioned. It's far better to catch mistakes and make tweaks before you've burned a DVD than after. That's where iDVD's Preview function comes in handy. Always preview your projects before burning them to disc.

Menus in Motion
Some iDVD themes include animated menu backgrounds called *motion menus*. To see these backgrounds in action when you preview the DVD, make sure the Motion button at the bottom of the iDVD window is green. If it's not, click it.

Playing It Safe
To be sure the DVD's elements won't extend off the edge of the screen, choose **Advanced**, **Show TV Safe Area** before you click Preview. This command places a rectangle on the screen that defines the boundaries of older TV screens.

Burning a DVD

Start

1 In iDVD, click the **Burn** button twice.

2 If motion is turned off, click **Cancel** and turn it on; then go back to step 1.

3 Insert a blank DVD disc.

End

INTRODUCTION

After your DVD project is set up the way you want it and you've confirmed this by using the Preview feature, it's time to burn an actual DVD disc. You must have a Mac with a built-in SuperDrive to accomplish this with iDVD.

HINT

Make Way for DVDs
You should quit all other programs while you're burning a DVD. This ensures that no other program will take over the computer while the DVD is being created, which might cause an error in the DVD.

HINT

iDVD Without the Burn
Previously, iDVD wouldn't even install if your Mac was SuperDrive-less, but with iDVD 3.0.1 and later versions, you can create iDVD projects on a Mac that doesn't have a SuperDrive. To burn a project, copy it to a SuperDrive-equipped Mac.

Sharing Your Mac with Multiple Users

Mac OS X is designed to be a multiuser operating system, meaning each user of a single Mac has his own account. Each user is either a standard user or an admin user; admin users can change preferences, install programs, and modify files—changes that affect all users rather than just the user who implements them.

Your account can be customized with your choice of name, password, and login picture (used both in the login dialog box and for Internet messaging with iChat). You also get your very own home folder, named with the short version of your login name. Your home folder is where you can put all your documents, music, pictures, and so on, and you can keep other users from reading, moving, or even seeing what files are in your home folder. When you do want to share files, you can put them in specific places where other users have access to them. Because customizations—such as the desktop picture, screen saver module, monitor resolution, and clock settings—apply only to the user who sets them up, you can also use user accounts to create different configurations of your Mac for specific purposes, rather than for different people.

In this part, you'll learn how to create user accounts and change their attributes, as well as how to log in and log out. You'll also learn how to add startup items—programs and files that open when you log in—and how to manage security with passwords and the FileVault feature.

Account and Security Setup

Change your password

Change your login picture

Add login items

Control users' access

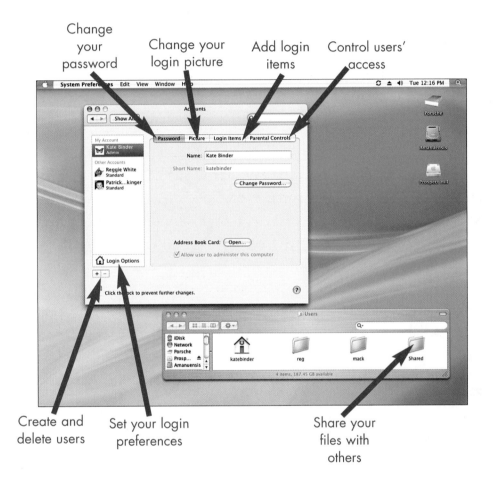

Create and delete users

Set your login preferences

Share your files with others

Creating and Deleting Users

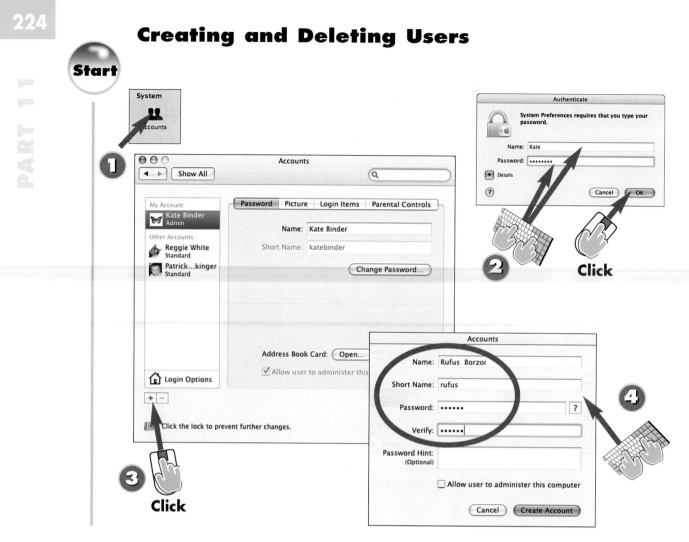

Choose **Apple menu**, **System Preferences**, and click **Accounts** to see the accounts preferences.

If the preferences are locked, click the closed padlock button to unlock them; then enter an admin name and password and click **OK**.

To create a new user, click the **Add User** button.

Enter the new user's name, a short version of the name (such as initials), and a password.

INTRODUCTION

Each user of a Mac gets her own account, with separate preferences, home folder, and login identity. You can also create accounts for different uses of your Mac—one that's all business, another for weekends that starts up your favorite game on login, and so on. Each account can have a customized level of access to system functions.

Setting Limits

When you create a new standard user account, you can determine how much access that user has to most of the Mac's functions, such as email and system preferences. In the **Accounts** pane, click **Parental Controls** and check the functions to which you want to limit access: Mail, Finder & System, iChat, or Safari. Then click the **Configure** button next to each function to make specific settings, such as whether the user can modify the Dock or visit specific websites.

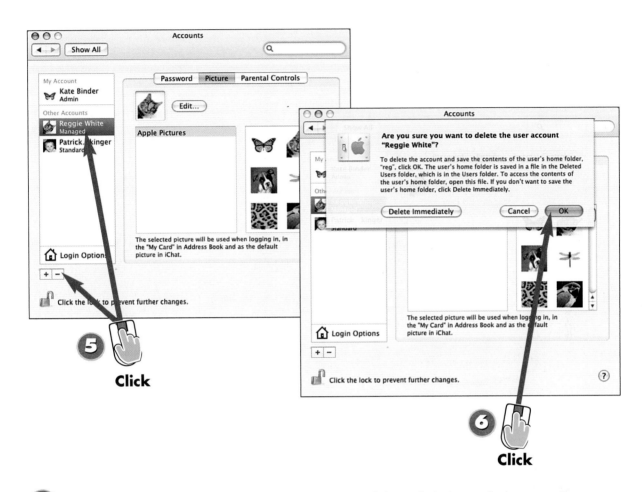

Click

Click

5 To delete a user, click a username in the list and then click the **Delete User** button.

6 Click **OK** in the confirmation dialog box.

The Stuff They Leave Behind

When you delete a user, you can save the user's files as a disk image that's placed in the Deleted Users folder in the Users folder. Double-click the disk image to see the saved files. If the user was using FileVault (see "Keeping Your Secrets," later in this part, to learn about FileVault), enter the user's password. FileVault or no FileVault, drag the disk image file to the Trash to delete the files. If you don't want to save the user's files in the first place, click **Delete Immediately** instead of OK in step 6.

Making a User an Admin

Start

Click

System
Accounts

1

Accounts

◄ ► | Show All | 🔍

My Account
🦋 **Kate Binder**
   Admin

Other Accounts
🦋 **Reggie White**
   Managed

🖼 **Patrick...kinger**
   Standard

| **Password** | Picture | Parental Controls |

Name: Patrick Fluckinger

Short Name: mack

(Reset Password...)

☐ Allow user to administer this computer

🏠 Login Options

+ −

🔓 Click the lock to prevent further changes.

2

Click

Auth...icate

🔒 System Prefere...ce requires that you type your
   password.

Name: Kate

Password: ••••••••

▼ Details

? (Cancel) (OK)

1 Choose **Apple menu**, **System Preferences**, and click **Accounts** to see the accounts preferences.

2 If the preferences are locked, click the closed padlock button to unlock them; then type an admin name and password and click **OK**.

Each Mac has at least one admin user—the first user identity created on your Mac is automatically an admin. You can make any other user an admin as well, so that user can control system preferences and make changes to the Mac's setup.

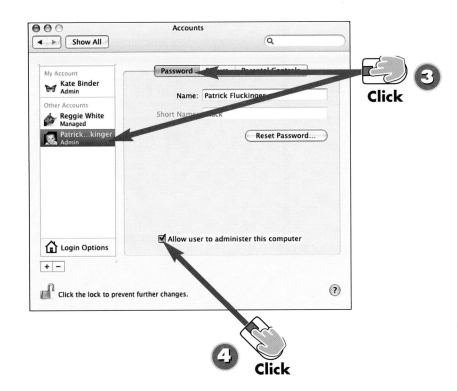

3 Click a username in the account list and then click the **Password** tab.

4 Click the **Allow user to administer this computer** check box.

Admins Beget Admins
Only admin users can create other admin users. If you're not an admin user, you'll need to have someone who is already designated as an admin on your Mac to give you that status.

Wherefore Admin, Anyway?
To home users the term *admin user* can seem strange. It's a result of Mac OS X's emphasis on accommodating multiple users of a single Mac. In most multiuser situations, such as computer labs, only authorized administrators should be able to change the Mac's setup.

Logging In and Out

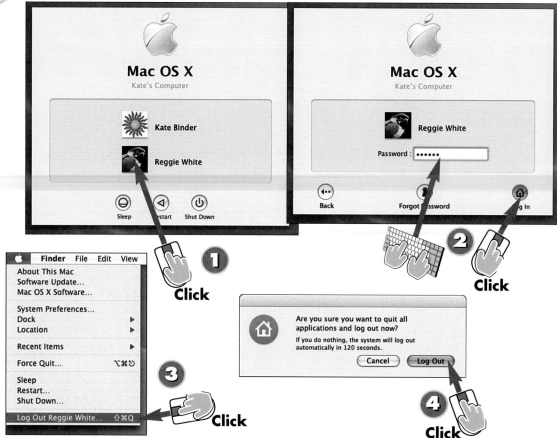

1. In the Login dialog box, click your username in the list of users.

2. Type your password and click **Log In**.

3. To log out, choose **Apple menu**, **Log Out**.

4. Click **Log Out** in the confirmation dialog box. All the applications quit, along with the Finder, and you're returned to the Login dialog box.

End

Depending on your preferences, you might need to log in to your Mac every day, or you might hardly ever see the login screen. Either way, you do need to remember your login name and password so you can log in when needed—after another user has logged out or after major changes are made to your system.

Skipping the Login

You can set your Mac so you're automatically logged in at startup. Click **Login Options** at the bottom of the Accounts preferences panel in System Preferences; then click the box labeled **Automatically log in as** and choose a user.

Faster Switching

Mac OS X's fast user switching feature displays a menu of users in the menu bar; choosing a new user switches instantly to that account. Click **Enable fast user switching** in the Login Options tab of the Accounts System Preferences panel.

Adding Startup Items

Start

Click

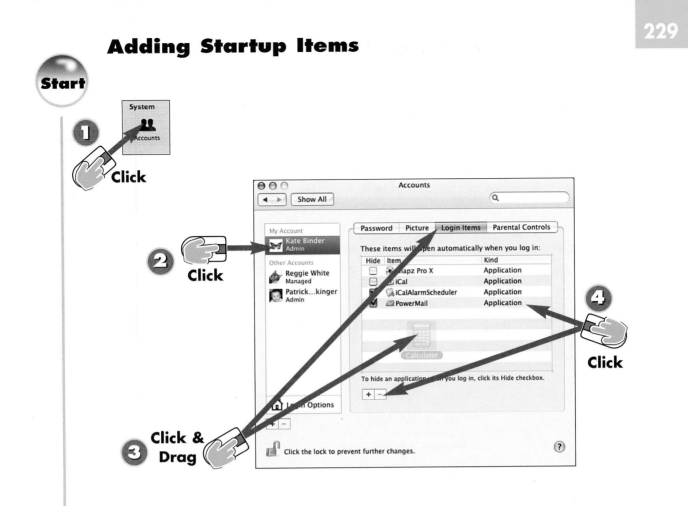

Click

Click

**Click &
Drag**

Click

1. In System Preferences, click **Accounts** to see the accounts preferences.

2. Click to select the account for which you want to add login items.

3. Click the **Login Items** tab and then drag programs, documents, bookmark files, or folders into the window from the Finder.

4. Click an item and click the **Remove** button to remove it from the list.

End

INTRODUCTION

When you log in, your Mac sets itself up the way you like things. One service it can perform for you when you log in is starting up programs you use all the time, such as your email client, your contact manager, and other constant companions. To make this happen, you add these programs to your login items.

TIP

What a Drag
Drag items up and down in the login list to change the order in which they start up when you log in to your Mac.

HINT

Be Creative
Login items don't have to be programs; you can open any file at login. Examples of files you might want to open every time you use your Mac include a sound file of your favorite song, the novel you're working on, or your recipe database.

Resetting Your Password

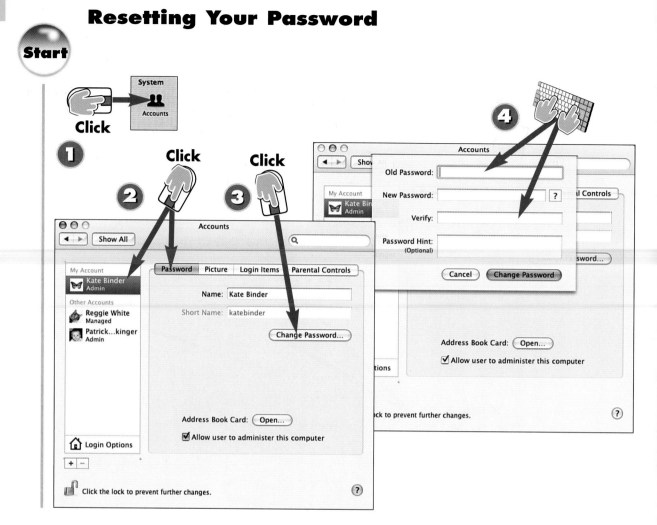

1. If you're logged in, choose **Apple menu**, **System Preferences** and click **Accounts** to see the accounts preferences.

2. Click your username in the list and then click the **Password** tab.

3. Click **Change Password**.

4. Type your old password and the new password in the **Password** and **Verify** fields.

Because you need a password to access files on your Mac, be sure to choose a password you can't forget, and take advantage of the Hint feature to provide yourself with a memory-jogging phrase when you need it. If the worst does happen and you just can't figure out your password, here's how to remedy the situation.

Don't Make It Too Easy
This might seem obvious, but if you enter a hint for your password, don't make the hint too obvious. Even if you're tempted to just use the password itself for the hint, don't!

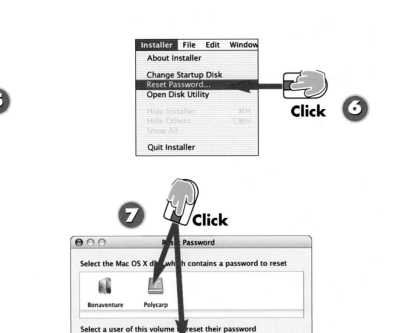

5

Click **6**

7 **Click**

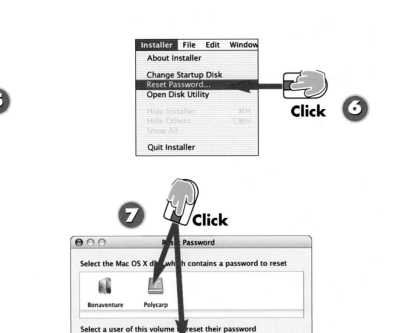

8 **Save**

---

5 If you have forgotten the Mac's main admin password (the one used by its first admin user), insert the Mac OS X Install Disc 1 CD and restart. Press **C** on your keyboard until you see the spinning gear symbol.

6 When the Installer starts up, choose **Installer**, **Reset Password**.

7 Choose the hard drive where your system software resides and then select your user-name.

8 Enter the new password twice and click **Save**.

End

A Little Help from a Friend

If you forget your password and can't log in or access your home folder (when you're using FileVault), an admin user can change the password for you.

Safe and Secure

Keep your system CD in a safe place so it's not accessible to people who might want to reset the password to gain access to files that aren't theirs.

Sharing Files with Other Users

Start

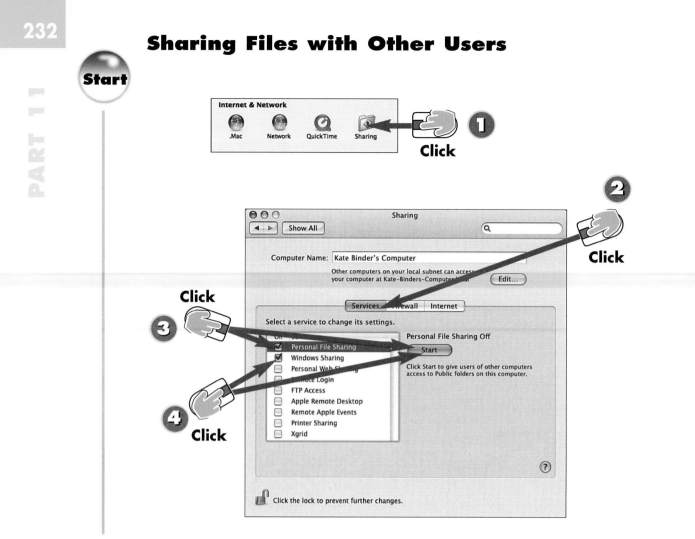

① To enable network users to access the Public folder in your home folder, open System Preferences and click **Sharing**.

② In the Sharing pane, click **Services**.

③ Check the box labeled **Personal File Sharing** to share files with other Mac users on your network, and then click **Start**.

④ Check the box labeled **Windows Sharing** to share files with Windows users on your network, and then click **Start**.

Some files are meant to be read and even modified by multiple users—a family calendar or a committee report in progress, for example. You can share these files in two designated places, with different results. And you can send copies of your files to other users via their Drop Box folders.

Skipping It
Why all this rigmarole, you ask? The point is to keep your files as safe as you want them to be. If you want to skip the security routine and share with everyone, you can keep your Mac logged in with a single user account and give all users the password.

Making the Connection
To learn how to connect to other Macs on a network, turn to "Connecting to Networked Computers," p. 240.

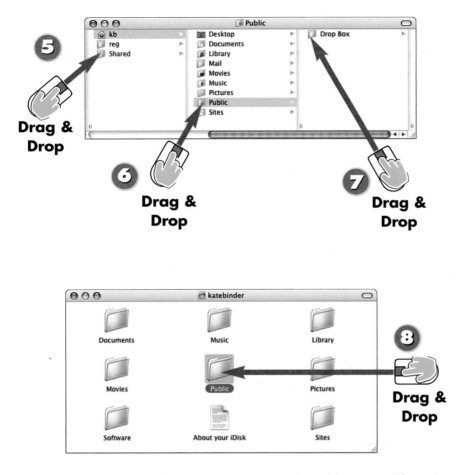

5. Put files you want all your Mac's users to be able to modify in the Shared folder in the Users folder.

6. Put files that you want all your Mac's users to be able to read but not change in the Public folder in your home folder.

7. To give another user of your computer a copy of a file, put the file in that user's Drop Box folder inside her Public folder.

8. To share a file with other Mac users on the Internet, copy it to the Public folder on your iDisk.

It's Good to Share
Files you might share in a Public folder or in the Shared folder within the Users folder include databases (of recipes, addresses, or clients, for example), templates for letters or memos that everyone uses, and logo graphics.

Large Attachments
Many email providers limit the size of file attachments. If you want to send someone a larger file than will fit through your provider's email gateway, put it on your iDisk (step 8) and create a File Sharing web page where she can snag the file.

Flying Blind
When you drag a file into another user's Drop Box, the Mac warns that you won't be able to see the result of the operation. This is its way of saying that you can't open the Drop Box folder to see what's in it.

Keeping Your Secrets

Start

System Preferences

◄ ► Show All   Q

Personal

Appearance | Dashboard & Exposé | Desktop & Screen Saver | Dock | International | Security | Spotlight

1 Click

Click

2 Click

Security

◄ ► Show All   Q

FileVault

FileVault secures your home folder by encrypting its contents. It automatically encrypts and decrypts your files while you're using them.

WARNING: Your files will be encrypted using your login password. If you forget your login password and you don't know the master password, your data will be lost.

...aster password is **not set** for this computer.   Set Master Password
...is a "safety net" password. It lets you unlock any
...ault account on this computer.

...Vault protection is **off** for this account.   Turn On FileVault...
...ing on FileVault may take a while.

...equire password to wake this computer from sleep or screen saver

...all accounts on this computer:

...Disable automatic login

...equire password to unlock each secure system preference

...og out after 60 ⬍ minutes of inactivity

...Use secure virtual memory

...ck to prevent further changes.   ?

A **master password** must be created for this computer to provide a safety net for accounts with FileVault protection.

An administrator of this computer can use the master password to reset the password of any user on the computer. If you forget your password, you can reset the password to gain access to your home folder even if it's protected by FileVault. This provides protection for users who forget their login password.

Master Password: ••••••••   ?

Verify: ••••••••

Hint:

Choose a password that is difficult to guess, ...e based on something important to you so that you never forget it. Click the Help ...tton for more information about choosing a good password.

?   Cancel   OK

3 Click

4 Click

1 In System Preferences, click **Security**.

2 Click **Set Master Password**.

3 Type the master password in the **Master Password** field, type it a second time in the **Verify** field, and click **OK**.

4 Click **Turn On FileVault** to set FileVault preferences.

FileVault encrypts the contents of your home folder so no one can read your files without entering your password. This includes all users, even admin users, under all circumstances—it's the ultimate protection for your files. You must be logged in to your account to turn on FileVault.

Coffee Break

While FileVault is being turned on or off, you are logged out and can't use your Mac. This could last just a minute or take longer, depending on how much data is in your home folder.

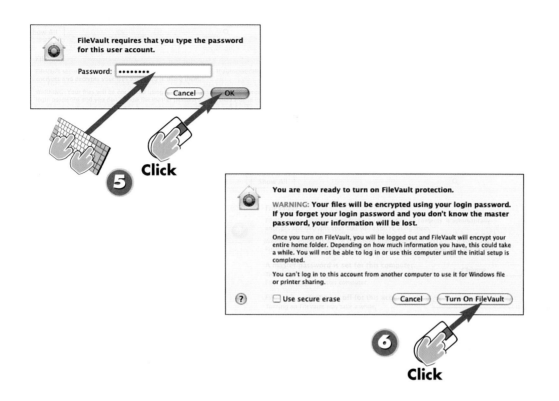

FileVault requires that you type the password
for this user account.

Password: ●●●●●●●

Cancel   OK

Click

5

You are now ready to turn on FileVault protection.

WARNING: **Your files will be encrypted using your login password.
If you forget your login password and you don't know the master
password, your information will be lost.**

Once you turn on FileVault, you will be logged out and FileVault will encrypt your
entire home folder. Depending on how much information you have, this could take
a while. You will not be able to log in or use this computer until the initial setup is
completed.

You can't log in to this account from another computer to use it for Windows file
or printer sharing.

? ☐ Use secure erase   Cancel   Turn On FileVault

6

Click

5 Type your login password and click **OK**.

6 Click **Turn On FileVault**. The system logs you out while it encrypts your home
folder; it then asks you to log in again.

End

How to Tell
HINT
When FileVault is turned off,
your home folder icon looks like
a little house. With FileVault
turned on, the folder icon
changes to a house-shaped
safe with a big combination
lock dial on its front.

Deceptive Appearances
CAUTION
FileVault makes your home
folder appear to some programs to be a single, constantly
changing folder or file, which
can interfere with backup software. If you use FileVault, be
sure to check that your backups
are working correctly.

Creating a Home Network

A network, whether it's composed of physical cables or wireless, connects your computer with other computers so you can share files, play network games, and all use the same printers and Internet connection. The Internet, in fact, is simply a huge network comprising many smaller networks. With Mac OS X, setting up your own network in your home or office is easy.

Creating a network has two basic components. First, you need to make the connection by either hooking up your Macs (and Windows PCs, if you like) with Ethernet cables or installing AirPort cards and an AirPort base station so they can talk to each other wirelessly. Then, you need to tell your Mac how your network is set up so the system knows which connector and language to use to communicate with the other computers it's connected to.

In this part, you'll learn how to set up your network and turn on file sharing so both Windows users and other Mac users on your network can exchange files with you. You'll also learn how to share printers connected to your Mac with other users on your network. And you'll find out how to share a single Internet connection among all the computers on a network, as well as how to connect to an AirPort network and get online via a wireless AirPort connection.

Setting Up and Using a Network

Get online

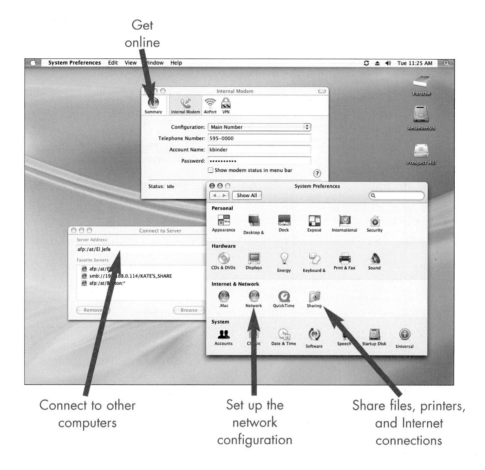

Connect to other computers

Set up the network configuration

Share files, printers, and Internet connections

Getting on the Network

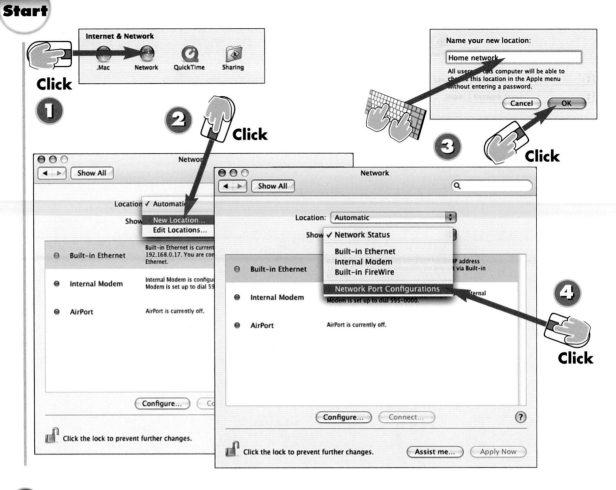

1. Open System Preferences and click the **Network** button.

2. In the Network pane, choose **New Location** from the **Location** pop-up menu.

3. Enter a name for the network configuration you're about to create and click **OK**.

4. Choose **Network Port Configurations** from the **Show** pop-up menu.

INTRODUCTION

The first step to setting up a wired home network is this: Connect your computers with Ethernet cables (a regular one for newer Macs and a crossover cable for older Macs). If you have more than two computers, buy a hub and connect each computer to the hub; otherwise, connect your two Macs directly to each other.

An Even Easier Way

If network settings completely befuddle you, try using the Network Setup Assistant to get connected. Start up System Preferences and click **Network**; then click **Assist Me** and follow the instructions.

Looking It Up

Start up System Preferences and click **Network**; then choose **Network Status** from the **Show** pop-up menu. Click the **Built-in Ethernet** or **AirPort** entries in the list to see your IP address.

5 Check the box next to the network port you want to use (usually either Built-in Ethernet or AirPort).

6 Choose the active network port from the **Show** pop-up menu.

7 To turn on TCP networking, click the **TCP/IP** tab and make sure that **Configure IPv4** is set to either **Using DHCP** or **Manually** (check with your network admin).

8 To share files with older Macs that can't do TCP networking, click the **AppleTalk** tab and check **Make AppleTalk Active**.

End

Going Both Ways
If other users want to connect to your Mac via AppleTalk, both your Mac and their Macs must have AppleTalk turned on as directed in step 8.

By the Manual
When you choose Manually in the Configure IPv4 pop-up menu, you must enter your Mac's IP address, your router's IP address, and the subnet mask. If all this is gibberish to you, go to Threemacs.com (www.threemacs.com) to learn about creating networks.

Connecting to Networked Computers

Start

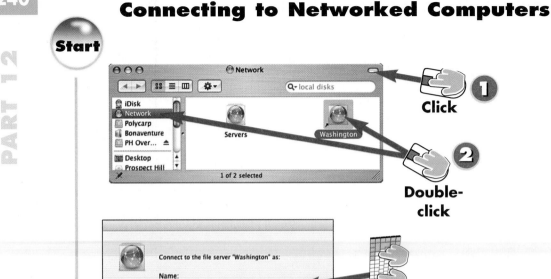

Click 1

Double-click 2

Double-click

3 **Click**

4

① In the Finder, click the transparent button to display the Places sidebar if it's not already visible.

② Click **Network** and double-click the computer to which you want to connect.

③ Enter your username and password and click **Connect**.

④ Double-click a drive or folder to connect to.

End

Networking has always been easy with Macs, but now the system's networking features are easier to use and more powerful than ever. You can connect to any Mac or Windows computer on your network using either AppleTalk or TCP networking, but all you need to know is the computer's name or IP address.

Invisible Friends
If the computer to which you want to connect isn't visible, you need to find out its network address (available in the Sharing section of System Preferences). Then choose **Go**, **Connect to Server** in the Finder and enter the address.

Connecting with the Other Side
To connect to a Windows computer, assign it an IP address (refer to Windows documentation). Then enter its address in the Connect to Server dialog box in this form: **smb://192.168.0.102**.

Sharing Files on a Network

Start

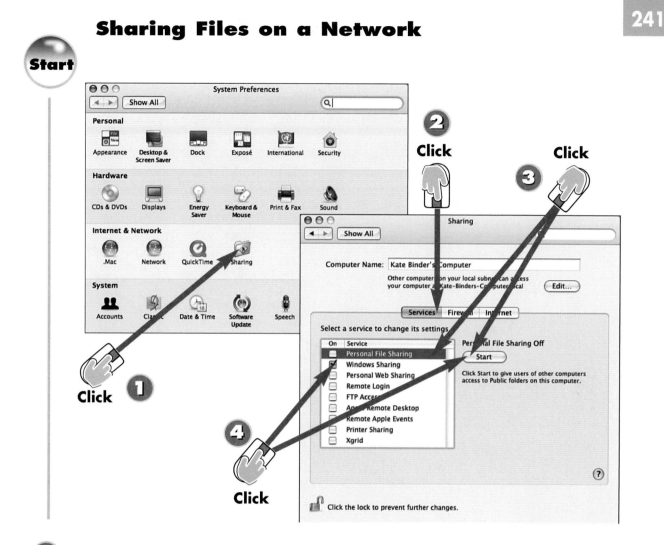

Click ②

Click ③

Click ①

Click ④

① Open System Preferences and click **Sharing**.

② In the Sharing dialog box, click the **Services** tab.

③ Click **Personal File Sharing** and click **Start**.

④ To share files with Windows users as well as Mac users, click **Windows Sharing** and click **Start**.

End

When computers aren't networked, sharing files requires the use of sneakernet: physically walking a removable disk to another machine. Fortunately, creating a network is easy enough (see "Getting on the Network," earlier in this part) that Mac users rarely have to resort to sneakernet. Here's how to share your files on a real network.

TIP

When You Get There
To connect to another Mac on your network, see the preceding task, "Connecting to Networked Computers." When you connect to another Mac, you'll see the home folders of that Mac's users. If you log in as a registered user of that Mac, you'll be able to access the same folders as if you were sitting in front of the Mac. Otherwise, you must connect as a Guest; in this case, you'll be able to see only the contents of the user's Public folder (see "Sharing Files," in Part 11, "Sharing Your Mac with Multiple Users").

Sharing a Printer on a Network

Start

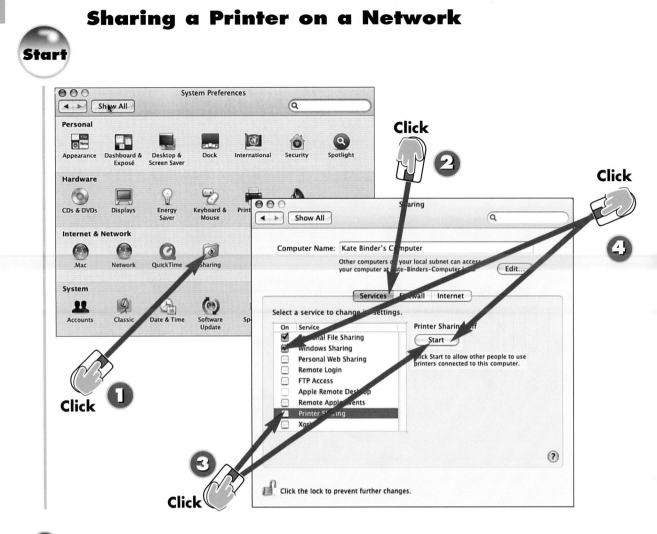

Click 2

Click 4

Click 1

Click 3

1 Open System Preferences and click **Sharing**.

2 Click the **Services** tab.

3 Click **Printer Sharing** and click **Start**.

4 To share printers with Windows users as well as Mac users, click **Windows Sharing** and click **Start** (if it's not already started).

End

INTRODUCTION
You can share printers connected to your computer with other computer users on your network. Starting up printer sharing is simple; you can choose to restrict it to Mac users or enable Windows users to use your printers as well. Network users can add shared printers to their Print dialog boxes just like network printers.

TIP
Where in the Office...?
To let other people know where shared printers are physically located, start **Printer Setup Utility** (in the Utilities folder in Applications). Select the printer and click **Show Info**; then add a description (such as "Kate's office") in the **Location** field.

HINT
What It's For
Printers on your network are already shared with other users on the network, even if the printers are located in your office. Printer sharing gives network capabilities to devices such as USB inkjets, which don't usually have network connectors.

Sharing an Internet Connection

Start

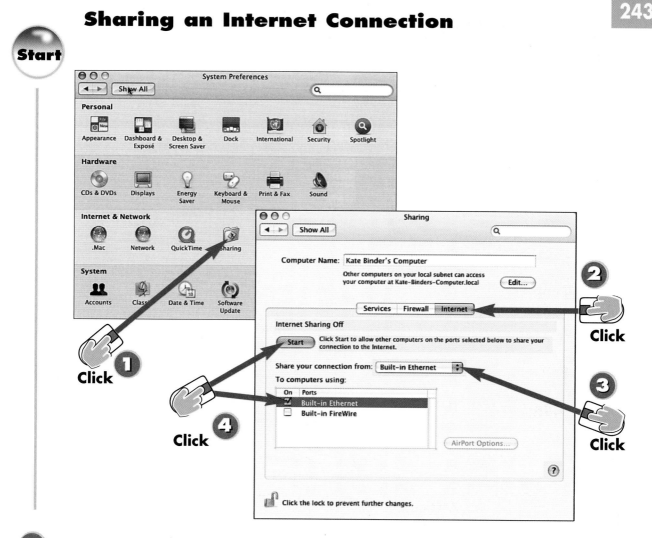

1. Open System Preferences and click **Sharing**.

2. Click the **Internet** tab.

3. Choose a connection to share. For direct cable modem and DSL connections, choose **Built-in Ethernet**; if you have a wireless connection to the Internet, choose **AirPort**.

4. Check the box next to the connection method the other computers on your network use; then click **Start**.

End

INTRODUCTION

If you've ever suffered through life with two Internet-capable computers and only one phone line, you'll appreciate the ability to share an online connection with all the computers in your house or office. And life gets even better when your connection is broadband, such as a cable modem or a DSL line.

When Not to Share

If you connect to the Internet and your network via the same port, sharing your Internet connection can disrupt the network by telling other computers to access the Internet through it when they shouldn't (such as when you take your laptop to the office).

Another Way to Share

If you're sharing an Internet connection through another Mac, you'll be able to get online only when that Mac is up and connected. If that doesn't work for you, consider buying a hardware router that can keep you online all the time.

Joining an AirPort Network

Start

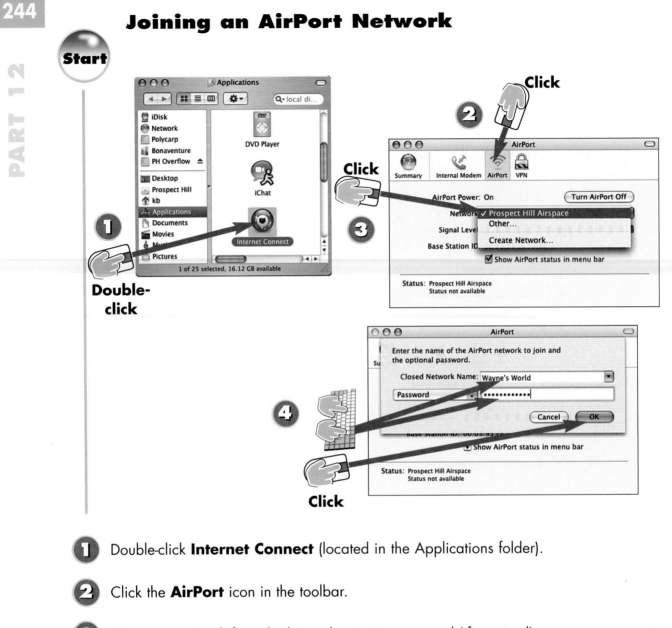

Click

Click

Double-click

Click

1. Double-click **Internet Connect** (located in the Applications folder).

2. Click the **AirPort** icon in the toolbar.

3. Choose a network from the list and enter its password (if required).

4. If the network you want isn't listed, choose **Other** and enter the network's name and password in the login dialog box, then click **OK**.

End

INTRODUCTION

With an AirPort card, you can get rid of those annoying network cables and connect to your network from wherever your computer happens to be, as long as you're close to an AirPort base station. AirPort is great for PowerBooks and iBooks, but you can use it for desktop Macs, too.

TIP

AirPort in Your Menu Bar
With the AirPort status menu, you can switch networks, turn AirPort on or off, open Internet Connect, or connect to AirPort-equipped Macs. Check the **Show AirPort status in menu bar** box in Internet Connect's AirPort settings.

HINT

Close to Home Base
If AirPort is turned on in Internet Connect but you can't get in touch with the network, you might be out of range. AirPort base stations have a range of about 150 feet; you must be within that area to connect to the base station.

Getting Online with AirPort

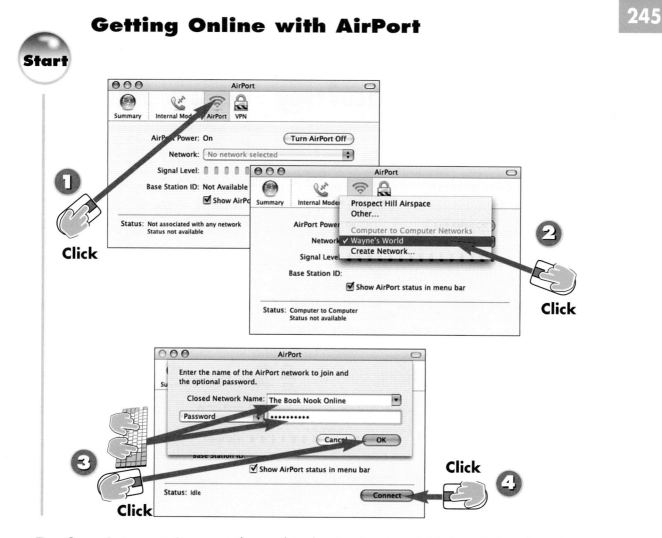

1 Open **Internet Connect** (located in the Applications folder) and click the **AirPort** icon in the toolbar.

2 If you're not already connected to an Airport network, choose a network from the list and type its password (if required).

3 If the network you want isn't listed, choose **Other** from the Network pop-up menu and type the network's name and password; then click **OK**.

4 Click **Connect**.

If you're connected to an AirPort network, you can share the Internet connection on that network. It might be configured to connect automatically when you need it (such as when you start up your web browser), but if it's not, you'll need to know how to tell it you want to get online.

Closing the Connection
You can disconnect AirPort from the Internet manually, too. Just open Internet Connect again, click the **AirPort** icon in the toolbar, and click **Disconnect**.

How About My PC?
Yes, Windows PCs can connect to AirPort networks, too. AirPort cards work only in Macs, but there are third-party wireless cards made for PCs; what you're looking for, says Apple, is a "802.11b Wi-Fi certified wireless card."

PART 13

Maintaining Your Mac

Most of the time your Mac just hums right along, cheerfully complying with your requests and sitting quietly in the corner when you're not using it. Every once in a while, however, even the best-behaved Mac needs a little maintenance or a minor repair. This part covers the basics of keeping your Mac happy and healthy.

In this part you'll learn how to fix disk errors and reformat disks—both removable disks and hard drives—as well as ways to remedy problems with Classic. Also covered are updating and installing system software, setting the date and time automatically, and calibrating your monitor for accurate color. Some of these techniques are one-time jobs (calibrating your monitor), and others are things you'll do on a regular basis (formatting removable disks).

Along the way, you'll learn a variety of useful tricks, such as displaying system information, rebooting from a different system, and force quitting programs when necessary. Whether you're a power user or a weekends-only Macster, the tasks in this part will teach you things every Mac user should know.

Mac Maintenance and Repair Kit

Get information
about your Mac

Repair
disks

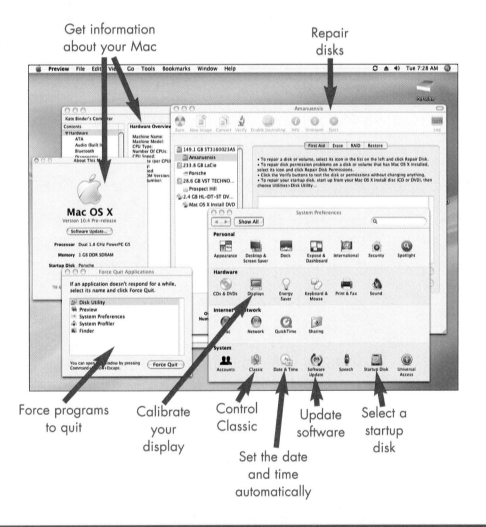

Force programs
to quit

Calibrate
your
display

Control
Classic

Update
software

Select a
startup
disk

Set the date
and time
automatically

Fixing Errors with Disk Utility

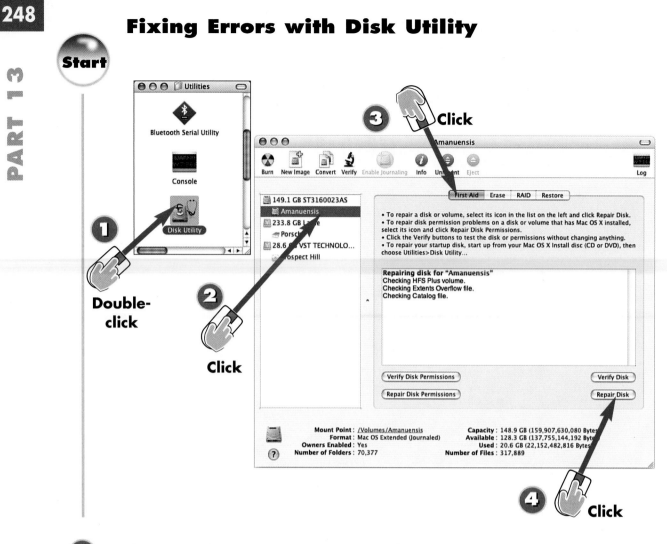

1. Double-click **Disk Utility** to start it (it's in the Utilities folder within Applications).

2. Select the disk to be repaired in the list.

3. Click the **First Aid** tab.

4. Click **Repair Disk**.

End

Over time and with use, the formatting structure of a disk can become scrambled, either slightly or seriously. If you have trouble reading files from or saving files to a disk, or if you experience other mysterious problems, it's time to run the repair program Disk Utility. (To use Disk Utility on your startup disk, see the next task.)

Verify or Repair?
Usually, you should click Repair Disk Permissions or Repair Disk right off the bat. If, however, you're concerned about modifying a disk in any way at all, you can check its status without making any repairs by using the Verify commands.

What Are Permissions?
Disk Utility can repair permissions. Each program, document, and folder in a Mac OS X system has permissions describing who can open and modify it. Incorrect permissions can prevent programs from running or cause them to malfunction.

Repairing the Startup Disk

Start

1 Mac OS X Install Disc 1

2 Click

Installer | File | Edit | Window
About Installer

Change Startup Disk
Reset Password...
Open Disk Utility

Hide Installer ⌘H
Hide Others ⌥⌘H
Show All

Quit Installer

4 Click

Porsche

Burn | New Image | Convert | Verify | Enable Journaling | Info | Unmount | Eject | Log

First Aid | RAID | Restore

- To repair a disk or volume, select its icon in the list on the left and click Repair Disk.
- To repair disk permission problems on a disk or volume that has Mac OS X installed, select its icon and click Repair Disk Permissions.
- Click the Verify buttons to test the disk or permissions without changing anything.
- To repair your startup disk, start up from your Mac OS X Install disc (CD or DVD), then choose Utilities>Disk Utility...

Repairing disk for "Porsche"
Checking HFS Plus volume.
Checking Extents Overflow file.
Checking Catalog file.

2.3 GB HL-DT-ST DVD-...
Mac OS X Install DVD
149.1 GB ST3160023AS
Amanuensis
233.8 GB LaCie
Porsche
28.6 GB VST TECHNOLO...
Prospect Hill

3 Click

Verify Disk Permissions | Verify Disk
Repair Disk Permissions | Repair Disk

Mount Point : /
Format : Mac OS Extended (Journaled)
Owners Enabled : Yes
Number of Folders : 164,395
Capacity : 233.8 GB (250,999,500,800 Bytes)
Available : 187.5 GB (201,355,444,224 Bytes)
Used : 46.2 GB (49,624,104,960 Bytes)
Number of Files : 665,997

1 Restart from the Mac OS X Install CD (see "Starting Up from a Different System," later in this part).

2 Choose **Installer**, **Open Disk Utility**.

3 Select your hard drive in the list.

4 Click the **First Aid** tab and click **Repair Disk**.

End

Disk Utility can't repair the startup disk because the program can't modify the section of the disk where it resides. If you have a second hard drive with a Mac OS X system installed, you can start from that drive to run Disk Utility or use your installation CD, as described here.

What's Going On?
The Open Disk Utility command (located in the Installer menu when you start up from your installation CD) isn't anything special. It simply starts up the Disk Utility program that's installed on the CD, which is the same as the one installed on your hard drive.

Updating Programs with Software Update

Start

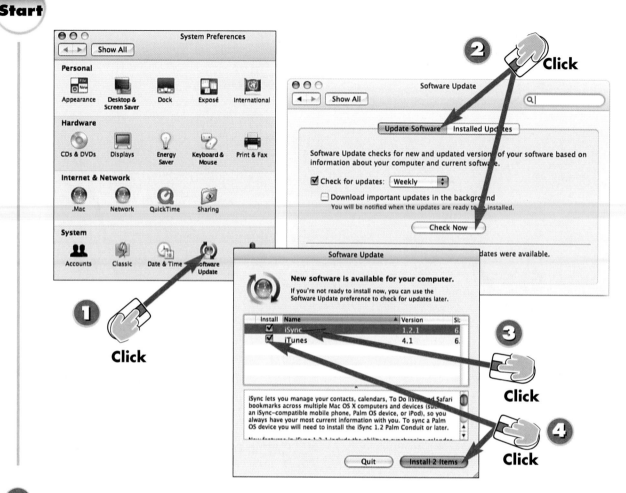

Click

Click

Click

Click

1 Start System Preferences and click the **Software Update** button.

2 Click the **Update Software** tab and click **Check Now**.

3 If updates are located, click the name of each update to see information about it.

4 Check the boxes next to each update you want to install and click **Install**.

INTRODUCTION

Software Update checks with Apple over the Internet to see whether it finds updated versions of your system software and preinstalled programs. Then it can download and install updates for you. You enter an admin name and password when you update your software. Mac OS X assumes only admin users are authorized to change software.

TIP

Behind the Scenes
If you have a broadband Internet connection, check **Check for updates** and choose an interval. Do this at the time of day when you want the check to occur—Software Update starts counting the time interval from the time you make this setting.

TIP

Keeping Track
If you want to know which updates have been installed and when, click the **Installed Updates** tab to see a list. Click the column headers to sort the list by the date, the update's name, or the version number.

Authenticate

Software Update requires that you type your password.

Name: Kate

Password: ••••••••

▼ Details

OK

Click

Software Update

New software is available for your computer.

If you're not ready to install now, you can use the Software Update preference to check for updates later.

Install	Name	Version	Si:
✓	iSync	1.2.1	6.
✓	iTunes	4.1	6.

Quit   Install

License Agreement

Apple Software

ENGLISH

Apple Computer, Inc.
Software License Agreement

PLEASE READ THIS SOFTWARE LICENSE AGREEMENT ("LICENSE ") CAREFULLY BEFORE PRESSING THE "AGREE" BUTTON BELOW. BY PRESSING "AGREE," YOU ARE AGREEING TO BE BOUND BY THE TERMS OF THIS LICENSE. IF YOU DO NOT AGREE TO THE TERMS OF THIS LICENSE, PRESS "DISAGREE" AND (IF APPLICABLE) RETURN THE APPLE SOFTWARE TO THE PLACE WHERE YOU OBTAINED IT FOR A REFUND.

1. License. The software (including Boot ROM code), documentation and any fonts accompanying this License whether on disk, in read only memory, on any other media or in any other form (the "Apple Software") are licensed to you by Apple Computer, Inc. or its local subsidiary, if any ("Apple"). You own the media on which the Apple Software is recorded but Apple and/or Apple's licensor(s) retain title to the Apple Software. The Apple Software in this package and any copies which this License authorizes you to make are subject to this License.

2. Permitted Uses and Restrictions. This License allows you to install and use the Apple Software on a single Apple-labeled or Apple-licensed computer at a time. This License does not allow the Apple Software to exist on more than one computer at a time. You may make one copy of the Apple Software (excluding the Boot ROM code) in machine-readable form for backup purposes only. The backup copy must include all copyright information contained on the original. Except as expressly permitted in this License, you may not decompile, reverse engineer, disassemble, modify, rent, lease, loan, sublicense, distribute or create derivative works based upon the Apple Software in whole or part or transmit the Apple Software over a network or from one computer to another. This license allow you to install or operate the Apple Software only on a computer system that came bundled with a licensed version of the

Disagree   Agree

Click

Click

Click

5️⃣ Enter an admin name and password and click **OK**.

6️⃣ If a license agreement appears, click **Agree**. Software Update downloads and installs the update.

7️⃣ Click **Quit**.

End

Updating a New System
Some updates don't show up until after other updates are installed. After installing system software from your original CDs (see "Installing the System Software," later in this part), run Software Update repeatedly until it doesn't show any updates.

Don't Go First
If you're not sure whether to install a system update, take a quick trip to MacFixit (www.macfixit.com) to see whether other users who've already updated their Macs have reported any problems with the update.

Using the Date & Time Preferences

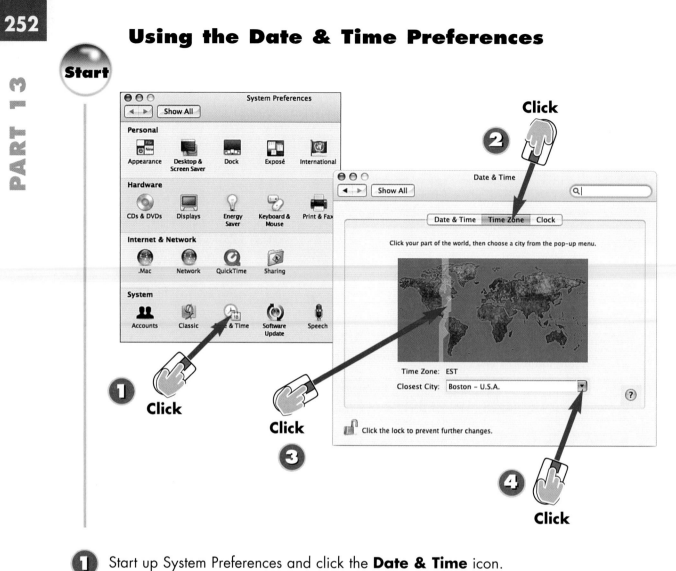

1 Start up System Preferences and click the **Date & Time** icon.

2 Click the **Time Zone** tab.

3 Click the map near where you live.

4 Choose the nearest city from the **Closest City** pop-up menu.

INTRODUCTION

It's important that your Mac know what time it is. Every file on your hard drive is time-stamped, and the system uses that information to determine which files contain the latest data. Using the Date & Time preferences, you can ensure that the date and time stamps on your computer are accurate.

TIP

Blink Blink
Another useful setting in Date & Time preferences is located on the Clock tab. Check the box marked **Flash the time separators**. Then, if the colon stops blinking, you'll know your Mac is frozen and you can restart it.

HINT

Today's Date Is...
To see the full day and date, click the menu bar to reveal its own menu. You can also open the Date & Time preferences from this menu, as well as changing the menu bar clock to an analog icon instead of the standard digital alphanumeric display.

Click

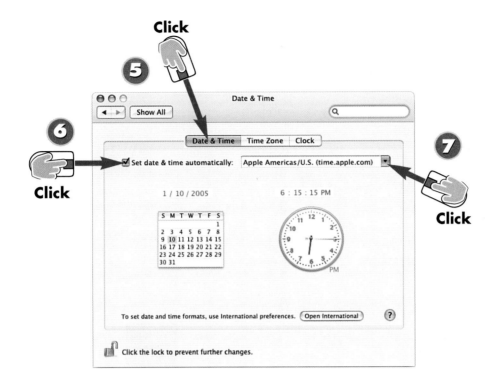

Click

Click

Click

5 Click the **Date & Time** tab.

6 Check the box marked **Set Date & Time automatically**.

7 Choose the nearest timeserver from the pop-up menu.

End

More About NTP
To learn more about how network timeservers work, you can visit the Network Time Protocol website at www.ntp.org. There you'll also find links to lists of alternative timeservers, including servers around the world.

Calibrating Your Monitor

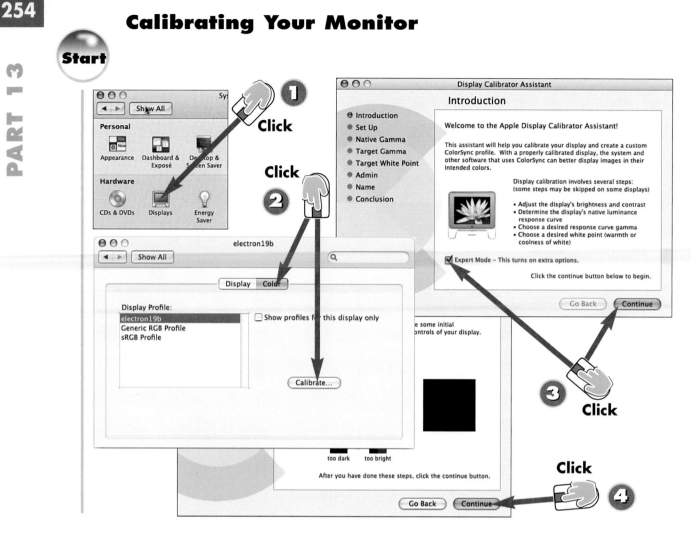

1️⃣ Start System Preferences and click the **Displays** icon.

2️⃣ Click the **Color** tab and click **Calibrate**. The Display Calibrator Assistant opens.

3️⃣ Click the **Expert Mode** box to create a more precise profile; then click **Continue**.

4️⃣ Make the monitor settings shown in the window and click **Continue**.

INTRODUCTION

It wasn't all that long ago that computers had grayscale monitors, but now it's all about color. To make sure color looks right on your screen, however, you need to calibrate your system. Here's how to create a color device profile that tells your Mac how your monitor displays color and makes appropriate adjustments.

HINT

Managing Color
The software components that translate color between your Mac and your monitor comprise a color management system (CMS). In its full-fledged form, a CMS ensures consistent color throughout your system, from scanner to monitor to printer.

HINT

Where to Start
The Color tab of the Displays preference pane includes a list of profiles. If one of those matches or is close to the monitor you're using, click to select that profile before you start the calibration process. You'll get a more accurate profile that way.

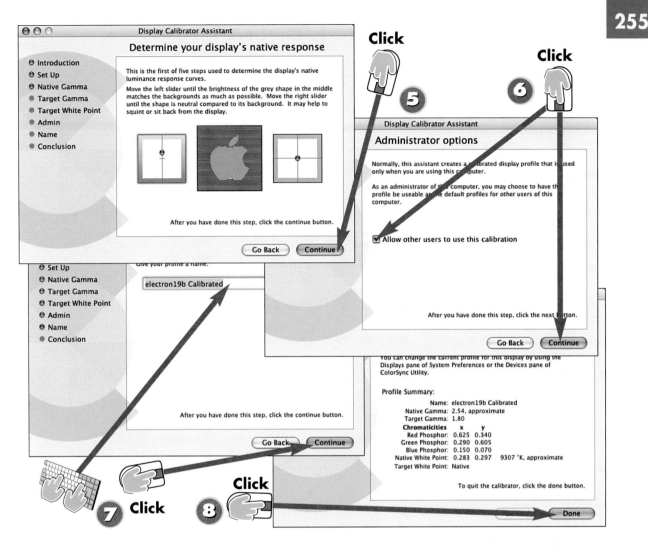

5. Follow the instructions on the Native Response, Target Gamma, and Target White Point screens, clicking **Continue** after each screen.

6. If you're an admin user, check the box to make the profile available to all users of this Mac; then click **Continue**.

7. Enter a name for the profile and click **Continue**. The Display Calibrator Assistant saves the profile.

8. Click **Done**.

End

HINT
Native Gamma, Target Gamma, and Target White Point, used in the Display Calibrator Assistant, might sound very technical, but they simply refer to how your eye perceives the lightness, darkness, and overall color cast of your monitor's display.

HINT
A Step Further
If you're in the market for truly accurate color, you'll have to spend a little to get it. Look into a color profiling application such as MonacoEZColor (www.monacosys.com), which can create custom scanner and printer profiles for your system.

Starting Up from a Different System

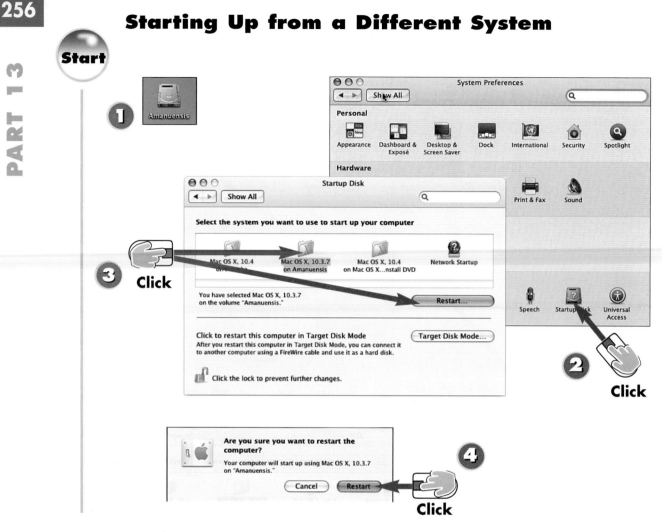

1. If needed, insert or hook up the disk that contains the system from which you want to start up.

2. Start up System Preferences and click **Startup Disk**.

3. Click to select the system installation you want to use; then click **Restart**.

4. Click **Restart** again.

INTRODUCTION

You can start your Mac by using a different version of the system software. You might use this feature to restart in Mac OS 9 because some older programs won't run in Classic. Or you can play it safe by installing a new Mac OS X system update on an external drive and test it before installing it on your main hard drive.

TIP

Getting Back Where You Belong
If you restart using a Mac OS 9 system, you can get back to Mac OS X by choosing **Apple menu, Control Panels, Startup Disk in Mac OS 9**. The control panel doesn't look the same as in Mac OS X, but it works the same way.

Forcing an Application to Quit

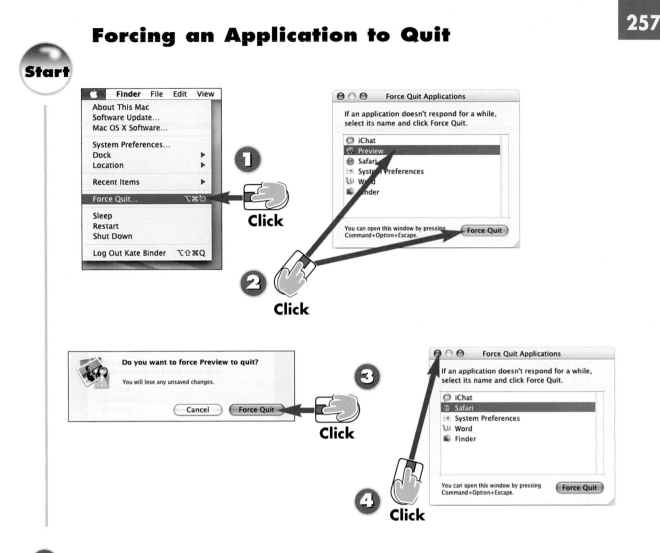

1 Choose **Apple menu, Force Quit**.

2 Choose the program you want from the list and click **Force Quit**.

3 Click **Force Quit** again.

4 Click the **Close** button to dismiss the Force Quit dialog box.

INTRODUCTION

When a program isn't working right, your first tactic should be to quit and restart it. But sometimes a program is so off-track that the Quit command doesn't work. Then you can force the program to quit. It doesn't affect the other programs that are running, but unsaved changes in documents within the problem application are lost.

HINT

In the Olden Days
Apple used to recommend that you restart your Mac after force quitting an application. But Mac OS X uses protected memory; each program runs in its own area of memory so that when it malfunctions, no other program is affected. No need to restart!

HINT

Classic Quitting
If you force quit an application running under Classic (see "Starting and Stopping Classic" in Part 3), Classic itself might quit. If this happens, you lose any unsaved changes in all Classic programs.

Displaying System Information

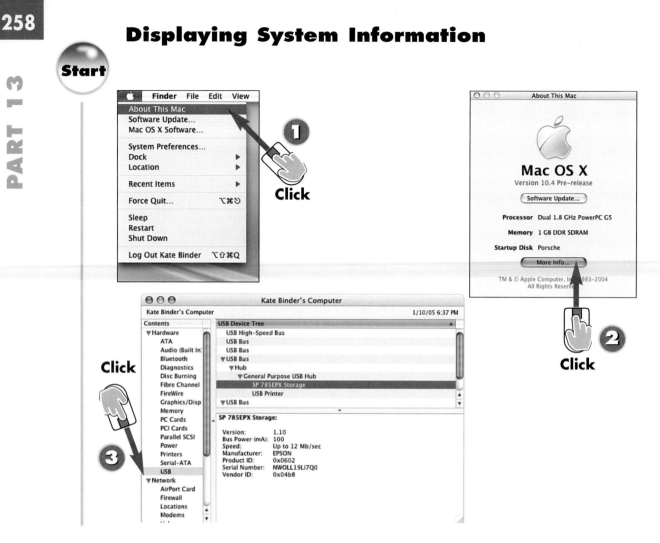

1. Choose **Apple menu**, **About This Mac** to see the system version, your Mac's processor speed and type, and the amount of RAM your Mac has.

2. Click **More Info** to start up System Profiler.

3. Click each entry in the **Contents** column to view that category of information.

End

Sharing Is Good
To share your system information with another person (such as a network administrator or technical support specialist), save a System Profiler report as a text file. Choose **File**, **Export**, **Rich Text**; then enter a name and choose a location.

Breaking News
If you make changes to your system configuration while System Profiler is open, you can force the program to update its report to include your changes by choosing **View**, **Refresh**.

Formatting a Disk

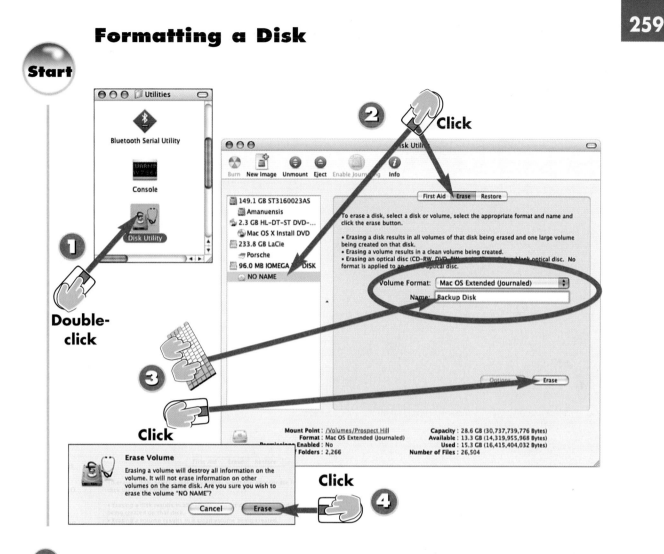

Start

1 Double-click

2 Click

3

Click

4 Click

Click

Erase Volume
Erasing a volume will destroy all information on the volume. It will not erase information on other volumes on the same disk. Are you sure you wish to erase the volume "NO NAME"?

Cancel   Erase

---

1 Double-click **Disk Utility** to start it (it's in the Utilities folder within Applications).

2 Choose the disk to be formatted in the list on the left and click the **Erase** tab.

3 Choose a **Volume Format** option, type a name for the disk, and click **Erase**.

4 Click **Erase** again.

End

INTRODUCTION

There are three good reasons to reformat a disk. First, if you want to use the disk on a Windows or Unix computer, it will need a different format. Second, formatting a disk erases all data completely. And finally, reformatting a disk is a last resort if you're having problems opening or saving files on it.

TIP

Lowest Common Denominator
Because Macs can read DOS disks but Windows PCs can't read Mac disks, you usually should choose the MS-DOS File System option when you're formatting removable disks such as Zip disks that might get used on either system.

Installing the System Software

Start

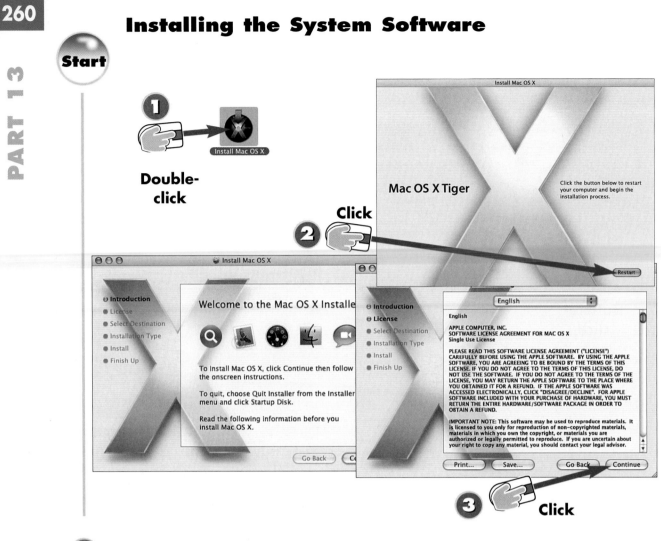

Double-click

Click

1

2

3

Click

Install Mac OS X

Mac OS X Tiger

Click the button below to restart your computer and begin the installation process.

Restart

1 Insert the CD labeled Mac OS X Install Disc 1 and double-click **Install Mac OS X**.

2 Click **Restart** and enter an admin name and password. Then click **OK**. Your Mac reboots using the system on the CD.

3 In the Installer's first screen, choose a language and click **Continue** to see the subsequent screens; click **Continue** again on the Introduction, Read Me, and License screens.

INTRODUCTION

When you install a new hard drive (a bigger one, of course!) or want to upgrade an older Mac to Mac OS X, you must install Mac OS X. Using the installer is easy, but it takes a bit of time, and you should be sure your documents are backed up onto another disk before you get started.

TIP

Getting a Fresh Start

Software Update (see "Updating Programs with Software Update," earlier in this part) makes updating your system every time a new version comes out easy. But if you start seeing strange behavior in your system and running Disk Utility doesn't fix it, your best bet is to start fresh with new system software.

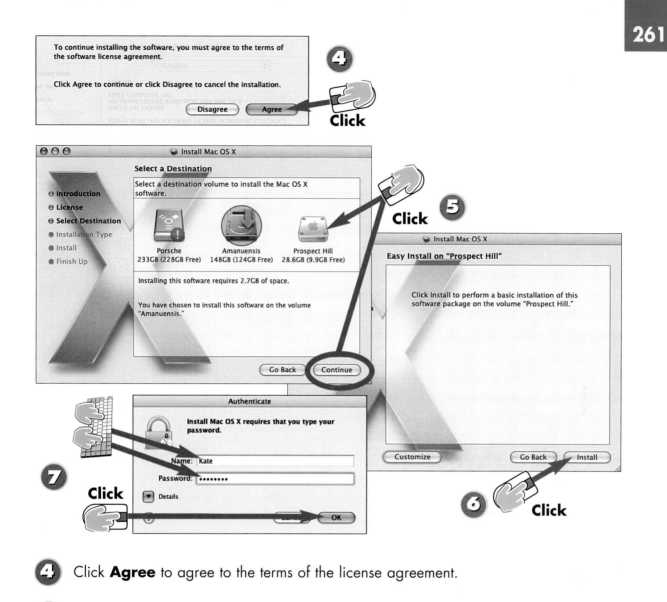

4 Click **Agree** to agree to the terms of the license agreement.

5 Choose a hard drive and click **Continue**.

6 Click **Install**.

7 Type an admin username and password and click **OK**.

Your Options

In step 6, if the hard drive you choose already has a Mac OS X system installed, you'll see an Options button. Click it to set whether you want the Installer to erase the hard drive before installing, archive the existing system so you can access its files later if you need to and install a fresh system, or just upgrade the existing system (the default choice).

Glossary

A

access permissions   Settings that determine who can read, write, or move a file or folder.

accessibility   The degree to which a device or program is usable by people with disabilities.

Action menu   A pop-up menu that appears in dialog boxes and windows in the form of a gear icon. It provides access to commonly used commands.

admin user   An administrative user of Mac OS X; a user who can read, write, and move some files that do not belong to him and who can change locked System Preferences settings and install new software.

AIFF   Audio Interchange File Format is a sound file format used by iMovie and other multimedia programs.

AirPort   An Apple-branded combination of hardware (AirPort cards and the AirPort base station) and software with which computers can form a network and communicate with each other and the Internet without wires.

alias   A small file that, when double-clicked, opens the original file from which it was created.

Apple ID   A username for the Apple Web site and the iTunes Music Store.

Apple menu   The menu at the left end of the Mac's menu bar; it contains commands such as Shut Down that can be used no matter which application you're using.

AppleTalk   A proprietary Apple system for network communication, used primarily by Macs and Mac-compatible devices such as printers.

Application menu   The menu that appears to the right of the Apple menu in each program; it's always named with the name of the program.

archive   A compressed version of a file that must be dearchived before it can be opened.

B

base station   A device that creates a wireless AirPort network in conjunction with Macs equipped with AirPort cards.

Bluetooth   A wireless technology that enables computers to communicate with other devices such as PDAs, keyboards, and mice.

bookmark   A record of a web page's location, saved for future reference.

boot   To start up a computer.

broadband   A high-speed Internet connection such as DSL or a cable modem.

burn   To write data to a disc; it usually refers to a CD or DVD.

burnable folder   A folder whose contents will be burned to a CD-R disc when the user chooses.

C

cable modem　A high-speed Internet connection that operates over your cable television line.

CD-R　Recordable CD, which can be recorded only once.

CD-RW　Rewritable CD, which can be erased and recorded again several times.

check box　Interface equivalent of the real-world object used to select options in a list or dialog box.

Classic　A special program that enables Mac OS 9 to run within Mac OS X so you can use old Mac OS programs that won't run under Mac OS X.

clip　A short section of video that can be combined with other clips in iMovie to create a movie.

Clip Shelf　The area of iMovie's window where individual video clips are stored before they're used in a movie.

Clip Viewer　The area of iMovie's interface where clips are combined with transitions, effects, and each other to form a movie.

collection　A group of fonts.

color management　The science of translating and adjusting scanned, displayed, and printed colors to produce consistent color from original art to final printout.

Column view　A Finder view in which columns of file and folder listings are placed from left to right, with the left columns representing folders closer to the root level of a drive.

compressed　Refers to a file that's reduced in size by manipulating its underlying data.

contextual menus　Menus that pop up wherever you click if you use a modifier key—specifically, the Control key. Their commands vary according to the context in which you're working.

D

Dashboard　An interface for using small, desk accessory programs called *widgets* without switching out of the current program or document.

database　A data file in which each type of information is delimited in a field so the data can be sorted or otherwise manipulated based on categories.

desktop　The visual workspace in the Finder.

desktop printer　An icon that provides quick access to a printer's features.

device profile　A file that describes the color reproduction characteristics of a printer, scanner, or monitor.

DHCP　The Dynamic Host Configuration Protocol is a method of automatically configuring a desktop computer's Internet connection.

dialog box　A window in which you can click buttons, enter text, choose from pop-up menus, and drag sliders to determine the settings you want to make in a program or your system software.

dial-up　An Internet connection over a standard telephone line.

disclosure triangle   A button to the left of a folder or category name in a list; clicking it reveals the folder's or category's contents.

DNS server   A computer that translates URLs (such as www.apple.com) into the numeric addresses where web browsers can find the files that make up websites.

Dock   The panel at the bottom of your Mac OS X Desktop that contains an icon for every running program, as well as icons for any other programs, folders, or documents you want to access quickly.

download   To copy files from the Internet to a local computer.

dragging and dropping   Clicking a file's icon and dragging it into a dialog box, on top of an application's icon, into the Dock, or elsewhere.

Drop Box   A folder within your Public folder that other users can use to give files to you; you are the only person who can see the contents of the Drop Box folder.

DSL   A high-speed Internet connection that operates over your phone line.

DVD   Digital video disc; a CD-like medium that holds several times as much data as CDs and that is generally used to distribute movies.

E

email   Electronic mail that travels from your computer to another computer across the Internet or over a local network.

Ethernet   A networking technology that enables you to transfer data at high speeds.

export   To store data in a new file, separate from the currently open file.

Exposé   A set of Mac OS X 10.3 features for moving windows temporarily out of the way.

extension   See **filename extensions**.

F–G

file sharing   A system feature that enables you to transfer files from your Mac to other computers and vice versa; it can also enable other users to access your files if you allow it.

filename extensions   Three-letter (usually) codes placed at the end of filenames to signify the type of file.

FileVault   A feature that encrypts the contents of a user's home folder so it can't be accessed without a password.

Finder   The part of Mac OS X that displays the contents of your hard drives and other drives in windows on your Desktop.

FireWire   A type of connector for digital camcorders, hard drives, and other devices.

folder   A system-level equivalent of a real-world file folder, in which you can store files and other folders to help you organize them.

font   The software that enables your Mac to represent a particular typeface.

format To prepare a removable disk or hard drive to accept data.

function keys The "F" keys at the top of a keyboard are used for performing special functions that vary depending on the program being used.

H

hard drive A device for data storage, usually found inside a computer.

hardware router A device that shares an Internet connection across a local network.

home folder The folder in your Mac OS X system in which you can store all your personal files.

HTML Hypertext Markup Language, which is the coding language used to create web pages.

hub A device that connects multiple individual computers to form a network.

I-K

icon A picture indicating a file's contents or type.

Icon view A Finder view in which files are represented by graphic icons rather than just lists of names.

iDisk A storage space on Apple's website that's available to any Mac user who registers for .Mac.

iLife Apple's bundle of programs, including iMovie, iPhoto, iTunes, and iDVD.

IMAP The Internet Message Access Protocol, which is a less common method of connecting to a mail server.

import To retrieve data from a file using a format other than the program's own format.

instant messaging A method of communicating over the Internet in which users type short messages and instantly send them to other users.

IP address A numerical code that identifies the location of each computer on the Internet, including your Mac.

iPod Small, portable Apple device for playing music in MP3 format.

ISP Internet service provider, which is a company that provides access to the Internet.

JPEG A graphic file format commonly used for photos displayed on the World Wide Web.

L

label A color applied to a file icon in the Finder.

LAN Local area network, which is a small network enclosed entirely within one building.

List view A Finder view in which each window displays the contents of a single folder or drive in the form of a list of files.

local network address An identifier of a computer on a LAN.

log in   To identify yourself as a partic-ular user by entering a username and password.

login icon   A picture representing an individual user that is displayed when that user logs in or uses iChat.

M

.Mac   An online service available to any Mac user that includes an email address and web storage space, among other features.

mail server   A computer that directs email to and from a local computer on the Internet.

memory   *See* **RAM**.

menu bar   The wide, narrow strip across the top of the screen that con-tains drop-down menus in the Finder and in applications.

menu screens   Screens on a DVD containing buttons that lead to other screens or open movies.

minimized   A folder or document window that has been placed in the Dock, where you can see a thumbnail view of it.

modem   A device that enables your computer to connect to the Internet over a standard phone, DSL, or cable line.

modifier keys   Special keys (such as Shift, Option, Command, and Control) that enable you to give commands to your Mac by holding them down at the same time as you press letter or number keys or the mouse button.

monitor   A computer's display.

motion menus   DVD menu screens that incorporate moving video in their backgrounds.

mount   To connect to a disk drive (either one connected to your Mac or one connected to a network computer) so you can access its files in the Finder.

MP3   A compressed music file that's very small but that retains very high quality.

multiwindow mode   Finder mode in which double-clicking a folder dis-plays its contents in a new window rather than in the same window.

N–O

network locations   Groups of net-work settings for specific situations or locations, such as an office LAN.

network port   Computer hardware interface used to connect the computer to a network.

NTP server   *See* **timeserver**.

operating system (OS)   The soft-ware that enables a computer to run.

P

pane   A separate page in a dialog box, usually accessible by choosing from a pop-up menu or (as in the case of System Preferences) clicking a button.

pathname   The address of a file on a hard drive; it lists the nested folders in which the file resides.

PDF   *See* ***Portable Document Format****.*

peripheral   A device that connects to your Mac, such as a printer, scanner, tape backup drive, or digital camera.

permissions   File attributes that determine which user owns each file and which users are authorized to read it and make changes to it.

pixel   Picture element; a square on the screen made up of a single color.

Places sidebar   A column of disk and folder icons that appears on the left side of each Finder window in multi-window mode.

playlist   A collection of songs in iTunes.

PNG   The Portable Network Graphic format is a graphic file format used on the World Wide Web.

POP   The Post Office Protocol, which is the most common method of connecting to a mail server.

pop-up menu   A menu that appears in a dialog box or other interface element rather than dropping down from the menu bar at the top of the screen.

Portable Document Format   The file format used by Adobe Reader (formerly Acrobat Reader) and its related software. PDF documents look just like the original documents from which they were created.

PPP   The Point-to-Point Protocol, which is a method of connecting to the Internet via a phone modem.

PPPoE   PPP over Ethernet, a method of connecting to the Internet via a DSL modem.

printer driver   A file that describes the characteristics of a printer and enables programs to use the printer's features.

processor   The core of a computer; its brain.

profiles   Data files that characterize how a device reproduces color. *See also* ***color management****.*

project   A collection of files used to produce a movie in iMovie or a DVD in iDVD.

protected memory   An operating system feature that places barriers around the areas of a computer's memory (or RAM) being used by each program, so that if one program crashes, the other programs are unaffected.

proxy preview   A thumbnail version of a document, usually in a dialog box, that can be manipulated to change the real document in the same way.

Q–R

queue   The list of documents waiting to be printed.

QuickTime   Apple's proprietary video format.

RAM Random access memory, which is the part of a computer that stores the currently running programs and the currently open documents so you can work with them.

reboot To restart the Mac.

removable disk Any media that can be ejected from its drive and used in another computer.

resolution The number of pixels per inch contained in a graphic or displayed on a monitor.

rip To convert songs on a CD to files on a hard drive.

router address The IP address of the computer or device that is providing a shared Internet connection.

RSS Really Simple Syndication, an XML format for distributing web content such as news headlines, events listings, and excerpts from discussion forums.

RTF Rich Text Format, a format for word processor documents that retains information about bold, italic, and other formatting in a form that almost all word processors can understand.

S

screen name A nickname by which iChat users are identified.

screen saver A moving display that covers the screen to prevent burn-in.

screen shot A picture of the computer's screen.

search field Text entry field at the top of a window where users enter search parameters.

select To choose or designate for action; for example, the user must click a file to select it in the Finder before he can copy the file.

Services A set of ways to access programs' features while those programs are not running.

Sherlock The Mac OS's built-in utility for searching the Internet to find a variety of types of information.

single-window mode The Finder mode in which double-clicking a folder displays its contents in the same window rather than in a new window.

sleep A state in which the Mac is still powered on but consumes less energy because it's not being used.

slider A dialog box control for choosing a value along a continuum.

smart folder A folder that collects files from all over the user's hard drive based on search criteria set by the user.

smart group An Address Book group whose contents are updated automatically based on user-determined criteria.

smart mailbox A mailbox in Mail that displays email messages that are actually filed in other mailboxes, based on user-determined criteria.

spam Junk email.

speech recognition A technology by which the Mac can understand spoken commands.

startup items Programs or documents that open automatically when a user logs in.

storage media A type of computer media used for data storage rather than active information exchange.

submenu A menu that extends to the side from a command in a drop-down menu.

SuperDrive An internal drive for writing CDs and DVDs.

sync To synchronize data between a computer and a device such as a PDA or cell phone.

system software *See operating system (OS)*.

T

TCP/IP Transmission Control Protocol over Internet Protocol, the networking method Mac OS X uses; it is an industry standard.

text buttons Buttons in iDVD that don't have video images.

themes Sets of menu and button designs that can be applied to iDVD projects.

thumbnail Miniature image.

TIFF A graphic file format used for images destined to be printed.

timeserver A computer on the Internet that transmits a time signal your Mac can use to set its clock automatically.

title bar The part of a window that displays the folder's or document's title.

toolbar A row of buttons for common functions that appears at the top of a window in Preview or another program.

track A component of a song in GarageBand, consisting of the part played by a single instrument.

transition A special effect inserted between scenes in iMovie.

Trash The holding location for files or folders you want to delete.

U–V

URL An alphanumeric address that points to a specific location on the Internet, such as www.apple.com for Apple's website.

USB Universal serial bus, a type of computer connector.

username An alphanumeric identifier of a single user.

vCard A small file containing contact information that can be attached to an email message.

video buttons Buttons in iDVD that have video images.

virus A program that damages a computer or the computer's files in some way and then reproduces itself and spreads via email or file transfers.

Glossary

W-Z

web browser A program used to view websites. Safari is the web browser that comes with OS X.

webcam A small, digital camera used with iChat or to provide a constantly updated image over the World Wide Web.

WebDAV A type of server that makes iCal calendars available to subscribers over the Internet.

widget A small program that can be accessed using Dashboard.

wireless The capability to communicate without cables; for example, AirPort is Apple's technology for creating a wireless network between multiple Macs. *See also* **AirPort** and **Bluetooth**.

word processor A program used for composing, laying out, and printing text.

Zip disk A removable disk larger than a floppy disk that holds at least 100 times as much data as a floppy.

Index

SYMBOLS

A

How can we make this index more useful? Email us at indexes@quepublishing.com

windows

X-Y-Z